Agile!

Bertrand Meyer

Agile!

The Good, the Hype and the Ugly

 Springer

Bertrand Meyer
ETH Zurich,
Zurich, Switzerland

Eiffel Software,
Goleta, USA

ITMO,
Saint Petersburg, Russia

ISBN 978-3-319-05154-3   ISBN 978-3-319-05155-0 (eBook)
DOI 10.1007/978-3-319-05155-0

Library of Congress Control Number: 2014936182

p. 13   (Tintin), Le Lotus Bleu by Hergé, © Hergé/Moulinsart 2014 , © Reprinted with Permission
p. 24   CALVIN AND HOBBES © 1988 Watterson. Reprinted with permission of UNIVERSAL UCLICK. All rights reserved.
p. 55   (I Musici), I Musici di Roma, www.imusicidiroma.com
p. 63   (lasagne), Kit James, finefettleguide.blogspot.ch
p. 127 (story card), Steven Thomas, itsadeliverything.com
p. 128 (task board), Gareth Saunders, blog.garethjmsaunders.co.uk
p. 129 (burnup chart), Alistair Cockburn in [Cockburn 2005], © 2005 Addison-Wesley
p. 1, 50 (Agile Manifesto) © 2001, the authors. This declaration may be freely reproduced in any form, but only in its entirety, through this notice.
p. 118 Design by Contract is a registered trademark of Eiffel Software.
p. 131 (Gantt chart) from the documentation of "GanttView for WinForms", used with permission from Microsoft (www.microsoft.com/en-us/legal/intellectualproperty/Permissions/default.aspx), © Microsoft

Springer International Publishing Switzerland is a brand of Springer
Springer is part of Springer Science+Business Media (www.springer.com)

Short contents

The full table of contents appears on page xv.

Preface

This is not a philosophical, theoretical or motivational book, but a practical one. Its purpose is to enable readers — software developers, managers involved in IT, and educators — to benefit from the good ideas in agile methods and stay away from the bad ones.

Agile methods are undeniably one of the important recent developments in software engineering. They are also an amazing mix of the best and the worst. This is an extraordinary situation: usually, when a new set of concepts bursts forth, one can quickly assess its overall contribution as beneficial, neutral or detrimental. Agile texts, however, defy such a simple judgment: you may find in one paragraph a brilliant insight, in the next paragraph a harmless platitude, and in the one after some freakish advice guaranteed to damage your software process and products.

No wonder then that practitioners have massively disregarded injunctions to use this or that agile method — such as Scrum, Extreme Programming, Lean Software and Crystal, the most prominent ones today — in its entirety. Industry knows better, and every agile team in the field makes up its own cocktail of agile practices, rejecting the ones that do not fit. Until now, however, each organization and project has had to repeat for itself the process of sorting out the gems from the gravel. What a waste of effort. This book spares you the trouble by presenting a comprehensive **description** and **assessment** of the key agile ideas.

DESCRIPTION AND ASSESSMENT

The first goal is *description*: you can use this book as a primer on agility, presenting the approach concisely, coherently and comprehensively. If agile development is new for you, this presentation will, I hope, teach you what it is about, enable you to apply to your own projects the agile ideas you decide to retain, and prepare you if you wish to read the more specialized literature (such as the texts advocating a particular agile method) in the most effective and profitable way. If you have already read about agile methods, and perhaps practiced them, I hope it will help you put all the concepts in place, understand them in depth, and apply them better.

What makes this descriptive component of the book necessary is that until now, in spite of the already enormous literature on agile methods, there was no place, as far as I know, where you could find a complete yet concise presentation of the essential agile ideas and techniques, not tied to a particular agile method, not drowned under anecdotes, and not interspersed with a constant exhortation to join the cult. Sermons have a role, but for most people, I think, it is more interesting to find out what exactly is meant by "velocity", "continuous integration", "user story", "self-organizing team", "sprint review", "planning game", "mob programming" and so on. That is what I have tried to provide — in 162 pages.

The second goal is *assessment*: we take an even-handed look at agile methods and sort out what helps, what is not worth the attention, and what harms — the good, the hype and the ugly. The assessment is unbiased (I have no horse in this race) but that does not mean it is the only possible one, since empirical software engineering, the objective study of software processes, is still a science in progress. So you will not necessarily agree with all the conclusions, but I think you will agree with most, and where you disagree you will be able to appreciate rational arguments on both sides.

The two aspects — "news" and "editorial"— are separated: you are entitled to know at any stage whether you are reading the factual presentation of an agile technique or a discussion of its merit. Judgmental elements are marked by the icon shown here on the right. The scope of its application will be clear from its position: at the start of a paragraph, it generally applies to the remaining part of the current section; at the start of a section, to the full section; and in the case of the final assessment, to the full chapter.

KEEPING A COOL HEAD

Anyone trying to gain a clear, cool-headed understanding and appreciation of agile methods has, so far, faced three difficulties that I hope this book removes: partisanship, intimidation and extremism.

Most of the existing texts are **partisan**. At issue here is not just the normal phenomenon of inventors arguing for their inventions, but a lack of restraint that sometimes borders on religious fervor and demands from the reader a suspension of disbelief. The first presentations of structured programming, object technology and design patterns — to cite three earlier developments that each imprinted a durable mark on how the world builds software, as agile methods have already started to do — were enthusiastically promoting new ideas, but did not ignore the rules of rational discourse. With agile methods you are asked to kneel down and start praying. This is not the right way to approach solutions to engineering problems involving difficult technical and human aspects.

The agile literature is often **intimidating**. It dismisses previous approaches as passé, scornfully labeling them "waterfall" (even though no company applies a strict waterfall process), and leaving the impression that anyone supporting them is a rigid, pointy-hair-boss type. We will encounter the typical example of an author for whom any objection to agile methods is a mark of *"bureaucracy"*, *"incompetence"* and *"mediocrity"*. The very name for the approach, "agile", a brilliant marketing decision — no, a stroke of genius! —, is enough to make any would-be skeptic think twice: who wants to → *See "Intimidation", 2.2.3, page 23.*

be cast as *not* agile? If you search the dictionary for antonyms to "*agile*", you will find such niceties as "*awkward*", "*lumbering*" and "*ungraceful*". If those are the alternatives, you, I and everyone else want to be agile! This name is just a name, however; we must unemotionally assess, one by one, the concrete principles and practices that it covers.

Clear, no-nonsense assessment is also complicated by **extremism**: the insistence of some method designers that you must apply their prescriptions entirely. There are exceptions; Crystal, for example, is more of a flexible, your-mileage-may-vary approach. But the prevalence of the all-or-nothing view in many of the foundational texts further complicates the task of identifying which techniques will work for your own project, and which will not.

PREVIOUS ATTEMPTS

Among the many books on agile methods, I know of only three that have not taken an adoring tone. The first is McBreen's *Questioning Extreme Programming*, whose "questioning" is plaintive, leaving the reader uncertain about any serious problems with XP. *Extreme Programming Refactored: The Case Against XP* by Stephens and Rosenberg does not suffer from such angst; it is a pamphlet, both funny and enlightening, but like any pamphlet it does better at highlighting absurdity than at performing a fair pro-and-con analysis. The book that made the most serious attempt at such an analysis, Boehm and Turner's *Balancing Agility with Discipline*, contrasts agile approaches with traditional plan-driven software engineering techniques. Its great strength is that it relies on empirical data from studies comparing the effectiveness of agile techniques to their classical counterparts. For my taste it tilts a trifle too much to the side of cautiousness; perhaps because Boehm is such a respected figure in software engineering and feared being branded as a proponent of the old order, the authors avoid sounding too critical. *[McBreen 2002].* *[Stephens 2003].* *[Boehm 2004].*

Do not expect such timidity in the present book (mentioning this just in case you were worried). Respect yes, deference no. It will highlight and praise the good ideas, and when it encounters balderdash it will call it balderdash.

STRUCTURE OF THE BOOK

The book has a simple structure and is intended for sequential reading.

The opening chapter, entitled "overview", presents a summary of agile ideas and a first overall assessment. It sets the stage for the rest of the book and serves as a summary of it.

The second chapter is a short foray into the style of agile descriptions, serving as a form of immunization against the risk of unjustified generalization. Working from examples in the agile literature, it analyzes the intellectual devices that agile authors use to convince the world.

Chapter 3 is a sketch of everything that agile methods do not want to be and agile texts love to lambast: traditional plan-based software engineering methods, including the derided "waterfall".

The next five chapters, the core of the book, review agile ideas: **principles** in chapter 4, **roles** (in the sense of personnel roles, such as managers and users) in chapter 5, **practices** in chapters 6 and 7, and **artifacts**, both material and virtual, in chapter 8. Here we do not focus on any specific method but look instead at the concepts and tools shared by all or most. This approach illuminates the many commonalities between the various methods. It will allow you to examine agile ideas by themselves, in a non-denominational way, so that you can decide which ones are suitable for your context. When some of them apply more specifically to one method, the discussion points this out, and includes in the margin one of the icons shown here on the right. The focus in those chapters remains, however, on individual methodological concepts and techniques.

That focus moves to the methods themselves in chapter 9, which studies four of the principal agile methods in existence today, the four already cited: Scrum, Lean, XP and Crystal. Since the constituent ideas have been presented in the preceding chapters, 4 to 8, we can in the presentation of each method concentrate on the particular combination of principles, roles, practices and artifacts that it has chosen, and just as importantly on the characteristic *spirit* of that method. The analysis shows that each of them has "one big idea" that sets it apart, supported by a number of auxiliary concepts.

These symbols were designed for the present book and are not official logos of the methods.

Chapter 10 is brief; it describes precautions that organizations should take when adopting agile methods, in particular when some are more agile than others. It warns that the laws of software engineering continue to apply, and cautions against the "either-what-or-when" fallacy that works well for consultants but not for their clients.

Chapter 11 is the final assessment: an overall examination of the agile canon, appraising which ideas stand up and which just do not make sense. It shows indeed that, as the book's subtitle indicates, agile ideas can be classified into three categories:

- *The good* (including the "*brilliant*"): principles and practices — some new, some not — that agile authors rightly present as helpful to software quality and productivity.

- *The hype*: widely touted ideas that will make little difference, good or bad, to the resulting software.

- *The ugly*: agile-recommended techniques that are just plain wrong, contradicting proven rules of good software engineering, jeopardizing the success of projects, and harming the quality of the resulting software.

PERSPECTIVE AND SCOPE

Any book is colored by its author's experience. What mostly characterizes mine is the mix of industrial practice (for most of my career) and academic work (for the past decade).

It is also useful to note what this book does *not* include: a comprehensive approach to software development. My previous books describe techniques of quality software development and argue for specific approaches, particularly object technology, formal specification and Design by Contract. This one, in contrast, studies other people's work. Even when I felt that my own work is relevant to the discussion or predates some of the successful agile ideas I have (except for a hint or two) refrained from talking about it.

Analysis: instinctive, experiential, logical or empirical?

Software methodology is a tricky business because it is difficult to prove anything. Many ideas get adopted on the strength of an author's powers of conviction. It does not mean they are good, or bad.

Authors use four kinds of argument: gut feeling, experience, logical reasoning and empirical analysis.

Do not laugh at **gut feeling** as a means of persuasion; after all, the mother of all software methodology texts, Dijkstra's 1968 *Go To Statement Considered Harmful*, largely relied on it:

> *Recently **I discovered** why the use of the go to statement has such disastrous effects, and **I became convinced** that it should be abolished from all higher-level programming languages.*

[Dijkstra 1968], emphasis added.

But if you are not Dijkstra your gut feeling will not take you very far in a quest to convince the community.

Experience was also part of Dijkstra's rationale:

> ***For a number of years I have been familiar** with the observation that the quality of programmers is a decreasing function of the density of go to statements in the programs they produce.*

Experiential arguments are among the favorite tools of agile authors. The typical agile book is a succession of alternating general observations and personal anecdotes of project rescues (rescued, remarkably, by the author) and project failures (failed, remarkably, after not following the author's advice). These anecdotes are usually entertaining and sometimes enlightening, but a case study is only a case study, and we never know how much we can generalize. One can, after all, summon an experience in support of almost any recommendation.

Anecdotes and individual cases, by the way, can have force of proof, but only in one case: *disproving* a general law. If such a law has been proposed, it suffices of a single experiment to negate it (the technical term is "falsify"). For example if someone — say, Aristotle — told you that bodies fall at a rate that depends on their mass, just go up that tower in Pisa, drop a light ball and a heavy ball, and see them reach the ground at the same time.

Logical reasoning is a powerful tool; it played a significant role in Dijkstra's advocacy (and for Galileo too, who according to some authors proved his hypothesis solely by thought experiment). But it is only as convincing as the hypotheses from which it starts, and there is the risk that it will remain academic.

Ideally, we should use **empirical analysis**. Does pair programming lead to better results than code inspections? Is constant customer interaction preferable to a solid requirements process? Credible answers to questions of software methodology require systematic, rigorous, realistic studies of projects. This book relies on such results when available, but there are not enough of them; the burgeoning field of empirical software engineering has not yet provided answers to many fundamental issues. This has been perhaps the biggest obstacle in the preparation of the book. Where not enough empirical evidence was available, the discussion largely relies on analytical reasoning.

I have not completely avoided anecdotes and personal experience, but have tried to confine them to the illustration of points supported by logical argument and to the task, mentioned above, of disproving undue generalizations.

FREE CRITICAL INQUIRY

Given that this work includes critical comments, a word is in order to explain the spirit in which it has been written.

Progress in science and engineering relies on free, critical inquiry of previous work. In reviewing the agile literature, I have found a number of reasons to disagree with its authors, and a few reasons to be shocked; I have not been coy about taking their claims to task. I have also, however, found elements to admire, and learned new insights about software development. This observation is worth remembering whenever you encounter criticism in the following pages.

I would not have spent a good part of my last three years immersing myself in agile methods and the supporting texts if I had not felt that I had something important to learn. The path has been tortuous at times; with this book I hope to spare you the path and share the lessons.

In no case does the criticism mean disrespect; the agile pioneers are experienced professionals, passionate about software. Even when I find them to be wrong, I value their views and share the passion. We are all in the same boat.

Bertrand Meyer
January 2014

ACKNOWLEDGMENTS

Since this book makes a number of judgments, the customary caveat that its content commits only the author is more than perfunctory: by acknowledging sources of influence and help I do not mean to imply that anyone listed endorses the views expressed. This caveat particularly applies to the first group of people to be thanked, some of whom may be expected to disagree: the authors of the best agile books. I have learned a lot from reading about agile methods, and am particularly indebted to the books and articles of Kent Beck, Barry Boehm with Richard Turner, Alistair Cockburn, Mike Cohn, Craig Larman, Mary and Tom Poppendieck, and Ken Schwaber with Mike Beedle. I credit my first encounter with agile ideas to a presentation of Extreme Programming by Pete McBreen at the Le Bréau EDF/CEA summer school in 1999. I am grateful to Mike Cohn for clarification of the origin of two of his citations. I also benefited from a lively Scrum workshop by Jeff Sutherland in Moscow, enabling me to become a proud Certified Scrum Master.

I have given several industry seminars at ETH on the theme of this book and gained from the participants' comments. I am grateful for the advice of Ralf Gerstner at Springer on refining the focus of the book, and am also indebted to his colleague Viktoria Meyer. Patrick Smacchia brought some recent agile practices to my attention. Claude Baudoin, Kent Beck, Judith Bishop, Michael Jackson and Ivar Jacobson were kind enough to encourage me after seeing a draft. Paul Dubois and Mark Howard sent me important comments which helped focus and refine the text. Claudia Günthart and Annie Meyer helped with editing. Carroll Morgan sent me particularly perceptive comments on both form and content. I have a special debt to Raphaël Meyer's for his thorough reading of the text, which led to essential improvements.

If I ever felt like pontificating abstractly about software engineering, I would quickly be brought back to earth by the development group at Eiffel Software; we are fighting the battle every day. Together we have seen it all: successes as well as those less glorious moments, the development iteration that seemingly will never end, the critical bug that surfaces two days after a release, the amorously crafted feature that turns out to interest nary a user. We are agile, in the best sense of the term, but we are learning all the time.

I have drawn on some material published on my personal blog, at bertrandmeyer.com, and on my blog at *Communications of the ACM* (cacm.acm.org/blogs/blog-cacm). I am grateful for reader comments on blog articles.

I am indebted to members of the Chair of Software Engineering at ETH Zurich for many discussions on software engineering issues. I cannot cite everyone but should mention that a remark by Till Bay was the spark that led to switching the EiffelStudio development to an agile-style time-boxed release process, and that Marco Piccioni first brought Scrum to my attention. He also made a number of important suggestions on the draft of the present book. In the ETH course "Distributed Software *se.ethz.ch/dose.* Engineering Laboratory", where students from a dozen universities around the world work together on a challenging distributed project, my co-instructors of many years, Peter Kolb and Martin Nordio, contributed numerous insights, as did the assistants (Roman Mitin, Julian Tschannen, Christian Estler) and the students and instructors from the participating universities. The course led to a number of published empirical studies which significantly helped my understanding of the field.

BOOK PAGE

Further material associated with this book is available at

bertrandmeyer.com/agile

Contents

1

Overview

Agile ideas date back to the development of Extreme Programming in the 1990s, but reached fame with the appearance in 2001 of the "Agile Manifesto": *[Agile 2001]*

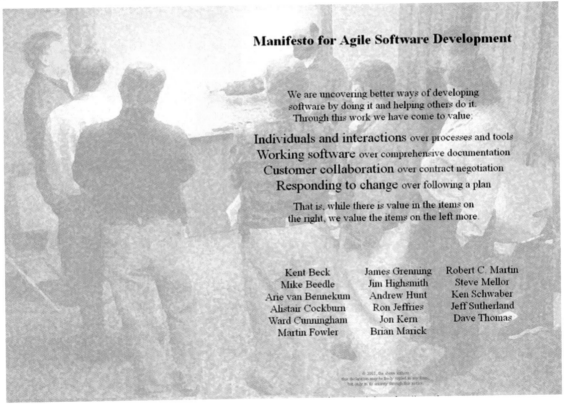

The sight of a half-dozen middle-aged, jeans-clad, potbellied gentlemen turning their generous behinds to us appears to have provided the decisive sex appeal. Personally, had I wanted to convey the suggestion of agility, I might have turned to something like the cover photograph of this book — which only demonstrates how out of tune I am with the times, since the above picture was successful beyond anyone's dreams. Agile ideas have

B. Meyer, *Agile!*, DOI 10.1007/978-3-319-05155-0_1,
© Springer International Publishing Switzerland 2014

become the buzz of the industry, the darling of the technical press, the kind of argument companies use in the fierce competition to attract the best programmers: *Come to us! Our development is agile!*

Rather than a single development method, "agile" denotes a compendium of ideas, which a number of full-fledged methods — particularly Extreme Programming (XP), Scrum, Lean Software and Crystal — apply in various subsets and combinations; many people also use some of the ideas without embracing a complete method. In this chapter we get into the mood, if not the details, of agile methods, by reviewing their core characteristics:

The abbreviation XP comes from the alternative capitalization "eXtreme Programming".

- *Values*: general assumptions framing the agile view of the world (1.1).

- *Principles*: core agile rules, organizational and technical (1.2).

- *Roles*: responsibilities and privileges of the various actors in an agile process (1.3).

- *Practices*: specific activities practiced by agile teams (1.4).

- *Artifacts*: tools, both virtual and material, that support the practices (1.5).

The principles follow from the values; the practices, roles and artifacts follow from the principles. The last section (1.6) provides a first assessment of the approach.

This chapter serves as a concentrate of the rest of the book, surveying the key ideas concisely. Except for the last part, it is descriptive, presenting the agile ideas neutrally. For brevity, it does not cite (with one exception, below on this page) from the agile sources describing the techniques summarized here; the following chapters include numerous citations from agile texts, where the authors explain their rationale in detail.

1.1 VALUES

Reading the Agile Manifesto on the previous page is enough to show that "Agile" is not just a collection of software techniques but a movement, an ideology, a cause. Going even further, one of the creators of Scrum declares that *"Agile is an emotion"*. To describe the fundamental underlying assumptions, agile proponents like to use the term "values". Before looking at specific principles, practices, roles and artifacts, we must get a feel for the agile philosophy, in the form of five general tenets:

[Sutherland 2009], at 5:59.

Agile values
1   Redefined roles for developers, managers and customers.
2   No "Big Upfront" steps.
3   Iterative development.
4   Limited, negotiated functionality.
5   Focus on quality, understood as achieved through testing.

The first tenet affects a fundamental feature of project development: the **role of developers and managers**. Agile methods redefine and limit the manager's job by transferring many of the duties to the *team* as a whole, including one of the most important responsibilities: selecting tasks to be performed and assigning them to developers. It is possible to give a sociological interpretation of the agile movement as a *"revolt of the cubicles"*: the rejection of rigid, top-down, Dilbert's-boss-like techniques for managing software projects. Programmers in the trenches — the cubicles — often resent these attempts as ignorant of the specific nature of software development. The Dilbert types know that documents and diagrams do not make a system: code does. Agile methods are, in part, the rehabilitation of code.

The redefinition of roles also affects *customers*, who in the agile world are not passive recipients of the software but active participants. Most methods advocate including a customer representative in the development team itself.

The second tenet is the **rejection of "Big Upfront Anything"**, a term used derogatorily for standard software engineering techniques involving extensive planning at the beginning of a project; the principal examples are *requirements*, to define the goals of the system, and *design*, to define its architecture. In the agile view:

- Requirements cannot be captured at the beginning of a project, because users do not know what they want. Even if one managed to write a requirements document, it would be useless because requirements will change through the project.

- Building a design upfront is a waste of time because we do not know what will work and what will not.

Instead of a requirements document, agile methods recommend constant interaction with the customer — hence the benefit of a customer representative in the team — to get both insights into the problem and feedback on what has been produced so far. Instead of design, the recommendation is to build the system iteratively, devising at each step the "simplest solution that can possibly work" (an Extreme Programming slogan) for the task at hand; then, if the solution turns out to be imperfect, improving its design through a process known as *refactoring*.

Agile development, as a consequence, is **iterative, time-boxed development**. The agile alternative to a requirements document is, at the beginning of each iteration, a prioritized list of functions from which the team will select for implementation the function that has the highest *Return on Investment* (ROI). In the absence of big upfront tasks, this choice will be made in successive steps, called "sprints" in Scrum, each taking a fixed time — a few weeks — hence "time-boxed". The development thus proceeds by iterative addition of functionality.

By addition, that is, of **limited, negotiated functionality**. The agile literature laments the effort that traditional projects devote to building program features that hardly anyone will use. It advocates limiting features to the most important ones, as measured by their business value: their ROI. The "Lean Software" school draws on comparisons with other industries (notably car manufacturing) to treat unused functionality as the software equivalent of "waste" in an industrial production process, and "waste minimization" as a core concern. "Kanban", influenced by processes developed for Toyota, seeks to minimize "work in progress".

The "negotiation" occurs at the step of choosing the functionality for each iteration. Just as it is impossible, in the agile view, to determine full requirements in advance, it is unrealistic to commit to both *functionality* and *delivery time*. With time-boxed development, any tradeoffs ("do you want it all or do you want it next month?") will tend to be resolved in favor of the second criterion: if not all the functions planned for an iteration can be delivered by the deadline, it is the functionality that goes; the deadline stays. The missed functionality will either be reassigned to a subsequent phase or — if further analysis deems its ROI insufficient — dropped. This process of planning and adjusting requires constant negotiation with the customer.

The final tenet is the **focus on quality**, which in the agile view essentially means continuous testing (rather than other approaches to quality, in particular those based on design techniques, formal programming methodology, or whatever smacks of "Big Upfront"). The agile approach has little patience with what it sees as the lackadaisical attention to quality in traditional development; it especially dislikes the practice of continuing to develop functionality even when the code already developed does not pass all the tests. One of its contributions is to emphasize the role of a project's *regression test suite*: the set of tests that must pass, including all tests that at some point did *not* pass and hence revealed faults that were then fixed. Regression testing has been known and applied for a long time, but agile methods have given this task a central place in the development process.

1.2 PRINCIPLES

The rest of this book considers that the following eight principles (three of them with sub-principles) constitute the core of the agile canon.

Agile principles
Organizational
1   Put the customer at the center.
2   Let the team self-organize.
3   Work at a sustainable pace.
4   Develop minimal software:
4.1   Produce minimal functionality.
4.2   Produce only the product requested.
4.3   Develop only code and tests.
5   Accept change.

> **Technical**
>
> 6 Develop iteratively:
>
>   6.1   Produce frequent working iterations.
>
>   6.2   Freeze requirements during iterations.
>
> 7 Treat tests as a key resource:
>
>   7.1   Do not start any new development until all tests pass.
>
>   7.2   Test first.
>
> 8 Express requirements through scenarios.

These principles follow from the five general "values" of the previous section, turning them into actual prescriptions.

They are not the principles — twelve of them — listed in the Agile Manifesto. Those official principles, discussed in a later chapter, are less appropriate for analysis: they are redundant and combine ideas at different levels, ranging from generous but hardly earth-shattering intentions ("*Build projects around motivated individuals*" — who would disagree?) to specific rules such as releasing software at specific intervals of two weeks to two months, which are practices rather than principles. They also omit key ideas such as the primacy of tests. The eight presented here provide a better overview.

→ *"The official principles"*, *page 50.*

1.2.1 Organizational principles

Five principles guide agile project organization and management.

Agile development is **customer-centric**. The goal of software development is to deliver the best Return On Investment to the customer; as part of the redefinition of roles, customer representatives should be involved throughout the project.

Agile teams are **self-organizing**, deciding on their own tasks. A corollary of this empowerment of the team is, as noted, a severe curtailment of the manager's responsibilities.

Agile projects work at a **sustainable pace** by refusing so-called "death marches", periods of intense pressure forcing a team to work exceptionally hard in preparation for an upcoming deadline. "Sustainability" requires that programmers work reasonable hours, preserving evenings and week-ends. The sociological undercurrent mentioned above — agile methods as empowerment of programmers and consultants against managers — is again apparent here.

Agile development is **minimalistic** in three ways: building only the essential functions (*minimal functionality*); building only what is requested, excluding extra work to prepare for future reuse and extension (*minimal product*); and building only two kinds of software, programs and tests, at the exclusion of anything that will not be delivered to the customer and hence is considered waste (*minimal artifacts*).

Agile development **accepts change**. In software projects, full requirements cannot be determined at the beginning; needs emerge as the project develops, and evolve as customers and others try intermediate releases. Such change is considered a normal part of the development process.

1.2.2 Technical principles

Agile development implies an **iterative development process**, consisting of successive iterations. Each is fairly short — a few weeks — and produces a *working release* of the software, even a very partial one, which customer representatives can try out to provide reactions that will fuel the next iteration. Scrum introduced the important rule that *functionality is frozen during iterations*: if an idea for a new function arises during development, it is postponed to the preparation of the next iteration.

→ *"Freeze requirements during iterations", page 71.*

The **primacy of tests** embodies the approach's focus on quality. This principle has two consequences, both significant enough to be considered sub-principles on their own:

- **No new development may start until all current tests pass**. This rule reflects a strict approach to quality and a refusal to compromise on bug-fixing.

- **Test First**. This principle, introduced in connection with Extreme Programming, prescribes that no code may be written unless there is already a test for it. It makes tests the first part of the replacement for requirements and specifications in agile development. The *test-driven development* practice, introduced in a later section, takes the idea even further.

→ *"Technical practices", page 9.*

The last principle gives us the second part of the replacement for requirements: **use scenarios to define functionality**. A scenario is a description of a particular interaction of a user with the system, for example (if we are building mobile phone software) a phone conversation from the time the caller dials the number to the time the two parties get disconnected. "Scenario" is not a common agile term, but covers variants such as *use cases* and *user stories* which differ by their level of granularity (a use case is a complete interaction, a user story an application of a smaller unit of functionality). Scenarios are obtained from customers and indicate the fundamental properties of the system's functionality as seen from the user perspective. Collecting scenarios, usually in the form of user stories, is the principal agile technique for requirements; it differs from traditional requirements elicitation in two fundamental ways:

- A scenario is just one example; unlike requirements, it cannot lay claim to completeness. A set of scenarios, however large, cannot come even close to achieving this goal, in the same way that no number of tests of a program can replace a specification.

- In agile development, requirements are not collected at the beginning of the project but throughout, as development progresses. Note, however, that this difference is not as absolute as the agile literature suggests when it blasts "waterfall approaches": while the traditional software engineering view presents requirements as a specific lifecycle step, coming early in the process, it does not rule out — except in the imagination of agile authors — a scheme in which the requirements are constantly updated in the rest of the lifecycle.

Chapter 4 discusses the organizational and technical agile principles in detail.

1.3 ROLES

Agile methods define roles for the various actors of a software project.

Key agile roles
1   Team
2   Product owner.
3   Scrum Master.
4   Customer.

The first and most important role is the **team**: a self-organizing group of developers and others (such as customer representatives), responsible for the ongoing assignment of development tasks to individual members.

Scrum has gone the furthest among agile methods in defining new roles that take over some of the traditional manager responsibilities. The definition of the properties of the product under development is the responsibility of a **product owner**; it includes the right to change these properties, but not while a sprint (a development iteration) is in progress. For the manager's job as coach, mentor, guru and method enforcer, Scrum defines a special role of **Scrum Master**, who cannot also be the project owner.

Common to all agile methods is the emphasis on involving **customers**. Defining "customer" as an explicit project role is part of the agile rejection of up-front requirements and general distrust of documents — "*valuing customer interaction over contract negotiation*", as the Manifesto puts it. Instead of couching the requirements on paper, the project involves customers directly. Extreme Programming, at least in its early versions, prescribed the embedding of "a customer" in the team, as a full-fledged project member; this practice, although simple to state, raises problems that we will analyze. Even when one does not go that far, every agile project reserves an important role for customers.

Chapter 5 discusses these and other agile roles in detail.

1.4 PRACTICES

To achieve the principles presented above, agile methods promote a set of practices. Here are the principal ones, again with more coming up in the chapter on the topic:

→ *Chapter 6 discusses agile practices.*

Key agile practices

Organizational

1 Daily meeting.
2 Planning game, planning poker.
3 Continuous integration.
4 Retrospective.
5 Shared code ownership.

Technical

6 Test-driven development.
7 Refactoring.
8 Pair programming.
9 Simplest solution that can possibly work.
10 Coding standards.

1.4.1 Organizational practices

All agile methods advocate frequent face-to-face contact, but Scrum specifically includes a requirement for a **daily meeting,** held at the beginning of every working day and known as the "daily Scrum". The meeting must be kept short: 15 minutes is the standard. This goal is reachable, with a typical group of a dozen or two people, because the scope of the meeting is strictly limited to every member of the team answering three questions: "What did I do in the previous working day?", "What do I plan to do today?", and "What impediments am I facing?". Anything else, such as *resolving* non-trivial impediments, must occur outside of the meeting. The daily meeting — which is only applicable in its basic form to a team located in a single place — helps teams remain cohesive, know what everyone is doing, and spot problems early.

Any software development project faces the issue of planning, in particular of estimating delivery times and functionality. Agile methods propose the **"planning game"** (Extreme Programming) and the **"planning poker"** (Scrum). Both are group estimation techniques which ask the participants to come with initial estimates independently, then examine each other's estimates and iterate until a consensus is reached.

More convincing is the concept of **continuous integration**. A decade or two ago, it was not uncommon for software projects to split into sub-developments and only try to put them together ("integrate") at intervals of months or more. This is a terrible approach: when attempting integration, projects often discover that the subsystems have made incompatible assumptions and have to undergo substantial rewriting. Modern development practice calls for frequent integration, at intervals not exceeding a few weeks. Agile methods apply this principle too and some of them actually advocate integrating several times a *day*.

Another agile practice is the **retrospective**, in which a team having finished a development iteration takes time off further development to reflect on the experience and the lessons learned, with the goal of improving its development process.

In many groups, the various units of the software are each "owned" by a particular developer, not in any legal sense but in the sense that this person ultimately decides what may and may not change in the unit. This practice is, for example, common at Microsoft. Agile methods instead advocate **shared code ownership**, where all of the team is responsible for all of the code. The goal is to avoid undue dependence on individuals, to emphasize that all team members have a personal stake in the product, and to avoid territorial battles when a change or new development straddles several parts of the system.

1.4.2 Technical practices

Test-driven development turns the "Test first" principle into a specific practice. Applied iteratively, this practice consists of: writing a test corresponding to a new functionality; running the program, which should not pass the test since the functionality is new; fixing the program; running the program again, and continuing to fix it until it does pass the test (and all other tests, to prevent any regression); examining the code and performing refactoring, as discussed next, to make sure the design remains consistent. This sequence of steps, applied from the start (when the program is empty and hence will fail any non-trivial test) and repeated from then on, is the central form of software development in Extreme Programming.

XP

Refactoring is the process of critically examining a design or implementation and applying any transformations that may be needed to improve its consistency. Catalogs of standard refactoring transformations exist; they include such typical examples, in object-oriented programming, as moving a feature of a class (field or method) up or down the inheritance hierarchy, to another class where it fits better conceptually. Refactoring is particularly necessary in connection with test-driven development: a process consisting solely of adding a code element for every new test would yield programs with a messy, ad-hoc structure; refactoring is necessary to maintain a clean design. Just as scenarios and tests are the agile replacement for Big Upfront Requirements, refactoring is the agile answer to Big Upfront Design.

E.g. [Fowler 1999].

Pair programming has been particularly promoted by Extreme Programming. In this practice, code is systematically developed by two people sharing a workstation, one controlling the keyboard and mouse and explaining his thought patterns as he types, the other commenting, criticizing and making new suggestions. The pilot-and-navigator metaphor is often used to explain that process. The goal is to catch possible mistakes at the source: since the "pilot" is forced to explain his thinking aloud, he will often realize right away that something is wrong, and otherwise the navigator will catch it when trying to understand. Extreme Programming presents pair programming as the only mode of development, to be applied systematically and universally. It figures less prominently in other agile methods.

Extreme Programming also popularized the practice of **the simplest solution that can possibly work**. An application of the minimalistic principles described earlier, in particular "produce only the product requested", it shuns any work that is intended to make the solution more extendible or more reusable, as software engineering principles would normally recommend, in particular the principles of object-oriented development. In the agile view such work is illusory anyway, because we may not need reuse, and we do not know ahead of time in which direction the software may have to be extended.

Finally, agile methods promote the use of **coding standards**: defined style rules that a team should apply to all the code it produces.

1.5 ARTIFACTS

The application of agile methods relies on a number of supporting tools; some of them are conceptual, such as the notion of a user story, and others material, such as a story card used to write such a story.

<table>
<tr><td colspan="2" align="center">**Key agile artifacts**</td></tr>
<tr><td colspan="2">**Virtual**</td></tr>
<tr><td>1</td><td>Use case, user story.</td></tr>
<tr><td>2</td><td>Burndown chart.</td></tr>
<tr><td colspan="2">**Material**</td></tr>
<tr><td>3</td><td>Story card.</td></tr>
<tr><td>4</td><td>Story board.</td></tr>
<tr><td>5</td><td>Open room.</td></tr>
</table>

1.5.1 Virtual artifacts

Use cases and particularly **user stories** are scenarios that represent user interactions with a system. Use cases were popularized, pre-agile, by a book due to Ivar Jacobson; user stories have emerged as part of the agile movement. The difference is in granularity; a *[Jacobson 1992]* use case covers a full run through the system, going for example from browsing for a product on an E-commerce site to completing the order; a user story is a smaller unit of functionality expected by users, such as

> *"As a customer, I want to see a list of my recent orders, so that I can track my purchases with a particular company."*

The **burndown chart** is a record of a project's *velocity*: how fast it processes — "burns down" — the items in its task list. The chart plots against time (in the example, up to a certain day in a given iteration) the number of unimplemented tasks:

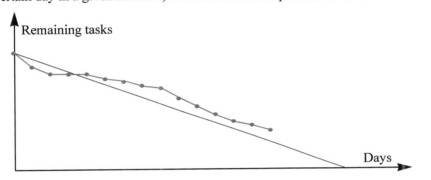

Burndown chart (red)

If the task list is fixed for the iteration and no completed task is re-opened, the curve will be non-increasing. The velocity is the number of tasks discharged; the blue line is the constant-velocity line. Where the burndown chart is below that line, the project is progressing faster than expected; above the line, it is progressing more slowly. Maintaining the burndown chart is a way to make the team aware of its progress and alert it when it is not discharging tasks fast enough.

1.5.2 Material artifacts

The remaining artifacts are, in their default form, material objects; for all of them, however, various companies and open-source projects offer software tools providing partial support or full replacement.

The **story card** is a paper-card (agile advocates even prescribe the size: 3 by 5 inches, presumably to be adapted to the local format when working under metric climes) used to write down a user story. Story cards are meant to be pinned to a **story board**, a large board which can host many of them; the team then moves them around the board to group them into categories.

The story board is often refined into a **task board**, which complements the burndown chart to show the progress of the project:

User stories | Tasks | *Task Board*

Post-it notes on the board represent individual tasks. As work gets done, the team moves them towards the right.

Another recommendation of agile methods addresses the physical layout of the offices in which programmers work: rather than closed offices, it should be set up as an **open room** to favor constant interaction between team members.

1.6 A FIRST ASSESSMENT

We have not gone into enough detail for a full-fledged analysis of the pros and cons of the agile approach (the good, the hype and the ugly); it will come in the final chapter. But we can take a first cut.

> Remember that this section only provides a general view, and that the comprehensive assessment of agile methods is the one that comes after the study of agile methods.

→ *Chapter 11: The Ugly, the Hype and the Good: an assessment of the agile approach.*

Samuel Johnson allegedly responded thus to an aspiring author:

> *Your work, Sir, is both new and good, but what is new is not good and what is good is not new.*

This statement (although apparently apocryphal!) provides us with a useful grid to evaluate agile ideas in four categories, resulting from two possibilities each for newness and goodness. In each category we will consider only a few examples.

See *www.samuel-johnson.com/apocryph.html.*

1.6.1 Not new and not good

The agile approach to requirements is based on user stories: units of functionality corresponding to interactions of users with the system. User stories, like use cases, are a valuable tool for *validating* requirements, to check that the identified functionality covers the most common scenarios. As a tool for defining requirements, they are inadequate because they only document *examples* of system execution. The task of requirements is to go beyond these individual examples, which can only cover a fraction of the possibilities available, and identify the more general functions of the system. If you forgo this step of generalization and abstraction, you get systems that do a few things — the user stories — and little else.

When using software systems, for example web applications, have you ever felt like Tintin the day he was being marched in a straightjacket? As soon as you dare to depart from the exact scenario that the designers, in their supreme wisdom, have planned for you, nothing works any more. This kind of system is the direct result of requirements based on the sole analysis of use cases or user stories.

© Hergé/Mou-linsart 2014.

Good requirements shoot for more abstract specifications, subsuming many different scenarios and supporting the development of flexible, extendible applications.

1.6.2 New and not good

Pair programming was introduced by the XP. To characterize it as "not good" is a bit strong since pair programming can be an effective technique if applied with reason. XP's insistence that it should be the absolute rule, however, makes little sense conceptually, as it neglects the role of programmer personality (some excellent developers like to concentrate alone and will resent having to be paired), and practically, as studies show pair programming to be no superior to other classical techniques such as code reviews.

Code reviews are also known as inspections.

To a certain extent pair programming can be dismissed as folklore, since many projects that try it stop after a while. Worse consequences of agile methods come from the injunction to develop minimal software, stated earlier as principle 4. Its component rules 4.2 (produce only the product requested) and 4.3 (develop only code and tests) may appeal to inexperienced project managers as a way to combat programmer perfectionism and deliver results quickly, focusing on the essential. But from a software engineering perspective they are not good advice, since they discourage efforts that have proved to be among the most fruitful practices of software engineering: generalizing code for ease of extension and reuse, and developing tools to automate repetitive processes. In Lean terminology, the results of such efforts are "waste" since they are not delivered to the customer; in reality, when applied appropriately, they are the key to the continuous improvement of a company's software process and the professionalization of software practice.

← "Agile principles", page 4.

Worse yet is the rejection of upfront requirements. The basic observation is correct: requirements will change, and are hard anyway to capture at the beginning. In no way, however, does it imply the dramatic conclusion that upfront requirements are useless! What it does imply is that requirements should be subject to change, like all other artifacts of the software process. This point has been made by much of the software engineering literature and remains as valid as ever. Unfortunately, many projects in recent years have followed the simplistic agile advice of skipping the systematic requirements phase, replacing it by attempts to evolve the system iteratively with the help of occasional customer interactions. The results are often (predictably) disappointing; projects get delayed because requirements end up being collected anyway, but too late in the lifecyle, when some functionality has already been built; some it will have to be discarded.

The agile advice here is irresponsible and serious software projects should ignore it. The sound practice is to start collecting requirements at the beginning, produce a provisional version prior to engaging in design, and treat the requirements as a living product that undergoes constant adaptation throughout the project.

1.6.3 Not new but good

There is a charmingly adolescent quality to the agile literature: I am sooooo unique! Nobody before me understood what life is about! My folks are sooooo, like, 20-th century!

In reality, despite the scathing attacks on traditional software engineering — the irreparable insult, akin to shouting "liberal!" at a Republican candidate, is "waterfall!" — a number of the productive ideas of agile methods have long been advocated in the standard software engineering literature. We will see examples through the rest of the book; here are two.

The first is iterative development. The industry understood in the nineteen-eighties that the old model of diverging for months and then trying to bring all the pieces back together was a recipe for disaster. A 1995 book by Cusumano and Selby — New York *[Cusumano* Times best-seller, no less — publicized Microsoft's "daily build", a practice which as the *1995]* name indicates requires the project to produce a working version every day. Open-source projects, which have flourished for decades, have a practice of releasing early and often. The advent of the Web intensified this trend: Google tools and many other cloud-based applications undergo frequent updates, often without any officially advertised release process. The agile literature has helped anchor the idea of frequent releases into the mindset of the software industry, but agile methods did not invent it.

Another example is the recognition that change plays an important role in software. The better part of the software engineering literature has long emphasized this point. Object technology, which has taken the software world by storm, is successful largely because it supports change better than previous software construction methods. Agile methods may enhance software change through organizational practices, but they make no technical contribution in this area; in fact, as we will see, some of the agile precepts → *"Accept* work *against* making software easy to change. The agile approach is not entitled to its *change", 4.4.5,* blanket contempt of earlier methods of improving extendibility. *page 68.*

1.6.4 New and good!

If at this point you feel ready to throw away the agile bath water, extreme and lean babies included, do not remove the tub stopper just yet. You would be missing some surprisingly good stuff.

The first major contribution is **team empowerment**. Giving a central place to the team and insisting that it can handle many traditional management responsibilities is a plus for any software project staffed by competent people.

When using software systems, for example web applications, have you ever felt like Tintin the day he was being marched in a straightjacket? As soon as you dare to depart from the exact scenario that the designers, in their supreme wisdom, have planned for you, nothing works any more. This kind of system is the direct result of requirements based on the sole analysis of use cases or user stories.

Good requirements shoot for more abstract specifications, subsuming many different scenarios and supporting the development of flexible, extendible applications.

© Hergé/Moulinsart 2014.

1.6.2 New and not good

Pair programming was introduced by the XP. To characterize it as "not good" is a bit strong since pair programming can be an effective technique if applied with reason. XP's insistence that it should be the absolute rule, however, makes little sense conceptually, as it neglects the role of programmer personality (some excellent developers like to concentrate alone and will resent having to be paired), and practically, as studies show pair programming to be no superior to other classical techniques such as code reviews.

Code reviews are also known as inspections.

To a certain extent pair programming can be dismissed as folklore, since many projects that try it stop after a while. Worse consequences of agile methods come from the injunction to develop minimal software, stated earlier as principle 4. Its component rules 4.2 (produce only the product requested) and 4.3 (develop only code and tests) may appeal to inexperienced project managers as a way to combat programmer perfectionism and deliver results quickly, focusing on the essential. But from a software engineering perspective they are not good advice, since they discourage efforts that have proved to be among the most fruitful practices of software engineering: generalizing code for ease of extension and reuse, and developing tools to automate repetitive processes. In Lean terminology, the results of such efforts are "waste" since they are not delivered to the customer; in reality, when applied appropriately, they are the key to the continuous improvement of a company's software process and the professionalization of software practice.

← *"Agile principles", page 4.*

Worse yet is the rejection of upfront requirements. The basic observation is correct: requirements will change, and are hard anyway to capture at the beginning. In no way, however, does it imply the dramatic conclusion that upfront requirements are useless! What it does imply is that requirements should be subject to change, like all other artifacts of the software process. This point has been made by much of the software engineering literature and remains as valid as ever. Unfortunately, many projects in recent years have followed the simplistic agile advice of skipping the systematic requirements phase, replacing it by attempts to evolve the system iteratively with the help of occasional customer interactions. The results are often (predictably) disappointing; projects get delayed because requirements end up being collected anyway, but too late in the lifecyle, when some functionality has already been built; some it will have to be discarded.

The agile advice here is irresponsible and serious software projects should ignore it. The sound practice is to start collecting requirements at the beginning, produce a provisional version prior to engaging in design, and treat the requirements as a living product that undergoes constant adaptation throughout the project.

1.6.3 Not new but good

There is a charmingly adolescent quality to the agile literature: I am sooooo unique! Nobody before me understood what life is about! My folks are sooooo, like, 20-th century!

In reality, despite the scathing attacks on traditional software engineering — the irreparable insult, akin to shouting "liberal!" at a Republican candidate, is "waterfall!" — a number of the productive ideas of agile methods have long been advocated in the standard software engineering literature. We will see examples through the rest of the book; here are two.

The first is iterative development. The industry understood in the nineteen-eighties that the old model of diverging for months and then trying to bring all the pieces back together was a recipe for disaster. A 1995 book by Cusumano and Selby — New York *[Cusumano* Times best-seller, no less — publicized Microsoft's "daily build", a practice which as the *1995]* name indicates requires the project to produce a working version every day. Open-source projects, which have flourished for decades, have a practice of releasing early and often. The advent of the Web intensified this trend: Google tools and many other cloud-based applications undergo frequent updates, often without any officially advertised release process. The agile literature has helped anchor the idea of frequent releases into the mindset of the software industry, but agile methods did not invent it.

Another example is the recognition that change plays an important role in software. The better part of the software engineering literature has long emphasized this point. Object technology, which has taken the software world by storm, is successful largely because it supports change better than previous software construction methods. Agile methods may enhance software change through organizational practices, but they make no technical contribution in this area; in fact, as we will see, some of the agile precepts → *"Accept* work *against* making software easy to change. The agile approach is not entitled to its *change", 4.4.5,* blanket contempt of earlier methods of improving extendibility. *page 68.*

1.6.4 New and good!

If at this point you feel ready to throw away the agile bath water, extreme and lean babies included, do not remove the tub stopper just yet. You would be missing some surprisingly good stuff.

The first major contribution is **team empowerment**. Giving a central place to the team and insisting that it can handle many traditional management responsibilities is a plus for any software project staffed by competent people.

Some of the management practices of agile methods, which may seem simple-minded at first, can actually make a considerable contribution to project success. One of the most significant is Scrum's **daily meeting**; reinforcing programmer interaction, and requiring everyone to describe every morning what he just did, what he will do next, and what impediments he faces, is a brilliant idea, the kind of egg-of-Columbus insight ("*I could have thought of this myself*" — maybe, but you didn't!) that makes a real difference, at least when it can be applied, that is to say, when the whole team is in one place rather than distributed.

A particularly interesting idea is the **freezing of requirements during iterations**. While demonstrating that — whatever the Agile Manifesto says — change is not *always* welcome even in agile development, this principle brings stability to the software process, without seriously hampering the emergence of change requests: they are not rejected, just delayed, and typically not for long since agile iterations are short.

The **time-boxed iteration** is also a productive practice, particularly through its influence on the planning process, since it discourages unrealistic promises.

On the technical side, a major achievement of agile methods has been to establish the **practical importance of tests** and specifically of the regression test suite. The regression testing idea itself is old, but agile methods taught us that the regression suite is a key asset of the project, that many activities should be organized around it (whether or not the project applies test-driven development), and that it is futile to move on to new functionality as long as important tests do not pass. Here we have the agile school at its best, advocating professionalism and quality.

A similar observation applies to several of the ideas listed earlier as "Good but not new". Even if the agile movement does not deserve the credit for inventing these concepts, which previous authors had energetically advocated, it has succeeded in conveying them effectively to the software industry, a significant achievement in itself. The two principal examples are:

- **Short iterations**. While the more competent companies have relied on iterative development for a long time, it is partly thanks to agile ideas that this practice has become so widely accepted.

- **The central role of code**. Once again this is not new but the agile movement has been instrumental in reminding everyone that our primary product is code, not diagrams or documents.

In emphasizing and popularizing these principles, the agile movement places itself in the best tradition of software engineering — of the very compendium of wisdom, accumulated over several decades, that it so haughtily deprecates. When the dust has settled and the field has matured, this is how we will remember the self-proclaimed agile revolution: as an incremental step, which — aside from indulging in some lunacies that were not destined to last long — improved our understanding of existing concepts and introduced a precious few new insights.

2

Deconstructing agile texts

In its quest to convert the world, the agile literature resorts to various devices, some of them, let us say, intellectually less impeccable than others. As a preparation for the detailed study of the method, it is important to know these devices and be prepared to look beyond them. We start with a typical example and move on to a more detailed analysis.

2.1 THE PLIGHT OF THE TRAVELING SEMINARIST

The example comes from one of the important agile books, *Succeeding with Agile* by Cohn, widely used and cited in the agile world. The author, an experienced consultant, is one of the main figures in the movement. The extract comes at the start of a chapter extolling the advantages of verbal communication over written documents.

> *There is a grand myth about requirements — if you write them down, users will get exactly what they want. That's not true. At best, users will get exactly what was written down, which may or may not be anything like what they really want. Written words are misleading — they look more precise than they are. For example, recently I wanted to run a three-day public training course. My assistant and I had discussed this, so I sent her an e-mail saying* "**Please book the Hyatt in Denver**", *and reminded her of the dates. The next day she e-mailed me,* "**the hotel is booked**". *I e-mailed back* "**Thanks**" *and turned my attention toward other matters.*
>
> *About a week later she e-mailed me saying* "**the hotel is booked on the days you wanted. What do you want to me do? Do you want to try another hotel in Denver? A different week? A different city?**". *She and I had completely miscommunicated about the meaning of "booked". When she told me* "**the hotel is booked**", *she meant* "**The room we usually use at the Hyatt is already taken**". *When I read* "**the hotel is booked**", *I took it as a confirmation that she had booked the hotel like I had requested. Neither of us did anything wrong in this exchange. Rather, it is an example of how easy it is to miscommunicate, especially with written language. If we had been talking rather than e-mailing, I would have thanked her when she told me* "**the hotel is booked**". *The happy tone of my voice would have confused her, and we would have caught our miscommunication right then.*
>
> *Beyond this problem, there are other reasons to favor discussions over documents.*

Citation from *[Cohn 2010]*, page 236. Emphasis added, otherwise verbatim quote.

I am going to tell you what I think of this anecdote and its generalization, but before you turn the page please take a moment to form your own opinion; it should make reading the discussion more interesting.

B. Meyer, *Agile!*, DOI 10.1007/978-3-319-05155-0_2,
© Springer International Publishing Switzerland 2014

2.1.1 Proof by anecdote

We start with two observations, one immediate and the other less obvious:

- The argument would fit well in a seminar presentation (maybe this is where it originated); put in writing, it is so incongruous that the serious reader might dismiss it offhand. In other words it provides an excellent refutation of its own message, since the absurdity that might remain unnoticed verbally becomes obvious in writing.

- The senselessness of the intended lesson should not hide the gems of wisdom that the anecdote contains, even if they are not what the author emphasizes.

Let us start with the attempted argument. Its first problem is that it follows a form of logic that appears worryingly often in the software literature (particularly but not exclusively in agile books): proof by anecdote. An anecdote is not a proof; as we saw in the preface, all it can prove is that a generalization does *not* hold. It is not even an argument; if can help an argument, but only if it is backed by enough evidence of being generalizable. Here, for every story of a hotel booking that email messed up and verbal communication might have avoided, there is an equally fascinating anecdote "proving" the reverse truth. I could tell you, for example, of the time when I wanted to convince my future wife to go out with me and on the phone I said... I could but (relax!) I will not, first because my love life is none of your business, second because you got the point already. *← "Analysis: instinctive, experiential, logical or empirical?", page xi.*

Here in fact is another anecdote, this one software-related. I recently witnessed, in a project, a bug that took two weeks to understand and fix because a developer was away. Sometimes the program would not terminate. It turned out that the code was calling one of the developer's routines on a data structure that occasionally was cyclic; the routine was traversing the structure, assuming it was acyclic, and looping forever if not. On his return, the developer found out what was happening and remarked that *"everyone knew"* the assumption of acyclicity. Perhaps, but "everyone" else had forgotten; good thing for the project that at least one person remembered! Even without the benefit of writing in the code an explicit precondition (**require** *structure.is_acyclic*), as you can do in some programming languages, it would have been better, and probably would have avoided the bug and the waste of time, simply to write down this requirement somewhere.

While I find this anecdote more relevant to a software engineering discussion than the story of a hotel booking mishap, someone else may disagree; and neither of them proves anything. Advocates of verbal communication and written specification could endlessly throw such war stories at each other without convincing the other party. An anecdote is just an anecdote.

Paul Dubois tells the following anecdote about anecdotes. In World War II, the military commissioned his future psychology professor to study whether it was better to train troops directly on a new rifle, or start with the older model then explain the differences. The professor does the research. At the meeting, one general offers: *"Ya gotta crawl before you can walk"*. Another counters, *"You ride the horse you're gonna ride in the race"*. The discussion escalates into a war of aphorisms, a decision is made; no one asks about the study. Luckily, its conclusion was that it did not matter.

All that Cohn's story "proves" is that he should find himself a better assistant. Contrary to what he writes ("*Neither of us did anything wrong in this exchange*"), it was a mistake, after the first email response, not to write back "so, what do you want me to do?". Such mistakes, however, can happen in verbal as well as written communication.

2.1.2 When writing beats speaking

In the case of software projects, which after all are the focus, there are many reasons for writing down at least part of the requirements:

- The spoken word is notoriously ambiguous, much more than written requirements. If we bemoan that requirements "look more precise than they are", the conclusion should be that we need *more* precise forms of requirements; that would mean formal (mathematical) specifications, probably not what the author is suggesting.

- The difficulty of achieving precision in spoken communication is the very reason why so many verbal requirements or design discussions end up with the request "*please write this down!*", meaning that the person being asked to provide a mechanism cannot make a final pronouncement before having seen the request on paper.

- Many projects today involve people of different backgrounds and particularly different accents. It can be hard — say in a Skype discussion between teams in Germany and in India, both using English, or believing they are — to make out the details of what the other party is trying to say. Again the usual conclusion is "*email this to me please*". While people also make mistakes in written language, it is much easier in writing to stick to a common language subset that everyone understands in the same way.

- Verbal discussions are known only to those who attend them. A written description does not have the warm-and-fuzzy feeling of a verbally agreed decision, but it can be circulated to any number of people. When software people talk to a representative of the customer company, they often do not know whether that particular person has the expertise and authority to specify a property of the system, or is just expressing a personal preference. Company environments have many actors and many viewpoints; it is dangerous to follow the lead of the last person you heard. Anything written down can be checked by many stakeholders, who will raise an alarm, before it is too late, when they see a requirement reflecting a partial or biased view.

- People in a software project come and go. One of the benefits of consigning requirement elements to writing is that they survive the context of a conversation, when six months later no one remembers why a particular decision was taken; or, worse yet, key participants are no longer around.

The discussion extends beyond software. If verbally communicated requirements were truly superior to written ones, engineering of any kind could discard such old-hat techniques as design specifications and plans, relying instead on frequent interactions between engineers and other stakeholders. After all, our forebears did build pyramids and cathedrals that way. But modern engineering is possible precisely because the builders of houses, bridges, aircraft, circuits — and software — do not stop at a friendly chat and a handshake, but insist on consigning the specifications on paper and having all sides endorse the result. No one has ever argued that writing things down removes every risk of "miscommunicating"; but if speaking them was the solution, humankind would have spared itself the whole detour through written language.

Think of all that time we wasted in grade school learning reading and writing, while we could have been enjoying the park and at the same time honing our conversation skills!

2.1.3 Discovering the gems

Setting aside its method (proof by anecdote) and its exaggerations, Cohn's discussion does contain three software engineering lessons, even if they are not the ones advertised.

The observation that *"Written words are misleading — they look more precise than they are"* is a genuine insight. The authority of the written word can be dangerous. Human language, written or spoken, is treacherously ambiguous; a well-known example *See e.g. [IEEE* in requirements is "the system shall respond in real-time", which in the end means *1998].* nothing: a response coming after a tenth of a second is real-time for a banking terminal and eternity for a network router. But the alternative is not spoken language, which is even less precise.

The alternative, when precision is the goal, is mathematics. The requirement $answer.time - query.time \leq 0.1$ does not look more precise than it is: it looks precise and it is precise. But this is not what Cohn has in mind. He is concerned about taking written requirements too seriously just because they are written. This is a valid concern, and yields the first meaningful lesson from this text: **Do not let the written form of a requirement element impress you into believing that everything has been clearly defined. Written implies neither precise nor correct**.

Useful as it is, this observation describes a problem, not a solution. The solution, if one exists, is certainly not to switch to the spoken word.

The second lesson is that **communication is hard**. All right, you knew that before reading Cohn's text or the present discussion, but communication is a particular challenge for software development. In any large and ambitious project (and in many smaller ones) communication issues are just as important as technical issues, and can wreck the project if the leadership does not handle them properly and proactively. They are critical for geographically distributed projects, where the usual issues of communication are compounded by distance, time differences, and the team members' diverse mother tongues, accents and cultural assumptions. (As a hilarious illustration, a YouTube video recorded by an Indian engineer *[Dhawan 2008]* explains the various meanings of "yes", "no" and head nodding in India.)

What about *spoken* communication? The lesson here is that **written descriptions are not enough; the various project stakeholders should talk** (where "stakeholders" include the development team as well as customers and users). Cohn undoubtedly had in mind the kind of strict environment where documents are all that matters. Case in point (this time a milestone incident of software engineering history, not a minor anecdote): the $125-million loss in 1999 of NASA's Mars Orbiter Vehicle was due to a software error that escaped all review processes; while NASA has standardized on the metric system, one contractor used English Imperial units in one of the modules, passing along a measurement that another module then interpreted as if it were metric. The observation in this case is in line with Cohn's: documents are great, but they can miss essential and seemingly obvious information. Those people should have been talking to each other!

See the official report: [NASA 1999].

Verbal communication is, however, a complement to written documents, not a replacement.

2.1.4 Agile texts: reader beware!

This example is representative of what you will often find in the agile literature, and its analysis provides a good guide of how to use that literature.

This conclusion itself generalizes from one example. The generalization is, however, pretty safe: the emphasis on verbal and other informal forms of communication is common in agile circles and not specific to the cited book. Alistair Cockburn, for example, writes that "*typed-in, paper-based documentation is one of the most expensive, time-consuming and least communicative forms available (never mind that it is traditionally the most frequently requested)*". Well, there is a reason such documents are frequently requested: they can be organized systematically, archived and searched.

[Cockburn 2005], page 179.

As examples of replacement, Cockburn suggests that the team "*videotape one of their designers explaining a section of the design*" and states: "*paper napkins happen to be my favorite documentation medium. They can be posted on the wall or scanned*". Sure, but when the time comes to find out whether a key system property was decided one way or another and why, searching text beats sifting through hours of video recordings or heaps of scanned paper napkins.

Agile authors are on a mission to convince the reader; their zeal leads them to simplify complex matters and draw conclusions that are sometimes warranted and sometimes not. As the field progresses, future books and articles will apply higher intellectual standards (they might also become more boring in the process). Until then, you must keep your defenses up. You must also keep an open mind and be prepared to draw your own conclusions, even when the author's own do not hold up to examination.

2.2 THE TOP SEVEN RHETORICAL TRAPS

The textual deconstruction just performed is a good preparation for coping with other techniques, of similarly questionable soundness, used by agile authors to advocate their approaches. As training for the rest of our trip and for your own forays into agile literature, here is the Top 7 list of the most outrageous rhetorical devices, not unique to agile authors of course, but particularly popular in their texts:

1 **Proof by anecdote**, which we have seen at work in this example. An anecdote, or ten, are not a proof.

2 **Slander by association**: lumping together an idea that an author wants to criticize with one that everyone loathes. Non-agile ideas get that treatment.

3 **Intimidation**: labeling anyone who does not buy the agile gospel, chapter and verse, as a reactionary control freak.

4 **Catastrophism**: pretending that software development as currently practiced is a disaster (so that only your agile method can save it).

5 **All-or-nothing**. promoting an extremist method, not practicable in its entirety, so that project successes can be ascribed to agile techniques and failures to their incomplete application.

6 **Cover-your-behind**: advocating radical prescriptions; then as a footnote stating that they may not after all be always applicable; but never saying precisely when they should be used and when not.

7 **Unverifiable claims**. The Scrum literature in particular routinely touts enormous productivity improvements. Who would not want to multiply project effectiveness by an order of magnitude? In the absence of rigorous independent verification, you should take such assertions (depending on your benevolence on that particular day) as either a sign of charming youthful enthusiasm or irrelevant hype to be discarded. *[Schwaber 2012], page 6: "90% improvement".*

Dubious rhetorical techniques do not disprove the value of the ideas being proposed, but do invite the reader to exert caution. We should both keep an open mind and not lower our methodological guard. The first step is to be aware of the seven traps to be described now.

2.2.1 Proof by anecdote

Agile books largely make their point through anecdotes; the example at the beginning of this chapter is typical.

Anecdotes are good for books, and for teaching in general. They can also backfire: if the anecdote serves as the basis for a general statement, a reader whose own anecdotal experience does not match the author's will reject the generalization. We will see an example in a later chapter with Poppendieck's enthusiastic invocation of a role model who in hindsight looks like a less than fortunate choice: Lance Armstrong. *← "Lean Software: an assessment". 9.2.3. page 135.*

Another example from the same author is her heartrending story of a bus driver at Disneyland who spotted a little girl crying and managed to have a Mickey Mouse actor greet her; the anecdote is supposed to illustrate the importance of quality. For the reader who has been to Disneyland with children, and found that the whole place, smiling drivers or not, is grossly under-dimensioned, so that one spends most of the day waiting in lines, this is not a good omen; the obvious generalization to software is a Web site that features a pretty interface and pathetic response times. Raising analogies in your readers' mind is good, but beware of where they will take them.

[Poppendieck 2003], page 16.

The general problem with an anecdote is that it is to a principle what — in software — a test is to a specification: it gives you one example and you are never sure how much you can extrapolate from that example to the general case.

2.2.2 Slander by association

An effective — if not too commendable — way to criticize an idea is to associate it, in the reader's mind, with one that everyone dislikes.

The positive counterpart of this technique is honorable: choose for your own ideas a name that connotes a pleasant feeling, and leave it to your audience to get the opposite feeling for the opposing ideas, or just different ones. This is smart marketing, which one can only admire; as noted in the preface of this book, the choice of the word "*agile*" is brilliant.

The negative version, however, is a different matter: improperly associating competing ideas with terms or concepts that the audience is likely to find repulsive. Here the favorite butt of agile scorn is the "waterfall" process, something that everyone knows is bad. But of course not everyone who does not agree with all agile ideas is preaching a return to a nineteen-seventies-style waterfall process; in fact almost no one practices it, and absolutely no one advocates it. Still we will find, in the next chapter, leading agile authors repeatedly lumping any non-agile ("predictive") approach with the waterfall, as in "*the predictive, or waterfall, process is in trouble*". It is a cheap trick; do not fall for it.

→ *"Predictive is not waterfall", page 31.*

2.2.3 Intimidation

The next set of dubious arguments takes advantage of the positive vibes that the term "agile" immediately sends, and of the general good feeling elicited by the hipness of the agile movement, to cast anyone who raises questions as a reactionary moron.

A good concentrate of the kind of artillery that awaits the impartial observer is a 2012 *Forbes* magazine article by Steve Denning intended to refute "*Ten Management Objections*" to agile methods. The author, a former World Bank director, is a business guru with an impressive list of Fortune-500 customers.

[Denning 2012] (also source of other citations in this subsection except as otherwise marked).

As Agile harangues go, this is not the most subtle — it is a full frontal charge against anyone who might question the sacred world — but in its very exaggeration it provides a useful checklist of what to expect if you have the temerity to think for yourself.

You will be hooted down because you reject novelty. Denning's paper starts with the Einstein quote that

"If at first an idea is not absurd, there is no hope for it".

It is always good practice, for an author whose arguments are a bit shaky, to use a hackneyed Einstein citation. You will find lots of them around the Web, some even authentic. Against Einstein, what are we poor souls to do?

Settle for mediocrity, that's what!

Agile squeezes out mediocrity and requires high-performance. Hierarchical bureaucracy breeds incompetence and feeds off mediocrity: the organization performs accordingly. Faced with the choice between high-performance and the mediocrity, traditional management opts for mediocrity.

Wow! Just one insult at a time, please. Bureaucrats; mediocre; incompetent. Thanks.

Einstein's witticism can serve to justify anything. The particular intellectual device invoked here is a variant of the logical fallacy of deducing "B implies A" from "A implies B". We may call it the **Columbus syndrome**: people thought Christopher Columbus's project absurd, and he was onto something big; you think that *my* idea is rubbish, so I must be onto something big. Or as Calvin put it in his decisive argument (Einstein again):

One of the main arguments in Denning's paper is a textbook case of the Columbus syndrome: over four paragraphs, he recalls the story of the discovery by John Harrison, in the eighteenth century, of how to measure longitude precisely by building better clocks; but: *The story is taken from a best-seller, [Sobel 2007].*

The scientists refused to concede that they had been wrong and give John Harrison his well-deserved prize.

What does this have to do with agile methods, you ask? You mediocre, incompetent bureaucrat! Denning explains:

Something similar seems to be happening with Agile.

Now lots of people come up with ideas that "experts" reject; sometimes the experts are wrong, but often they are right to reject the new idea. If I start arguing that the earth is flat, I will be scorned by the experts: *"something similar"* will *"seem to happen"* and I will fail (what a scandal!) to get my *"well-deserved prize"*. Why are the experts more wrong in the agile case than in that one? No clue.

The invocation of expert rejection is another rhetorical device. Many defenders of a cause feel more comfortable if they can identify an enemy; or, if none is available, make one up. It particularly helps to argue that the Establishment is against your ideas. In this case, however, the enemy is rather gracious. The software engineering world has been receptive to agile ideas, giving them ample resonance in the community's most presti- *[Boehm 2004].* gious forums, including its top conferences (OOPSLA, ICSE, ESEC...). An important book that empirically assesses agile techniques, published shortly after agile ideas burst onto the scene, has as its lead author one of the most venerated figures of traditional soft- ware engineering, and provides an open and measured account of the approach. We are not talking about persecuted innovators facing an entrenched order. The establishment has been inclusive and welcoming.

Will it help if — in the footsteps of empirical studies as collected by Boehm and Turner — you perform an objective, empirical analysis of how agile methods work in your organization? No, that would be irrelevant. If you tried an agile method and found it did not work, what conclusion do you draw? Silly question. *You* are the problem:

> *When the culture doesn't fit Agile, the solution is not to reject Agile. The solution is to change the organizational culture. One doesn't even have to look at the business results of firms using hierarchical bureaucracy to know that they are fatally ill.*

(Brings to mind another quotation, not quite Einstein this time, sorry, just Brecht: *"The* *Brecht poem: see* *people have forfeited the confidence of the government; would it not be easier for the* *bit.ly/h1rKGS.* *government to dissolve the people, and elect another?"*)

Like others in Denning's paper this argument does not include any specific evidence, so it could serve to support any radical idea, useful or silly. Note how the reasoning slips into a faith-based argument: *one doesn't even have to look at the business results*. At that level of irrationality, it is not clear what we are supposed to do; if we will not look at busi- ness results, what is the point of discussing management techniques?

If you are not an enthusiastic promoter of agile approaches, you are by definition a dinosaur. The technical term is *"member of the command-and-control gang"*. Agile teams self-organize, use *"radical management"*, and non-followers are *"control-minded man- agement practitioners and theorists"*. I can think of a few people who fit this last descrip- tion. Steve Jobs, for example. Judging by the effects of his management — although admittedly this means that we *"look at the business results"* — he must not have been such an ineffective manager. Now his management style may not be to everyone's taste, but that is precisely the point: a large spectrum of styles exists, from the completely self-organized team to the military-style organization micro-managed by a control freak, and many variants in-between. More than one strategy can work, and a strategy that suc- ceeds in one environment may fail in another. Summary judgments against those who do not pliantly follow of the latest fashion are an obstacle, not a benefit.

The rest of the article, which you should read as a form of vaccine, is of the same flavor.

With such defenders, who needs enemies? Serious agile proponents should be wary of the damage caused by extreme propaganda of this kind: hype and intimidation can convince a company once, but every decision-maker will sooner or later "*look at the business results*" and is likely, if they do not live up to the hype, to throw away good ideas with bad.

The zealots of an idea are often more extreme than its creators — the phrase "more royalist than the King" captures that phenomenon — and you will find that foundational agile texts, such as those by Beck, Larman or Cockburn, occupy a higher plane of discourse; in particular they avoid below-the-belt hits at other approaches.

Such hits from the true followers are what you risk if you set out to define a measured, reasoned adaptation of agile ideas for your organization. Well, you have been warned. In this book we fearlessly (applause for the courage, please!) undertake to untangle the best from the not-so-good and the pretty bad.

2.2.4 Catastrophism

When you are advocating a new approach, it is natural to highlight flaws of the current ways of doing things. If everything were perfect, why should people listen to you? Certainly the state of software engineering leaves much to be criticized. To be credible, however, such criticism must be accurate.

Software engineering started around 1968 with the recognition of a "software crisis". For many years it was customary to start any article on any software topic by a lament about the horrible situation of the field; you would not *explicitly* write that the little contribution of your article — a methodological idea, a new programming language, a programming tool — was going to solve the "crisis"; it was enough to plant the suggestion in the reader's mind and let him draw the conclusion.

After the field had matured, this lugubrious style (everything is rotten in the kingdom of software) went out of fashion. It is indeed hard to sustain: in a world where every device we use, every move we make and every service we receive is powered by software, it sounds a trifle silly to claim that software development is all broken and everyone is wrong.

The apocalyptic mode has, however, made a comeback in the agile literature, which is fond in particular of citing the "Chaos" reports. Emanating from the Standish Group, a consulting firm, these reports purport to show that a large percentage of projects miss their goals or fail entirely. It was fashionable to cite Standish (I even included a citation in a 2003 paper), until the methodology and results were debunked starting in 2006 [Glass 2006] [Eveleens 2010]. To summarize, these results are inconsistent, not confirmed by other studies, and based on proprietary data that independent researchers are not permitted to see. Yet to this day they continue to be reverently cited as a justification for agile processes, including in the most recent book by the Scrum creators, who add

> *You have been ill served by the software industry for 40 years—not purposely, but inextricably. We want to restore the partnership.*   [Schwaber 2012], *page 1.*

No less!

I tried to imagine the kind of circumstance that might draw one to issue such a definitive indictment of an entire industry. You can find the result in a "postscript" to this chapter.

→ *"Postscript: you have been ill-served by the software industry!", page 30.*

Software engineering faces enough obstacles, obvious to anyone in the industry and to any user of software products, that we do not need to conjure up imaginary scandals.

The Standish episode also reminds us of the dangers of exaggeration — of either kind, aghast at others' failures or boastful of one's own triumphs — and of software engineering's dire need for sound, credible empirical results.

2.2.5 All-or-nothing

While some agile texts and methods take a measured approach, others, as noted in the preface, insist that to apply their methods you have to use all the associated practices.

While we cannot deny methodologists the right to specify a few incontrovertible principles defining their methods, the number of such absolute requirements has to be small. Otherwise the principles serve as a marketing gimmick, as one can see in the many agile presentations that claim to achieve balance by reporting on case studies of both successful and failed projects. The successful ones demonstrate the power of the method; and the failed projects failed because they dared to ignore one of the recommendations!

The trick is brilliant, but that does not mean we should fall for it. Industry, as noted, ignores such absolutism: every group devises its own selection, picking some practices and rejecting others. Software projects are too diverse, and software development too difficult, to allow for a single recipe that will work identically for everyone.

2.2.6 Cover-your-behind

Not all agile authors want to appear as extremists, but even those who try to shed that image often leave the reader in the dark about when to use the techniques they advocate and when to renounce them. The typical scheme is to extol radical ideas, then as a brief afterthought state that they are not always applicable, without presenting any criterion to decide. It makes the author look reasonable and even-handed, but is not of much help to the practitioner trying to make sense of the advice.

A typical example appears in the foundational book on Lean Software by Mary and Tom Poppendieck. After seven chapters calling for radical changes in software practice, each based on a strong principle, a final chapter humorously entitled "Instructions and warranty" suddenly brings in words of caution:

`Lean ▸`

> *Look for the balance point of the lean principles:*
>   • *Eliminate waste* [first Lean principle] *does not mean throw away all documentation.*
>   • *Amplify learning* [second principle] *does not mean keep on changing your mind.*
>   • *Decide as late as possible* [third principle] *does not mean procrastinate.*

[Poppendieck 2003], page 179.

and so on (four more "***does not mean***" bullet points, one for each of the remaining Lean principles). These comments are intended to demonstrate restraint, but they are useless since the chapter is only eight pages long and says almost nothing about what would actually help practitioners: *when* the principles are not or not fully applicable, and *how* they should be attenuated in such cases.

As software developers or managers, we do not need the blanket observation that extreme principles may need tempering. We figured that out by ourselves. What we do need are criteria for making exceptions. The exceptions and criteria should be specified *along with each principle*, not in a global cop-out which destroys the very credibility of the principles. Rather than "instructions and warranty", such a cop-out resembles the far-sweeping disclaimers attached to many consumer products. It is meant to help not the users of the method, only its authors, for whom it provides cover-your-behind protection. You applied my principle X and your project ended in disaster? Sorry to hear that! I did warn you, of course, that you should look for a balance point.

(Well, yes, thank you so much, but I would have preferred that you tell me what the balance point is.)

At work here is a common style of cover-your-behind: "A1-does-not-mean-A2", where A2 is hardly distinguishable from A1. For example, A1 is "*deciding as late as possible*" and A2 is "*procrastination*". If there is a difference, it is subtle. ("Procrastination" in the Oxford English Dictionary: "*the action or habit of postponing or putting something off; delay; dilatoriness*".)

The agile cover-your-behind device is not specific to the Poppendiecks or to the Lean method. We will encounter examples from many other sources, such as this gem: "*although project development teams are on their own, they are not uncontrolled*".

→ *See this example and others in "Let the team self-organize", page 53.*

When we discover the limits of applying an agile idea dogmatically, we must not fall into the same pitfall ourselves and just declare that one should exercise moderation. This book tries to explain *when* and *how* agile prescriptions should be replaced or combined with other techniques. An example is the balance point (in Poppendieck terms) between the agile rule of producing a running system at every step, and the software engineering benefit of building infrastructure even without immediately user-visible results. It does not help much to state blandly that both viewpoints may have a value depending on the circumstances. The discussion of this issue will present a concrete policy, **"Dual Development"**, combining them in a precisely specified way.

→ *"Dual Development", page 74.*

2.2.7 Unverifiable claims

A document by one of the creators of Scrum is entitled "*The Art of Doing Twice the Work in Half the Time*". If my arithmetic is correct, this means a productivity improvement by a factor of four. Wow. Who would not sign up? In presentations by agile method creators I have heard more extreme claims, of an order of magnitude improvements or more. In a comment we will encounter later, the Poppendiecks imply that applying just one of their recommendations will divide costs by a factor of ten.

[Sutherland 2013].

→ *"Produce only the product requested", page 58.*

We may accept that someone, somewhere, gave an agile method to a team — perhaps a badly demotivated team which suddenly gained both focus and enthusiasm — and stirred it into producing amazing results. The question is what it means for other teams, in particular those already using good software engineering techniques, agile or not.

It is notoriously hard to perform convincing large-scale studies of the effect of software development techniques. Obstacles abound:

- To work under realistic conditions you should take actual projects and collect precise measurements, but not all companies are willing to put in the effort, and even fewer to reveal the results.

- Sometimes two methods are applied in succession because the first project failed. This case is a frequent argument for new methods: "we succeeded where others failed". That may be true, but the comparison is biased: the second time around the team has learned from the first project, even if it was a failure. You can only really compare projects done in parallel, not one after the other.

- Even fewer companies, however, will be willing to fund two projects with the same tasks just to assess methods.

- Assuming such a setup, it remains just one case and does not permit drawing general conclusions since the results may be influenced by the specific task and teams. The experience should be repeated among several projects and ideally among several companies, making the whole prospect even less realistic.

While credible empirical industry results do exist, many empirical studies rely on experiments with university students, which have their value but also obvious limitations.

At the other extreme, you will find an IBM study assessing agile methods; reading the fine print reveals that it was conducted in collaboration with the Scrum Alliance, an advocacy organization for Scrum. Advocacy has its place, but not in empirical research. The study finds much good to report about Scrum; are you surprised? Agile seems to induce so much fever as to make such an organization as IBM, usually more responsible, toss all methodological caution to the wind. Do not toss yours. *[IBM 2012]; see also [Ambler 2012].*

Some company environments are truly messed up. Under-appreciated developers spend their time on repetitive tasks, subject to the whims of incompetent managers. Then a team that suddenly gains the confidence of upper management, the opportunity to try fashionable new ideas, and the benefit of an excellent agile coach, can almost overnight turn from torpor to torpedo. Such feats can even be sustained, showing that they are not just due to the "Hawthorne effect" (a phenomenon, named after the Western Electric plant where it was observed in the 1930s, under which workers perform better as soon as they are *told* that they are experimenting with a new approach, whatever it is, and even if they are not). Drawing general conclusions from such individual experiences is another matter.

Before you go tell your management that by switching to an agile method you will gain a four-fold productivity improvement, or more, think carefully. They might just believe you.

POSTSCRIPT: YOU HAVE BEEN ILL-SERVED BY THE SOFTWARE INDUSTRY!

After reading one description too many (***"you have been ill served by the software industry for 40 years — not purposefully, but inextricably"***) of how terrible everything was before the author rode his white horse to the rescue, I had some fun trying to imagine the circumstances that might lead someone to write such a sentence. Here is the result.

← "Catastrophism", page 26.

On a cold morning of February 2012, Mr. S woke up early. He had set up his iPhone's alarm to a favorite tune from Götterdämmerung, downloaded from a free-MP3 site. He liked his breakfast eggs cooked in a specific way, and got them exactly right since he had programmed his microwave oven to the exact combination of heat and cooking time.

Adapted from [Meyer 2013].

He had left his car to his daughter on the previous night; even though the roads were icy, he did not worry too much for her, since the automatic braking system was good at silently correcting the mistakes of a still somewhat novice driver; and the navigation system would advise her away from any impracticable street.

As for himself he was going for public transportation. He looked up the schedule on the Web and saw that he had a few minutes before the next bus, enough to check his email. He noticed that he had received, as a PDF attachment, the pay slip for his last consulting gig; as an Agile consultant, Mr. S was in high demand. He did not need to check the details since he knew his accountant's system would automatically receive all the information.

He went out and hopped onto the bus, all the way to the client's office continuing to check his email on his phone, even finding the time to confirm the online reservation for his next flight, while checking the large monitor in the bus to avoid missing his stop. On reaching the building, he slid his id into the elevator's slot, gaining access to the right floor.

He brought up his computer from hibernation, for some reason remembering — Mr. S was fond of such trivia — that the newest version of Windows reportedly consisted of over 50 million lines of code, and reflecting that the system now kind of did what he expected. Mr. S had thought of moving to a Mac, following many of his friends, but the advantages were not clear, and he liked the old Word text processing system with which he was writing his latest agile advocacy text, tentatively entitled "Software in 30 days".

[Schwaber 2012].

Mr. S — whose full name was either "Schwaber" or "Sutherland", although it might have been "Scrum" or perhaps "Sprint", as some of the details of the story are missing — opened up the document at the spot where he had left it the evening before. Like many a good author, he had postponed finalizing the introduction to the last moment. Until now inspiration had failed him and his coauthor: it is always so hard to discover how best to begin! Over the past months, working together in long Skype discussions from wherever each happened to be, they had tried many different variants, often simultaneously editing their shared Google Docs draft. But now he suddenly knew exactly what he had to say to capture the readers' attention.

The sentence sprang to his mind in one single, felicitous shot:

> ***You have been ill served by the software industry for 40 years — not purposefully, but inextricably.***

3

The enemy: Big Upfront Anything

Any cause needs a villain. Agile's villain is variously called "waterfall", "process-based methods", "predictive" (see below) and "Big Upfront Anything" where "Anything" particularly includes requirements and design. Boehm and Turner, in the title of a book *[Boehm 2004]* attempting to reconcile agility with traditional software engineering approaches, use "*discipline*"; in the body of the book, however, they note that agile methods can exhibit discipline too, and resort for the classical techniques to "plan-based" — not a bad name.

This chapter summarizes the main characteristics of plan-based approaches, focusing on those that agile proponents typically resent. Covering these approaches in detail would require an entire software engineering textbook; here we only need a bird's eye view of the principal ideas.

3.1 PREDICTIVE IS NOT WATERFALL

First, a word of warning, complementing the advice of the previous chapter. In their most recent book, the creators of Scrum write:

> *Although the predictive, or waterfall, process is in trouble, many people and organizations continue to try to make it work.*

[Schwaber 2012], page 29.

and later in the same paragraph:

> *[A customer was using] services from PricewaterhouseCoopers (PWC). The PWC approach was predictive, or waterfall.*

[Leffingwell 2011], pages 5-6, also presents "predictive" as a synonym for "waterfall".

The book's index entry for "*Predictive process*" reads "*See Waterfall*".

At play here is one of the intellectual devices identified earlier: slander by association — *repetitive* association. "*Waterfall*" means a specific lifecycle model, whose main role (since it hardly exists in the practice of software engineering) is pedagogical: it serves as a textbook example of how **not** to organize a software project. Even the 1970 article that *[Royce 1970].* first explicitly described the model did so to *criticize* it. Ever since, waterfall-bashing has been the favorite sport of software engineering authors. "*Predictive*" is something else. Engineering is by definition predictive: it tries to organize a greater or lesser part of the design and production process in advance, based on techniques of science and management. There are a myriad predictive approaches out there that are not the waterfall. Attempting by force of repetition to lump "predictive" in the reader's mind with the classic punching ball of software engineering, and hence to discredit anything that is not the authors' own approach, is a dubious device that does not help advance understanding.

B. Meyer, *Agile!*, DOI 10.1007/978-3-319-05155-0_3,
© Springer International Publishing Switzerland 2014

The discussion in this chapter summarizes approaches that are predictive to a greater or lesser extent. Not every one of them is to everyone's taste and some are subject to obvious criticism, but they have been widely used and helped make many projects successful. Just as agile methods, they are part of what we know about software engineering.

← *Unless you believe that until agile came around all projects were failures. See "Catastrophism", page 26.*

3.2 REQUIREMENTS ENGINEERING

Software engineering is not just programming but solving a problem of interest to some people, its "stakeholders". Defining what the problem really is, and what kind of solution will satisfy the stakeholders — a task known as requirements analysis — is one of the most important aspects of successful software development: building an otherwise perfect system that does not meet stakeholder needs is not very useful. Study after study has shown that requirements mistakes are among the worst to plague software projects. Much of software engineering is about building systems right; requirements are about building the right system.

3.2.1 Requirements engineering techniques

Requirements analysis has developed into a full-fledged discipline with many useful techniques, tools and methodological principles, described in software engineering textbooks as well as specialized books on the topic. An important part of requirements analysis is requirements *elicitation*: gathering user needs. Elicitation techniques include:

General textbooks: e.g. [Ghezzi 2002], [Pfleeger 2009]

- Stakeholder **interviews**: going around and asking people what they need.
- Stakeholder **workshops**: bringing together a group of stakeholders to discuss requirements. Workshops are particularly useful when various classes of stakeholders exist, with different and sometimes conflicting wishes; identifying the contradictions and discussing them openly helps understand and resolve them.

The result of a requirements process typically includes a **requirements document**, which summarizes the objectives of the system. Other important outcomes — sometimes integrated in the requirements document, sometimes yielding separate documents — are a **system test plan** (since the requirements define the conditions against which the system will have to be tested) and a **development plan**.

Traditionally, a requirements document was a single, sequential text, but the term also covers modern, more flexible formats such as a Web site, a wiki (advocated, in an agile context, by Larman) or a cloud-based collaborative document (e.g. Google Docs).

[Larman 2010], page 275

3.2.2 Agile criticism of upfront requirements

The agile school rejects the idea of upfront requirements. The rejection is common to all agile variants. Beck, arguing for XP, writes:

> *Requirements gathering isn't a phase that produces a static document, but an activity producing detail, just before it is needed, throughout development.*

[Beck 2005], page 137.

Cohn, in the Scrum context and as part of a broad-encompassing rejection of Big-Upfront-Anything:

> *Scrum projects do not have an upfront analysis or design phase; all work occurs within the repeated cycle of sprints.*   *[Cohn 2009].*

Agilists view requirements documents as a form of "waste", for two reasons:

- The **waste criticism**: a requirements document is not a useful deliverable, since it will not be part of what is given over to the customer. Poppendieck writes:

    > *If your company writes reams of requirements documents (equivalent to inventory), you are operating with mass-production paradigms. Think "lean" and you will find a better way.*   *[Poppendieck lean], 7 November 2002 and 24 June 2004.*

    In case you are wondering, "*operating with mass-production paradigms*" is not a compliment. Further:

    > *Inventory in the software development value stream is partially done work [such as] requirements that are not analyzed and designed.*

    The analogy here is with inventory in manufacturing, a form of waste.

- The **change criticism**: the agile view is that customers do not know what they want; if they think they do, it might be an unrealistic system; and they will change their minds anyhow. The only way to satisfy them is to start building some piece of the system, show it to them, gather feedback and iterate.

These two objections, the waste criticism and the change criticism, are often commingled into one. Beck, for example, writes:

> *Software development is full of the waste of overproduction, [such as] requirements documents that rapidly grow obsolete.*   *[Beck 2005], page 136.*

This is again a case of criticism by association: conflating the two arguments makes it easier to criticize upfront requirements. Note how Beck's earlier citation (at the bottom of the previous page) rejects the notion of a "*phase that produces a static document*"; but these are two different things: as we will see in more detail, requirements can both be a separate phase (in the software process) and produce a document that changes.

In reality the two arguments are distinct; we will review them in turn.

3.2.3 The waste criticism

The waste criticism is in principle limited to *unused* requirements ("*not analyzed and designed*" in Poppendieck's terms). This is not much of a restriction, since when you write requirements they are by definition not yet analyzed and designed, and you do not know whether they will be retained. In fact the purpose of writing requirements is precisely to have a sound basis, early in the project, to discuss the system's future functions, and in particular to decide which functions to drop.

Does this mean that the effort was "waste"? To decide, we must compare two techniques for weeding out unnecessary functions:

1   The plan-first approach: perform an upfront requirements process, rate the importance of the functions that come out of that process, decide which ones are not essential, and get rid of them.

2   The agile approach: select a few initial functions, start implementing them, and if the result is not satisfactory for customers get rid of the unnecessary stuff.

Each approach has merits. It is usually cheaper (approach 1) to kill a superfluous feature at the requirements stage, before it has wasted implementation resources. This is also better for the morale of the team: developers get frustrated when something they implemented gets discarded; that form of waste is worse than tossing out a requirement before anything has been done with it. On the other hand, agilists are right that sometimes the best way (approach 2) to find out if something will be useful is to build it, show it, and see whether it fits.

Sometimes, but not always. The problem here is dogmatism. Upfront requirements are useful; iterative development is useful. Condemning either of these two complementary techniques in the name of some absolutist ideology does not help projects, but actually harms them.

The agile criticism is right on target when it lambasts the huge requirements documents, sometimes running into the thousands of pages, that some bureaucratic environments demand. While describing every single detail in advance is necessary for some life-critical systems (typically embedded systems, for example in transportation), for most business systems such documents are overkill; they become so complex that it is hard to get them right (contradictions and ambiguities creep in), and so unwieldy that they end up forgotten on a shelf rather than being used for the development.

This criticism does not justify throwing away the notion of upfront written requirements. First, we should note that even a strict definition of "waste" as anything that does not get delivered to the customer does not necessarily exclude requirements documents, since requirements often provide a good basis for writing *system documentation*. But there are even more fundamental reasons to retain a certain dose of upfront requirements. Software, in spite of its specificities (its virtual nature, the ease of changing it), is an engineering artifact. There is no justification for renouncing the basic engineering technique of specifying what you are going to do, in writing and at the appropriate level of detail, before you do it.

In sum: there is a middle ground between one extreme, absurdly bureaucratic, and the other, absurdly informal.

That comment was not strong enough. Starting any significant software project (anything beyond a couple of months and a couple of developers) without taking the time to write some basic document defining the core requirements is professional malpractice.

I *once* let myself be swayed by a customer company's project managers, who said: "we do not need a requirements phase, we are agile, we can jump in right away". Spending a few weeks upfront just on defining the system's functions precisely would have saved the project many months of delay, and the team many sleepless nights. I will not repeat that experience.

3.2.4 The change criticism

The agile emphasis on change is correct: it is hopeless to try to freeze the requirements at the beginning of the project. Even if by some combination of talent, experience and luck you could get them right, the customers would change their wishes as they start seeing versions of the system, which will give them new ideas.

The resulting charge against requirements, however, is largely hitting at a strawman. No serious software engineering text advocates freezing requirements at the beginning. The requirements document is just one of the artifacts of software development, along with code modules and regression tests (for many agilists, the only artifacts worthy of consideration) but also documentation, architecture descriptions, development plans, test plans and schedules. In other words, **requirements are software**. Like other components of the software, requirements should be treated as an asset; and like all of them, they can change (and in practice should be put under the control of configuration management tools).

To invoke the changeability of requirements as a reason to reject upfront requirements makes no sense. The proper technical response to the observation that requirements will change is: "*so what?*". When you write an article, its structure will change as you go; most people still find it useful to start with a table of contents, knowing that it is not cast in stone. (One may even suspect that some of the best agile books started with a table of contents, too — just a conjecture, of course.) When a company launches a new product, it has a marketing plan, *and* is ready to adapt it as things evolve. These are only examples — among many possible ones — from fields other than software, but they do indicate that *writing* requirements does not imply *freezing* requirements.

> Military strategists like to quote Marshal Helmuth von Moltke: "*No battle plan survives contact with the enemy*". They quote it — and then they make plans! The situation is exactly the same in software: we know that plans are only plans and will have to be adapted to reality. That is not a reason for dumping the notion of plan altogether.

We note once again the confusion inherent in such agile criticism as Beck's comment that "*Requirements gathering isn't a phase that produces a static document*", as if having a requirements *phase* implied that the resulting requirements document will be *static*. The two matters are separate.

In fact the appropriate software engineering technique is to have a requirements phase *and* treat the resulting document as a dynamic product. Similarly, when Beck adds that instead of a phase, requirements gathering is "an activity", he invokes a non-existent contradiction: we should treat requirements gathering as a phase *and* as an activity that continues, after that phase, throughout the project.

Here as in many earlier cases, the lesson is to appreciate the validity of the agile observation and ignore its unwarranted extremist conclusions.

3.2.5 The domain and the machine

In comparing traditional requirements processes with the agile approach, an additional concept to consider is the distinction between *domain* and *machine* requirements, emphasized for many years by Pamela Zave and Michael Jackson. The idea is simple: *[Zave 1997], [Jackson 1995], [Jackson 2000].*

- Some requirements elements describe properties of a model of a part of the world, or "domain", in which the system will operate.

- Others describe desired properties of the system, or "machine", that the project wants to build.

In a banking application, rules on accounts, deposits and overdrafts are domain properties; specifications of how to process payments and other operations are machine properties. In software for phones, the laws of physics, defining for example limits on signal speed, and the company's call pricing policy, are "domain"; the functions of the system, which must be compatible with these constraints, are "machine". Although requirements documents often intertwine the two kinds, it is essential, say Jackson and Zave, to separate them because they are of a different nature: the project defines the machine, but it has no influence on the domain. Commingling them causes confusion and mistakes.

A frequent agilist comment is that "requirements are design", meaning that it is pointless to pretend that requirements exist as pure customer needs whereas they are in fact decisions on the system to be built. The Poppendiecks write:

> *And those things called requirements? They are really candidate solutions;* *[Poppendieck* *separating requirements from implementation is just another form of handover.* *2010], page 31.*

("Handover" is one of the kinds of waste.) Here requirements are viewed as equivalent not just to design, but directly to implementation; the authors argue elsewhere that design *Pages 54-55 of* and implementation are the same thing. *the same work.*

Justified or not, such comments can only apply to the *machine* part of requirements; the *domain* properties do exist independently of any system. Here are examples of rules that are clearly requirements and not "candidate solutions":

- In a business system: "Any transaction over $10,000 requires approval by a supervisor". This statement describes a business rule, perhaps a legal obligation; not something that the project decides, but a constraint that the implementation must satisfy. If it does not, the implementation is incorrect. What competent software manager would ever embark on a banking system, constrained by such rules, without setting aside time, *up front*, to write them down?

- In an embedded system: "All cell phone communications shall take place within the allocated frequency range" (also defined precisely in the requirements). Another example of a fundamental constraint imposed on the project by its environment.

It is the responsibility of the project to identify such domain properties *as requirements*, separate from design decisions. And it should do so early. Missing an important constraint means that when it is finally discovered some of the code developed so far will have to be thrown out. Here we are not talking about incremental development anymore, but about elementary professional competence.

As in many other cases, agilists identify a real issue: the risk of spending time too early on design or implementation decisions, camouflaged as requirements for respectability, whereas it would be better to defer them until more information becomes available. But from this observation on the excesses of some traditional projects, agilists embark on undue generalization and hasten to their own reverse excess, which is just as bad. Denying the existence of requirements as separate from design and implementation stands in the face of reason. That difference is simply the software engineering version of the difference between problem and solution.

The speed of light is not an implementation decision.

3.3 ARCHITECTURE AND DESIGN

If requirements analysis describes the problem, design is part of the solution. In software, the solution will be ultimately expressed by the code; but the code is concrete, containing all the details, whereas the design defines the overall modular structure, or *architecture*, of the solution. Examples of design decisions include: choices of *abstractions* (in object-oriented development these will be in particular *data* abstractions, expressed as classes); use of *design patterns*, which describe standard software structures for addressing specific problems, for example the "Visitor" pattern to support traversal of data structures; specification of *interfaces* between modules, and definition of *inheritance* structures to organize sets of related abstractions into coherent taxonomies.

See [Gamma 1994] on design patterns.

There is little meaningful difference between "design" and "architecture". For clarity, this discussion will use "design" for the process and "architecture" for its result (then we do not need "architect" as a verb). The same convention can be applied to "implementation" and "code".

3.3.1 Is design separate from implementation?

Many traditional software engineering methods present design as a separate phase, but there has been growing recognition that no clear boundary exists between design and implementation. As early as 1968, the conference that started software engineering as a scientific discipline included a session about the difference between design and "*production (or implementation)*" where Peter Naur said:

> *The distinction between design and production is essentially a practical one, imposed by the need for a division of the labor. In fact, **there is no essential difference between design and production**, since even the production will include decisions which will influence the performance of the software system, and thus properly belong in the design phase.*

[NATO 1968], page 31, emphasis added.

and Edsger Dijkstra:

> *Honestly, I cannot see how these activities allow a rigid separation if we are*
> *going to do a decent job. If you have your production group, it must produce*
> *something, but the thing to be produced has to be correct, has to be good.*
> *However, I am convinced that the quality of the product can never be established*
> *afterwards. Whether the correctness of a piece of software can be guaranteed or*
> *not depends greatly on the structure of the thing made. This means that **the ability***
> ***to convince users, or yourself, that the product is good, is closely intertwined***
> ***with the design process itself**.*

Same source,
emphasis added.
[Poppendieck
2010], page 54,
also cites from
this comment.

A 1992 paper by Jack Reeves, often cited by agilists, argues that in talking about design
as a separate activity in software construction the industry got it all wrong. Reeves notes
that "design" in engineering denotes the task of producing documentation that is then
used for the manufacturing process. In software, "manufacturing" corresponds to the
build process (collect, compile and link the various modules involved) and is largely the
task of computerized tools — "make" and such — rather than people. But then:

[Reeves
1992-2005].

> *After reviewing the software development life cycle as I [Reeves] understood it, I*
> *concluded that the only software documentation that actually seems to satisfy the*
> *criteria of an engineering design is the source code.*

Reeves is indeed right if the focus is on comparing the software process to the process
of other engineering disciplines. Then, as he points out, their "design" is our programming — writing the source code — and their "production" is our build process. That
insightful observation does not end the discussion, however, since the software community has long used the word "design" in its own way, without implying that it is the same
thing as design in — say — mechanical engineering or building construction.

In its specific software meaning, design denotes the process of defining the overall
structure of the code. The difference with implementation is not, as all three authors last
cited note, a matter of intrinsic nature: it is a matter of abstraction. If I show you

```
across subscribers as sub loop
    sub.item.update (arguments)
end
```

(i.e. code that applies the operation *update*, with the given *arguments*, to the value *item*
of every element *sub* of the list *subscribers*), I am giving you code. If I now mention that
I am using the "Observer" design pattern, I am telling you about the architecture: the concept behind the above code is, in that classic architectural solution, to signal a change in
some information (say, a stock price) to all the software elements that monitor it (the
"subscribers", for example a user interface element that shows the stock price, and a program module that updates the stock history database), so that each can execute its specific *update* operation.

On Observer see
[Gamma 1994],
or [Meyer 2009].

Clearly, the code is all that counts in the end, since we execute the code, not architectural elements (such as design patterns). But to obtain that code, and to understand it once it exists, the design is crucial. Once someone has said *"Let's use Observer here!"* a competent software engineer can derive the code. If the code already exists, knowledge that it is not some arbitrary loop but an implementation of Observer is critical to whoever has to work on it further. *Meaning "the Observer pattern".*

A big difference between software and other kinds of engineering is that there is no firm line between "design" documentation and code. "Program Design Languages" look suspiciously like programming languages; even UML diagrams, when precise enough to be useful, can be mapped to code. Implementation is (to paraphrase a famous quote by Clausewitz) design continued by other means; "by other means" means here "at a different level of abstraction".

Another interesting characteristic of software is that, more than in other fields, it may make sense to perform the design (to produce the "documentation") *after* writing the code — or partly before and partly after. A classic software engineering article explains this well: Parnas's and Clements's *A Rational Design Process: How and Why to Fake it*. *[Parnas 1986].* The title conveys the core idea: what matters is that we end up not only with the code but with a good architecture. What matters less is *how* we get that architecture, and particularly *when*: *before* implementation, as a rigid waterfall-like process would suggest; *during* the implementation, with the design and coding effort intertwined; *afterwards*, in an effort to document what was meant; or some combination of these approaches. This is what Parnas means by "faking" the design process. Something *[Parnas 1986].* similar is familiar from mathematics: a mathematical publication presents a polished path of reasoning, where every proposition follows from the previous one and implies the next one; but ask the mathematician how he derived the result, and he will describe (as Hadamard did in a classic book) a much more disorderly process where intuition *[Hadamard* plays as big a role as rigor. The end justifies the means. *1945].*

As the age of the cited articles indicates, the strong coupling between design and implementation in software has long been understood. The evolution of software technology in recent decades, particularly with the spread of object-oriented technology (emphasizing seamless development) and of high-level languages offering powerful abstraction mechanisms, has made that close relationship even move visible.

There probably remain companies that enforce a strict lifecycle model where design is an entirely separate phase from implementation, but this is not what any serious software engineering text promotes.

3.3.2 Agile methods and design

While agile methods are unanimous in their denunciation of any process that includes a separate design phase at the level of the full system lifecycle, there is no single articulated agile approach to design. Three key ideas, however, characterize the agile views of design. It is important to present them in a positive style (*"do this…"*), although we must note that agile presentations always introduce them as a reaction against adverse approaches ("*instead of* doing that…"):

1 If a specific design activity is needed, apply it at the level of individual system iterations, and alternate it with implementation phases.
    (*Instead of*: performing design at the level of the entire system.)
2 Focus on solving the problem at hand.
    (*Instead of*: trying to make your solution extendible and reusable.)
3 To obtain a good architecture, produce something that works, then examine its architecture critically and, if needed, improve it, a task known as *refactoring*.
    (*Instead of*: aiming for a perfect solution from the start.)

We will come back to both points 2 and 3 in later discussions. The general observation is that the agile de-emphasis of extendibility and reusability tends, like other prescriptions we have seen, to start from a correct observation and go too far. Refactoring, for its part, has emerged as an important software engineering technique, but is not a replacement for sound upfront design; if an architecture is decent you can improve it, but refactored junk is still junk.

Larman has been a particularly strong proponent of the idea that design should occur at the level of individual iterations (point 1). He advocates holding design workshops "*at the start of building each new item*" and "*just-in-time whenever else the team finds agile modeling at the walls useful*". The "*walls*" in this description are "*vast open wall spaces without borders, all virtually covered with whiteboard material*".

[Larman 2010], pages 289-290.

→ See "Open space", 6.6, page 96.

With remarkable openness, agile texts explain the limitations of the agile approach to design. A large part of Cohn's discussion of design is devoted to describing what can go wrong in a "life without a big design":

*   *Planning becomes harder.*
*   *Partitioning the work among teams and individuals becomes harder.*
*   *Not having an overall architecture may make people uncomfortable.*
*   *Rework will be inevitable.*

[Cohn 2010], pages 166-171. Only the bullet points headers are cited.

These are indeed obstacles to be taken into consideration.

Together with the idea of refactoring, what dominates agile discussions of design is the opposition to any kind of upfront system-level design. Larman, for example, dismisses the view that "*it is important to have the architectural foundation before you implement anything else*" as a "*false dichotomy idea*".

[Larman 2010], pages 287.

Once again this conclusion is going too far and (although he is no longer around to tell us) I am pretty sure that it is not what Dijkstra had in mind when he was arguing for the sameness of implementation and design. Two typical examples:

*   Security. A common phrasing in some security circles is that "*security cannot be an afterthought*". In that extreme form, such a statement is in fact as incorrect as the reverse view ("forget about security until late in the process") would be. What security experts will tell you is that you should include security concerns upfront, *and* keep them on the agenda throughout.

- Multi-lingual user interfaces. It makes a major difference to the construction of a system whether the user interface — dialogs, error messages etc. — has to support multiple languages. This property is fairly easy to ensure, through appropriate architectural techniques, if it is taken into account right from the start; it can be extremely expensive to retrofit if the system has initially been built monolingual.

> I was once involved as an expert — after the fact, unfortunately — in a legal dispute over a system which the customer rejected at the time of delivery, in part because the program had originally been designed for another country and the multi-lingual feature had been added as an afterthought. Every once in a while, the monthly bills for English-speaking customers included a sentence in another language; the company was not amused.

More head-scratching. Why can agile proponents not leave a good idea alone? The good idea is to avoid doing too much at the start: since not all necessary information is available, defer some of the design decisions to later iterations. There is no reason to turn this insight into a ban on *all* upfront design.

3.4 LIFECYCLE MODELS

Lifecycle models attempt to define and standardize the sequence of phases through which a software project typically proceeds, such as analysis, implementation, V&V (Verification and Validation) and others. The best-known models are the waterfall — the butt of everyone's scorn — and the spiral, an iterative variant of the waterfall. There are many others. They are usually depicted by some diagram where boxes denote phases and arrows the transitions between them. (The sophisticated reader of this book does not need diagrams. In fact let us start a tradition with what has to be, in the entire software engineering literature, the first-ever lifecycle discussion *not* supported by pretty pictures.)

→ *A picture of the "V-Model" variant of the waterfall does appear in a later section, on page 82.*

"*Define*" and "*standardize*". Lifecycle models play two distinct roles, often confused. One is purely **descriptive**: trying to capture how successful teams work. The other is **prescriptive**: saying how teams should work. This distinction is already present in uses of the word "model" in everyday language: a "mathematical model" is descriptive; presenting a person as "a role model" is prescriptive.

Lifecycle models, understood in the prescriptive sense, have taken considerable flak, starting with a 1982 article with the unambiguous title "*Lifecycle concept considered harmful*" by McCracken and Jackson; note once again how early the basic concepts were understood. The agile school also shuns traditional lifecycle models in favor of a more flexible kind of process.

[McCracken 1982].

Before joining the waterfall-bashing party, it is useful to understand three arguments *for* considering a waterfall-like model:

- **Historical** argument: in the early days of the software industry, strict lifecycle models were a healthy reaction against entirely informal approaches, which may be termed "code first, think later" or just "hacking" (in the non-security-related sense). By emphasizing the need for separate activities, in particular those before and after implementation, lifecycle models brought order into the process. Today the software industry is far more sophisticated — an observation that applies to agile methods, whatever limitations they may have — and has moved beyond simple lifecycle models. To reach the present stage, however, these models played a role.

- **Conceptual** argument: even if we stop talking of analysis, implementation, V&V etc. as temporally ordered *phases* of a project, it remains useful to understand their distinctive properties as *activities* of software development.

- **Pedagogical** argument: when teaching software engineering, it is convenient to explain these activities, discuss an idealized linear sequencing between them, and explain why successful software development requires more flexibility.

The remaining presence of the waterfall model in today's software engineering discourse is primarily a consequence of the pedagogical argument; the model survives mostly as a foil against which we can argue for better approaches. This role is important. Think of a political science course that talks about the monarchical, absolute-power system of government. The professor is probably not arguing for bringing in a Louis XIV-style monarch as head of state, but analyzing why people used to find such a system appropriate and what lessons it teaches us for applying more modern views.

Beyond that role, the waterfall is discredited today, and agile criticism of it is correct.

The notion of model, regardless of McCracken's and Jackson's 30-year-old critique, is not going away, whether in its descriptive or prescriptive role. For example a good deal of what we will learn in our study of Scrum is a lifecycle model: successive one-month sprints, accompanied by specific planning and review phases. A lifecycle model can help structure any engineering effort, as long as it is used as a guide for getting things organized, not a barrier to creativity.

Discussions of lifecycle models tend to oscillate between the two title words of a book by Sigmund Freud: *Totem and Taboo*. Neither is appropriate. Every project needs a temporal framework to predict and assess its progress. It can be more sequential, influenced by waterfall ideas, or more iterative, in the Scrum spirit, or some combination of these and other ideas. Defining and standardizing such a framework is only one of the components of project success.

3.5 RATIONAL UNIFIED PROCESS

An influential approach, the Rational Unified Process, promotes a waterfall-style but iterative lifecycle model, and combines it with a number of recommended software engineering practices. RUP was developed at Rational, a company that became part of IBM.

The most important contribution of RUP is a set of six recommended practices: develop iteratively; manage requirements; use component-based development; model software visually; verify quality continuously; and control changes. All but one correspond to widely accepted practices of software engineering. (The exception is the recommendation of visual representation, which describes a technique rather than a principle at the same level of importance as the others, and establishes a connection to the UML graphical notations, also developed by Rational.)

The lifecycle model involves four phases for a project: inception, elaboration, construction and transition. The first three sound very much like requirements, design and implementation under new names, and that is very much what they are. (The RUP literature says otherwise, with the help of a multi-colored diagram that you will find in any discussion of the approach, but the distinctions are too subtle for common mortals.) Transition is another name for deployment, which, although absent from the traditional models because software issues were much simpler in 1970, is indeed a critical aspect of any significant software project: imagine you are a bank and have just written your new program for handling ATMs; you are not out of the woods yet if the system is to be deployed on thousands of machines in dozens of languages and a hundred countries with different constraints and regulations. Assigning to deployment a role on a par with other essential project phases has been one of the contributions of RUP.

RUP is not popular in agile circles, and can in fact serve them as an example of a Big (Bad) Upfront Method. In spite of the "iterative" label, the lifecycle model is too sequential for agile tastes. The practices, however, do not cause any particular incompatibility. Even "manage requirements" has an agile interpretation where requirements, in the form of user stories, are defined iteratively throughout the project. RUP's continuous verification of quality is definitely in the spirit of agile approaches.

[Ambler 2001] discusses agile vs. RUP.

3.6 MATURITY MODELS

Rooted in the tradition of lifecycle models, but addressing more important problems, maturity models started in the nineteen-eighties with the ISO 9000 set of standards from the International Standards Organization and the more software-specific Capability Maturity Model (which the Software Engineering Institute, based at Carnegie-Mellon University, developed for the US Department of Defense). CMM has since been extended into a family of models applicable to a variety of industrial disciplines, CMMI (the "I" stands for "Integration"), which will be our reference for this discussion.

Warning: if you have seen other presentations of CMMI, you may not immediately recognize the description below. Official CMMI documents use a dreadful form of bureaucratese that obscures simple notions, resulting in 482-page documents for what could be comfortably explained in 30 pages. No wonder CMMI puts off so many people, agilists and others. It took me a long time to pierce the wall and realize that in spite of its pomposity CMMI actually introduces useful software engineering concepts. The following summary presents these concepts in plain English.

Such as [CMMI 2010]. I discussed how style hurts CMMI in a blog article: [Meyer 2013a].

3.6.1 CMMI in plain English

CMMI is a collection of best practices specified precisely enough to help reach identified goals and to allow assessing an organization's compliance. These three notions, **practices**, **goals** and **assessment**, are at the center of the approach. (A simpler but far better name for the approach would have been "**Catalog of Assessable Practices**".)

Most CMMI practices and goals are *specific* to a "**process area**": a clearly identified aspect of the software process, with its own set of issues and activities. Examples of process areas include configuration management, project planning, risk management and supplier agreement management (handling relationships with contractors). In addition, CMMI defines some *generic* goals and practices, applicable across process areas.

For examples of specific goals and practices, consider the "configuration management" process area, which we may define as the identification and tracking of the various items relevant to the software process, such as program modules, test cases, hardware assets etc., whose evolution will be subject to strict rules. In configuration management:

- One of the specific goals is "*Establish baselines*", where a baseline is a collection of items to be managed under the stated rules.
- One of the specific practices for that goal is "*Identify configuration items*": define the basic elements (program modules, test cases, hardware assets) that will be under the control of configuration management.
- Also for that goal, another practice is "*Establish a configuration management system*".

There are only a few *generic* goals. An example is "*The process is institutionalized as a managed process*", using words that have a special meaning in the CMMI context: a "managed process" is a process that is planned in accordance with a clearly stated policy, employs skilled people, and is subject to monitoring; a process is "institutionalized" if it is not just practiced but thoroughly supported by the organization, with a clear commitment. A generic practice supporting this generic goal is "*Plan the process*".

In addition, *specific* practices from particular process areas can support a *generic* goal. For example, "*Include the configuration management plan in the project plan*", a Configuration Management practice, supports the generic goal just cited.

The third major aspect of CMMI — complementing goals and practices — is **assessment**. The model allows an organization that develops software to submit to evaluation the quality of its corresponding process. Process, not product: the assessment only affects *how* the software is produced. Any conclusion about the quality of *what* is being produced has to be deduced indirectly: for example applying CMMI does not guarantee the absence of defects (bugs), but does assess whether procedures are in place to evaluate software quality, for example through precise policies for defect discovery and tracking.

There are two kinds of assessment, each with its corresponding scale of "capability" *[CMMI 2010], pages 22-23.* or "maturity". The *continuous* scale governs assessment for specific process areas; the *staged* version assesses the overall state of the processes of an organization. For this discussion we limit ourselves to the staged variant. Its scale defines five levels of increasing maturity for an organization, starting with little or no process at level 1.

You cannot just declare to the world that your organization is at CMMI level i (for $i > 1$) but have to qualify for it through an assessment process conducted by approved assessors. You cannot skip levels: to ask for assessment of level $i + 1$ qualification, you must already have been qualified at level i.

> It is serious business; moving from one level to the next is typically a matter of many months and hundreds of thousands of dollars. Like Scrum in the agile world, CMMI supports a small industry, in this case of assessors, who must themselves be certified, and consultants helping companies reach their desired level.

The successive levels (each, from level 2 on, including the properties of its predecessors) reflect an organization's increasing degree of understanding and control of its processes:

1 **Initial**, a level generally described in CMMI texts by negative characteristics, reminiscent of how agile presentations describe the detestable state of non-agile projects: *"processes are usually ad hoc and chaotic"*, *"success depends on the completeness* [CMMI 2010], *and heroics of the people involved, not on the use of proven processes"*. Time to get *page 27.* ready for serious CMMI implementation, defined by the subsequent levels.

2 **Managed**: processes exist for projects, supported by adequate resources and commitments from stakeholders.

3 **Defined**: the processes are specified precisely through documents, procedures and tools; and these specifications exist at the level of the entire organization, so that even if a project needs its own variants they will be tailored from that common base.

4 **Quantitatively managed**: the application of processes is subject to numerical criteria of quality and performance, and assessed through statistical control techniques.

5 **Optimizing**: the processes include mechanisms for their own evaluation and continuous improvement (a feedback loop).

Each level includes certain process areas; to reach that level you must have implemented the corresponding specific practices. For example (partial lists except at level 4):

• Some process areas for level 2: project planning, configuration management, supplier agreement management.

• For level 3: requirements development, validation and verification, risk management.

• For level 4: quantitative project management.

• For level 5: causal analysis and resolution (mechanisms for identifying the causes of observed deficiencies and removing them).

The assessment aspect of CMMI and in particular this 1-to-5 scale are the most visible part of the approach. They should not, however, detract from the core contribution: defining a catalog of generic and specific management practices.

> The original incentive for developing CMMI and its assessment methodology in the *At that time it* nineteen-eighties was to allow the US Department of Defense (DoD), the largest consumer *was just CMM.* of software products and services in the world, to choose its suppliers on an objective basis by forcing them to qualify at the appropriate level. CMMI also played a major if unintended role in the development of the modern software industry: it was seized upon by the then nascent Indian outsourcing industry to establish its credibility with Western customers. Many of the first companies to achieve level 5 were Indian, and outsourcers continue, along with DoD suppliers, to be among the main adopters of CMMI.

3.6.2 The Personal Software Process

CMMI is meant for organizations and more specifically — if not in intent, at least in practice, given the costs involved — to *large* organizations. Watts Humphrey, a former *[Humphrey* IBM manager who provided much of the inspiration for CMMI, was conscious of the *2005].* need to translate its core idea — the systematic application of recognized practices — into recommendations that every programmer could apply at the level of his or her individual work, whether or not as part of a company mandate. The result of this effort is the Personal Software Process. Along with PSP, Humphrey also introduced TSP, for Teams.

TSP and PSP have attracted only a modest level of commentary, usually dismissive, from agile authors, but the basic ideas are worth noting. It is easy to be turned off at first by PSP because it relies on a rigid and largely outmoded lifecycle model for individual programmers: plan-design-code-compile-test-postmortem. Other than the last phase and (agile buffs please close your eyes for a second) the first, we do not work like that any more. But the main contribution of PSP is elsewhere, not tied to a particular technology: encouraging programmers to work in the tradition of engineers by keeping logs, tracking time spent, recording bugs, and applying the methods of statistical quality control (also expounded by agile authors such as the proponents of Lean programming). This advice, not widely applied or even known in the industry, makes the studying of PSP useful for any programmer even in today's changed technology world.

3.6.3 CMMI/PSP and agile methods

No fundamental contradiction exists between the agile and CMMI ideas (or with PSP if we limit it to its better side as just noted). Agile methods prescribe certain processes and practices. CMMI requires a company to codify its processes and practices; it does not say what they should be, and the agile variants can qualify just as well as others.

The common perception is different: CMMI and agile are often considered incompatible ("*like oil and water*"). Culturally, the two communities are indeed different: one focused on control, planning, documents, the other rejecting all this "waste" and swearing by just code and tests. The planning-oriented parts of CMMI are indeed hard to swallow for an agilist, but most of the practices have turned out to be transposable to a CMMI context. The Poppendiecks have two main criticisms against CMMI-style models:

- That they "*may standardize on less than ideal practices and create a bias against* *[Poppendieck* *change*". But CMMI explicitly fosters a self-improving process, although that aspect *2003], page 97.* of the approach only becomes most prominent at the higher levels of the CMMI scale.

- That "a*s frequently implemented, these models tend to remove process design and decision-making authority from developers and put it under the control of central organizations*". But even though this phenomenon indeed happens with the models "*as frequently implemented*", nothing in them requires you to apply a particular model of management, centralized or not. That some companies interpret them to impose a bureaucratic structure is a problem with the companies, not the models.

CMMI is not for everyone; it requires a major commitment on the part of an organization, usually triggered by a regulatory obligation or commercial incentive to qualify at a certain level of the scale. It may not be your cup of tea. But if it is, and you find some agile ideas attractive, a number of existing experience reports — including one by a team *[Sutherland* including Sutherland, devoted to a CMMI level 5 effort using Scrum — show that it is *2010].* possible to combine ideas from both schools of thought.

Such a combination, refreshingly different from the stridently exclusionary style sometimes found elsewhere in the agile canon, confirms the observation that recurs throughout this book: that agile methods are not a tsunami that makes all classical techniques of software engineering suddenly obsolete, but an increment and extension — and, here and there, partial replacement — of what has been shown to work.

3.6.4 An agile maturity scale

Predictably, a number of authors have proposed "agile maturity models" with the requi- *See [Schweigert* site five levels, although at least one of them is ostensibly dated April 1st. They are little *2012] for a sur-* more than "me too" attempts to show that agilists can also have 5-step scales if they want *vey. The April* to. (If they were the result of genuine, unbiased analysis, why would they all have to end *1st article is* up with exactly five levels?) *[Ambler 2010].*

We saw that even though the assessment scale is the most publicized aspect of CMMI it is only one of three important components, along with practices and goals. Agile methods have their own practices and goals. There is no large-scale organization for assessing compliance of agile projects, although certification of individuals for titles such as Scrum Master plays an important role for Scrum.

Agile methods do refer to a scale that may be their closest counterpart to the CMMI *See [Cockburn* levels: Shu-Ha-Ri (or Shuhari), a three-step gradation. The terms come from the vocab- *2010] and* ulary of Japanese martial arts and denote successive steps in learning, which agile meth- *[Sutherland* ods transpose into steps that agile teams must climb towards mastery of the method: *2013], pages* *35-38.*

* In the Shu state, from a word meaning obeying, people just learn and apply recipes.

* In the Ha state, meaning detach, they are able to abstract from the core rules and combine them in various ways.

* In the Ri state, meaning surpass, they can go beyond existing rules and methods to devise their own solutions when needed.

You can also think of the bachelor's-master's-PhD scale, which admittedly lacks the exotic frisson of the Japanese characters that adorn agile presentations of Shu-Ha-Ri. (In education circles, similar ideas underlie a popular five-level scale, the Dreyfus model.)

The parallel with CMMI levels is clear; in particular the last level of Shu Ha Ri is comparable to level 5, "Optimizing", of CMMI.

4

Agile principles

Underlying the specific practices and artifacts of agile development, we find a number of general *principles*: methodological rules that express a general view of how software should be developed. We will now study these principles, the core of the agile approach.

4.1 WHAT IS A PRINCIPLE?

To clarify the methodological context it is useful to recall first what qualifies, or not, as a principle. A good methodological principle is both *abstract* and *falsifiable*. Abstractness differentiates principles from *practices*; falsifiability distinguishes them from *platitudes*.

Abstractness means that the principle should be a general rule, not a specific practice. "Build a solid financial foundation for the future" is a principle; "Put 10% of your earnings every month into a savings account" is a practice. Often, as in this example and as in the case of agile practices discussed in a later chapter, a practice exists to help satisfy a principle.

→ *Chapter 6 reviews agile practices.*

Falsifiability means that it must be possible for a reasonable person to disagree with the principle. If no one in his right mind would ever disagree with a proposed rule, as with "seek software quality" (who would advocate *not* seeking quality in developing software?), then it may be right but it is also uninteresting. For the rule to be a principle, you must be able — regardless of your own opinion — to envision someone supporting its negation. "Test first" satisfies this criterion: it is possible to argue that programs should be written before tests, or that *specifications* rather than tests should precede the program. A rule whose negation is unsustainable, such as "seek software quality", is not a principle but a platitude.

The principles reviewed in this chapter satisfy these requirements. Practices are important and have a separate chapter; platitudes occasionally arise in the agile literature (as elsewhere) but we will ignore them.

In addition, a principle should generally be **prescriptive**, not descriptive: rather than stating a fact or property, it directs action ("Do not covet thy neighbor's wife"). This requirement is not absolute for principles in non-technical areas ("the best is the enemy of the good" is a principle even though not expressed as a prescription), but for principles governing software development methodology it is a good idea to use a prescriptive style, as will be the case with the principles presented in this chapter.

B. Meyer, *Agile!*, DOI 10.1007/978-3-319-05155-0_4,
© Springer International Publishing Switzerland 2014

4.2 THE OFFICIAL PRINCIPLES

As noted in the introductory chapter, the Agile Manifesto itself lists twelve principles, *[Agile 2001]; numbers added.* which we should examine first since they represent the official view:

Official agile principles

A1 Our highest priority is to satisfy the customer through early and continuous delivery of valuable software.

A2 Welcome changing requirements, even late in development. Agile processes harness change for the customer's competitive advantage.

A3 Deliver working software frequently, from a couple of weeks to a couple of months, with a preference to the shorter timescale.

A4 Business people and developers must work together daily throughout the project.

A5 Build projects around motivated individuals. Give them the environment and support they need, and trust them to get the job done.

A6 The most efficient and effective method of conveying information to and within a development team is face-to-face conversation.

A7 Working software is the primary measure of progress.

A8 Agile processes promote sustainable development. The sponsors, developers, and users should be able to maintain a constant pace indefinitely.

A9 Continuous attention to technical excellence and good design enhances agility.

A10 Simplicity — the art of maximizing the amount of work not done — is essential.

A11 The best architectures, requirements, and designs emerge from self-organizing teams.

A12 At regular intervals, the team reflects on how to become more effective, then tunes and adjusts its behavior accordingly.

This list is useful to set the mood but — even though it comes straight from the source — we cannot work from it and our first task will be to clear the way for a more accurate and usable set of principles. The official list is not up to this role:

- Some of the points listed are practices: A6, A12.

- Others are platitudes: A5 — who would support building projects around *unmotivated* individuals? — and A9.

- Some are not prescriptions but assertions, which does not matter when they can readily be turned into prescriptions (A7 could have been phrased as "Use working software as the primary measure of progress"), but becomes problematic when the assertion is **wrong**. It is not true that, as taken for granted in A10, simplicity means "maximizing work not done": seeking simplicity is a meaningful principle; so is maximizing the amount of work not done; but they are different principles. (This is an → *"What is simplicity?", page 66.* important matter which we will examine in detail below.) Sticking to a prescriptive style might have avoided the confusion.

- Although we would expect a set of independent rules, the ones listed here are partly redundant: frequent delivery is mentioned in A1 and A3, the importance of working software in A3 and A7.

- On the other hand the rules are clearly incomplete: none of them mentions testing, even though the focus on testing to ensure quality is a core property of agile approaches, and among their principal contributions.

4.3 A USABLE LIST

To replace the official list, we will use the classification of agile principles introduced in the overview chapter. Here for ease of reference is the list again:

← *"Principles", 1.2, page 4.*

Agile principles

Organizational

1   Put the customer at the center.
2   Let the team self-organize.
3   Work at a sustainable pace.
4   Develop minimal software:
    4.1   Produce minimal functionality.
    4.2   Produce only the product requested.
    4.3   Develop only code and tests.
5   Accept change.

Technical

6   Develop iteratively:
    6.1   Produce frequent working iterations.
    6.2   Freeze requirements during iterations.
7   Treat tests as a key resource:
    7.1   Do not start any new development until all tests pass.
    7.2   Test first.
8   Express requirements through scenarios.

We look first at *organizational* principles, then at software-specific *technical* principles.

4.4 ORGANIZATIONAL PRINCIPLES

Organizational principles affect project management, scheduling and team organization.

4.4.1 Put the customer at the center

"We are customer-oriented" is a platitude in business. Agile development takes this idea seriously, requiring close involvement of customers throughout the development.

In many traditional approaches, customers intervene only at specified points: they provide input during the requirements — only as part of a strictly controlled process, in requirements interviews or workshops — and do not reappear until the final stages, in "user acceptance testing". Some organizations even forbid contact between customers and developers in-between these stages, although many do not go to such extremes.

In agile approaches the interaction with customers takes place throughout the project. In Beck's terms:

> *You will get [better] results with real customers. They are who you are trying to*   *[Beck 2005],*
> *please. No customer at all, or a "proxy" for a real customer, leads to waste as*   *page 62.*
> *you develop features that aren't used, specify tests that don't reflect the real*
> *acceptance criteria, and lose the chance to build real relationships between the*
> *people with the most diverse perspective of the project.*

Customers in an agile project are welcome at regular project meetings, can interact freely   → *"Onsite cus-* with developers and have the opportunity to try the project as it gets released in incre-   *tomer", 6.5,* mental versions. Some approaches go further and recommend "embedding" a customer   *page 96.* in the development team.

The emphasis on customer involvement addresses one of the principal dangers that threaten software projects: building a software system that does not properly address the users' needs. As early as 1981, Boehm's classic *Software Engineering Economics* cited   *[Boehm 1981]* software failures in which projects produced systems where everything was right — reliability, performance, ... — except for one detail: they solved a problem other than what users wanted, or needed. Lutz's empirical analysis of the sources of software-related safety errors in major NASA missions, also a classic, reports that

> *The primary cause of safety-related* functional *faults is errors in* **recognizing**   *[Lutz 1993],*
> **(understanding) the requirements** *(62% on Voyager, 79% on Galileo).*   *emphasis in*
> *Safety-related conditional faults, for example, are almost always caused by*   *original.*
> *errors in recognizing requirements.*

Such studies, however, can also be invoked to justify putting more effort into writing upfront *requirements*, precisely the kind of thing agilists dislike.

The encouragement to involve customers is an important agile contribution. The problem is the insistence that such interactions *replace* requirements. Such a move is dangerous because there is no such thing as "the customer". Any significant project involves many categories of stakeholders (a more general term than "customer"):

- Users of the future system — themselves of different kinds, such as, for an online event reservation system, the event staff, the owners of theaters and other venues, event attendees, artists, agents, producers.

- Executives — also working for the customer company, but particularly concerned about such matters as integration with company policies and future evolution.

- Purchasing agents, lawyers and so on.

These various constituencies often have conflicting needs and priorities, and it is precisely the role of a good requirements process to bring contradictions to light, resolve them if possible (this is why *requirements workshops* are often a good complement to individual requirements elicitation sessions), and obtain decisions from the person in charge — the "product owner".

If you replace this formal process by a practice of talking to stakeholders, you run the risk of skewing the result to fit the views of those who participate in these discussions. They may not be the best source anyway: the people whose perspective really matters may also be the most busy; they would find time for a focused requirements workshop, but will not keep their door open to any developer walking in for a question. Chances are you will be influenced by those who have too much time on their hands, precisely because their work may not be so important to the organization. The risk is particularly important with the methods that prescribe *embedding* a customer representative in the development team: if management is so willing to assign to your project a supposed → *See also* expert of the application domain, taking him or her away from tasks in that domain, you *"Customer",* may wonder whether the person is really the most qualified. *5.5, page 82*

Beck acknowledges the risk of listening to just one person:

> *The objection I hear to customer involvement is that someone will get exactly the* *[Beck 2005],*
> *system he wants, but the system won't be suitable for anyone else.* *page 62.*

He answers the objection by stating that

> *It's easier to generalize a successful system than to specialize a system that doesn't solve anyone's problem.*

This argument is debatable. The "*successful system*" might be so unique to the identified user's need as to require complete rework for anyone else, while the "*system that doesn't solve anyone's problem*" might have a solid foundation and a terrible user interface that can be fixed. Even if we accept Beck's view, it does not explain why talking to *some* users throughout the project excludes trying to collect the views of *all* stakeholder categories at specified stages of the project — a rejection that appears pretty irresponsible.

4.4.2 Let the team self-organize

The agile approach takes away from managers such traditional roles as assigning tasks to developers. It places considerable trust in the team's ability to organize its own work. Scrum is particularly systematic in this respect, replacing the traditional notion of project manager by an empowered team which makes its own decisions, under the control of a *product owner* who decides on the product functionality and a *Scrum Master* who supports the team and enforces the method. We will study these roles in the next chapter.

For many developers having previously suffered from bad project managers, this aspect is one of the great attractions of agile methods. In response to a long blog article critical of agile development, a defender of XP and Scrum wrote:

> *The most important aspect of these methods is to put the management of the* *[Yegge 2006],*
> *project squarely where it belongs: on the backs of the people doing the work.* *Reader com-*
> *When the people actually doing the work have the final say in what gets done and* *ment by "Dixie-*
> *when, then projects actually get done on time.* *Geek".*

The need for managers remains, of course, because this is how companies work and because in the words of the creators of the original (non-software) Scrum method "*subtle control is consistent with the self-organizing character of project teams*". Schwaber and Sutherland, creators of the software Scrum, also emphasize this concept of subtle control: *Cited in [Cohn 2010a]. See also [Nonaka 1995].*

> *Control through peer pressure and "control by love" are the basis of subtle control. The dynamic flow of the team surfaces the tacit (unconscious) knowledge of the group and creates explicit knowledge in the form of software.*

[Schwaber 2012], page 28.

Words somewhat scary if you have been told that your team is self-organizing and suddenly learn that you are in fact being "subtly" controlled through "tacit" and "unconscious" techniques. The part about love may be reassuring; or not.

Maybe it is a matter of taste. Personally, if I am to be managed, I would rather have a boss than be told I am self-organized only to be subjected to surreptitious control techniques.

In fact the role of the manager is murky in the agile literature; comments on this topic tend to be of the scandalized denegation style, as "*it is a common misconception that, in agile projects, …*", which may be true but does not tell us why the "misconception" arose in the first place and, more importantly, what is the proper (not misconstrued) role of the manager. Schwaber and Sutherland, for example, write:

> **Although** project development teams are on their own, they are **not** uncontrolled.

[Schwaber 2012], page 28, emphasis added.

And Cohn:

> A **common misconception** about agile project management is that because of [*the*] reliance on self-organizing teams, there is little or no role for team leaders. **Nothing could be further from the truth**. In "The Biology of Business", Philip Anderson **refutes** this **mistaken** assumption: "Self-organization **does not mean** that workers **instead of** managers engineer an organization design. It **does not mean** letting people do whatever they want to do. It means that management commits to guiding the evolution of behaviors that emerge from the interaction of independent agents **instead of** specifying in advance what effective behavior is."
>
> *Self-organizing teams* **are not** *free from management control. Management chooses what product to build or often who will work on their project,* **but** *the teams are* **nonetheless** *self-organizing.* **Neither** *are they* **free from** *influence. …* **That being said***, the fewer constraints or controls put on a team, the better.*

[Cohn 2010a]. Emphasis added.

In other words agile managers "control", except they do not or maybe they do but "*nonetheless*" not that much.

Agile texts abound with project anecdotes, illustrating the intended balance between too much and too little; but the manager in search of firm general principles will only find rules stating what managers should *not* do, for example deciding what functions to include (that is for the product owner) and who should work on what when (that is for the team).

Cohn's assertion that "self-organizing" does not mean "*letting people do whatever they want to do*" leaves one wondering. If there is a difference, it must be subtle. Derby, in an article again devoted to "*misconceptions*", emphasizes that "self-*organizing*" does not mean "self-*organized*":

> *That's because [self-organization] is a process and a characteristic, **not** something that is done once and for all. Self-organizing, from a social systems perspective **only** means that the team can create new approaches and adapt to meet new challenges in their environment.*

[Derby 2011], emphasis added.

"Create new approaches and adapt to new challenges" sounds underwhelming. What decently led project — including a traditional one led by a strong, "command-and-control" manager — would not allow its members, in fact encourage them, to do that? "Self-organizing" has to be more ambitious. Mittal writes that self-organizing teams

> ***still** require mentoring and coaching, **but** they **don't require** command and control.*

[Mittal 2013], emphasis added.

While mentoring and coaching are indeed important roles for agile managers (as we will see in the next chapter), the negative part of the observation is again disappointing: "command and control" is what managers traditionally do; as Cohn points out, they still have to do some of it, but it would be useful to know exactly what.

Although the answer is not to be found in the agile literature, in the end it is not hard to derive from plain common sense. Most projects need a manager to take care of "command and control". The drawback of a military-style scheme in which a single person performs that role is that it bridles the creativity of team members. At the other extreme, a talented and experimented team can completely self-organize, with or without a "mentor" and "coach".

In the music world, a famous example is the legendary I Musici ensemble, in continuous operation since 1952 and one of the best chamber orchestras in the world:

I Musici in concert

As the Wikipedia entry states, "*I Musici is a conductorless ensemble. But the relation-ships among the musicians enable great harmony in their music-making*". Indeed! If you put a group of top-notch software developers together they can manage by themselves, like I Musici, and resent any pointy-haired "suit" foolish enough to think he can order them around. At the other extreme, asking a group of inexperienced music students to play together will not work. Even seasoned professional musicians generally cannot work that way; that is why most orchestras, including smaller ensembles, have a conduc-tor. Most software development teams, similarly, need a project manager.

What we can learn in the end from the agile insistence on self-organizing teams is this:

- Exceptionally, an experienced and closely-knit team ("*I Programmatori*") may work without a manager. Most teams, however, need one.

- Some of the traditional manager roles, such as the selection of tasks for the next development iteration, may be assigned to other team members.

- The manager should encourage initiative from the team members and gradually move the team to a partially or totally self-organized mode of operation. (Here we may note Derby's notion that until that stage is reached the team is *evolving* towards self-management.)

4.4.3 Work at a sustainable pace

Agile methods emphasize the central role of programmers and the need to give them working conditions that enable them to deliver their full potential. A particularly forceful consequence of this view is the rejection of what Ed Yourdon, in a popular and useful book, calls *death marches*: the management practice of accepting an unrealistic commit- *[Yourdon 2003]* ment — a project with fuzzy and ever-growing requirements and tight deadlines — then trying to force the programming team to meet it through pressure, long working days and sacrificed week-ends.

Another influential book was DeMarco's and Lister's *PeopleWare* (first published in *[DeMarco 1999]* 1987), which explained in clear terms how programmers function and how important it is to provide them with a calm, respectful working environment.

Cockburn has been particularly vocal in promoting principles of "Personal Safety" for developers, enabling them to speak freely. In his words:

> *Personal Safety is being able to speak when something is bothering you without*   *[Cockburn*
> *fear of reprisal. It may involve telling the manager that the schedule is*   *2005], page 29,*
> *unrealistic, a colleague that her design needs improvement, or even that she*   *slightly abridged.*
> *needs to take a shower more often. With Personal Safety, the team can discover*
> *and repair its weaknesses. Without it, people won't speak up, and the weaknesses*
> *will continue to damage the team.*

More generally, agilism emphasizes, in the *PeopleWare* tradition, the respect due to programmers and the need to provide them with good working conditions. These ideas mesh well with other aspects of the method: its preference for personal communication over written documents; and its advice (discussed in a subsequent chapter) to use open spaces rather than cubicles. Schwaber describes the before-and-after of a company's atmosphere: → *"Open space"*, *6.6, page 96.*

> *The first tour of the engineering space at Service1st was downright depressing. People were either housed in offices with closed doors or exiled to cubicles... There was no conversation, no hum of activity, no feeling of a group of people undertaking work that they were excited to do.*

[Schwaber 2004a], pages 114-115.

The company hired him, however, and at the time of the second sprint review:

> *Everything felt different... People were talking and sharing laughter and lively conversation filled the workspace.*

The sociopolitical overtones are interesting. We noted in the first chapter that agile ideas have a sociological interpretation: "the revolt of the cubicles". The agile movement reflects programmers' self-assertiveness, extolling the primacy of code at the expense of "Dilbert's boss" artifacts such as plans, models and documents. ← *"Values", 1.1, page 2.*

The debate is not new: as early as 1977, a book by Philip Kraft, complete with Marxist analysis, denounced the forerunners of today's Big Upfront techniques (even including structured programming) as an attempt by management to taylorize software production and turn programmers into a voiceless proletariat. The Marxist analysis is gone — if anything, agilists emphasize ROI and other unabashedly capitalistic goals — but the push to bring the programmer to the forefront remains. *[Kraft 1977]*

There are nuances between the agile schools. They may all promote empowering programmers, but not necessarily for the same reasons. Between the four methods particularly covered in this book, two categories emerge:

- XP and Crystal are true programmer-pride movements; Cockburn's statement cited above is typical of these methods' focus on restoring programmers' dignity against management.

- The spirit of Scrum and Lean is different. These are methods rooted in the tradition of industrial production engineering; their authors keep citing Deming and Toyota, blasting waste and extolling productivity.

As an example of the second school, Schwaber proudly recounts how as the Scrum Master for a project he enabled the team to meet its next deadline: when it turned out that the project could not proceed without the input of a key developer who had gone incommunicado — or so he believed — to Yellowstone for his first vacation in two years (try that in Europe!), the diligent Scrum Master hired a private detective to track him down (try that in Europe!). Maybe this is "subtle control" again, leaving one nostalgic for the good old managers of yore, with their prerogatives but also the built-in limits on their power. Since the anecdote seems intended not only to boast about the author's fearless management style but to convey a general lesson, the befuddled reader wonders how to reconcile that lesson with principles of sustainable pace such as Crystal's Personal Safety. *[Schwaber 2004a], page 117.*

Also part of the emphasis on sustainability is the XP-recommended practice of *slack*, following the theme of another DeMarco book. Beck writes: *[DeMarco 2001].*

> *In any plan, include some minor tasks that can be dropped if you get behind.*

[Beck 2000],
page 48.

and

> *You can structure slack in many ways. One week in eight could be "Geek Week". Twenty percent of the weekly budget could go to programmer-chosen tasks.*

The twenty-percent allowance is, famously, part of Google's practices.

Although the company report-edly tried to kill it in 2013.

4.4.4 Develop minimal software

Agile methods emphasize simplicity. The goal is to get user feedback quickly by delivering software at short increments, even if it covers only a subset of the expected functionality.

The agile spirit of minimalism manifests itself in several forms: minimal functionality; produce only the product requested; produce only code and tests. Let us examine them in turn, then assess the virtues of minimalism.

Produce minimal functionality

A general agile view is that many software systems suffer from bloat: elements of functionality that are not needed, or needed by only a few users. During development, they take time away from the fundamental functionality and delay the releases; they harm the team's focus; they create a future maintenance burden (since once a feature is there someone is going to use it and demand that future versions continue to provide it); they may constrain the future evolution of the software.

A slogan made popular by XP is "You Ain't Gonna Need It" or YAGNI, which

> *reminds us always to work on the story we have, not something we think we're going to need. Even if we know we're going to need it.*

[Jeffries 2001],
page 190.

The Poppendiecks write:

> *Our software systems contain far more features than are ever going to be used. Extra features increase the complexity of the code, driving up costs nonlinearly. If even half of our code is unnecessary — a conservative estimate — the cost is not just double; it's perhaps ten times more expensive than it needs to be.*

[Poppendieck 2010], page 26, slightly abridged.

(I do not know whether the factor of ten is a wild estimate or is meant to be taken literally, and am not aware of published studies giving precise empirical values.) They add:

> *Our best opportunity to improve software development productivity is to stop putting features that are not absolutely necessary.*

In short,

> *If code is not needed **now**, putting it into the system is a waste. Resist the temptation.*

[Poppendieck 2003], page 6.

Produce only the product requested

Software engineering wisdom encourages developers to strive for two software qualities that produce long-term rather than immediate benefits:

- Extendibility: devise the architecture to support future extensions, in particular future user needs.

- Reusability: make software elements as general as possible beyond their immediate role in the current project, so that they can be reused elsewhere in that project and future ones. (When this happens they have been turned into software *components*.)

For agile methods, these are not important goals, and may not be goals at all. What matters is to develop software that works here and now. Here are two typical quotes illustrating the agilists' distrust of anything that addresses more than the needs of the moment. Ward Cunningham writes:

> *You are always taught to do as much as you can. Always put checks in. Always look for exceptions. Always handle the most general case. Always give the user the best advice. Always print a meaningful error message. Always this. Always that. You have so many things in the background that you're supposed to do, there's no room left to think. I say, forget all that and ask yourself, "What's the simplest thing that could possibly work?".*

[Cunningham 2004].

This phrase, "Do the simplest thing that could possibly work", has — like YAGNI but without an acronym — become an agile mantra. Ron Jeffries, explaining why designing for reuse is not worth it, states:

> *Unless the projects are being done by the same team, reuse is quite difficult to do effectively: there is a big difference between some part of the project that I can reuse, and packaging that part well enough so that others can do so. I have to do packaging work that I wouldn't do for myself, to document it, to make it more bulletproof, removing issues that I just work around automatically, to support it, answer questions about it, train people in how to use it. If I do those things, it's expensive. If I don't, using my stuff is difficult for others and doesn't help them much.*
>
> *I build the abstractions I need. If I need an abstraction again, in a different context, I would improve it. But unless my project's purpose is to build stuff for other projects, I try not to waste any of my time and money building for other projects.*

[Jeffries 2001], page 190.

Such statements are an occasion for head-scratching. (Yet another one. We encounter so many that maybe this book should include a discount coupon for hair-restoration treatment.)

As in many other cases, they start from correct, even insightful observations: designing for the future can detract from solving the problem of here and now; designing for reuse is hard. An example that I find convincing is that of a class defining points in a two-dimensional space: how do you make it more general? You could think of points in an *n*-dimensional space for any *dimension n*; or of any *objects* defined by two numerical coordinates (points, vectors, complex numbers…); or of any two-dimensional *figures* (points, lines, polygons…). There is no way to know which of these, if any, will be the useful generalization. In such cases, it is better not to try to guess where the future will take us.

But from this common-sense observation to deduce that we can forget about generality, "checks", "exceptions" and reuse? Such injunctions are an encouragement to use bad software engineering practice. A simple example is the use of built-in constants. You are writing software for a small company and need a data structure to represent the list of employees; well, an array of 1000 elements should be enough, right? Before you know it, the company has grown and suddenly the software mysteriously stops working. Historical catastrophes that caused billions of dollars of wasted effort resulted precisely from this kind of agile, let's-just-do-what-we-need-now approach: the MS-DOS 640-K memory limit, the Y2K mess, the initial size of IP addresses.

The myopic advice quoted above, enjoining you to worry only about what is needed here and now, is detrimental to your software process. Regardless of what you find useful in the rest of the agile canon, your best bet is to ignore it.

Develop only code and tests

One of the most radical principles of agile methods deprecates all the standard supporting products of a software development, in particular documents — requirements documents, design documents, plans, program documentation... — as diversions from the main acts, running code and tests. In Poppendieck's words:

> *The documents, diagrams, and models produced as part of a software development project are often consumables, aids used to produce the system, but not necessarily a part of the final product. Once a working system is delivered, the user may care little about the intermediate consumables. Lean principles suggest that every consumable is a candidate for scrutiny. The burden is on the artifact to prove not only that it adds value to the final product, but also that it is the most efficient way of achieving that value.*

[Poppendieck 2001].

"Consumables" covers anything that is not delivered to the customer. Other than code and tests, most traditional artifacts of software development can be considered consumables: feasibility studies, transcripts or videos of requirements interviews and workshops, requirements documents, PowerPoint presentations about the future system, emails, design documents, UML diagrams...

Similarly, to describe the role of architects, Beck has this to say:

> *Architects on an XP team look for and execute large-scale refactorings, write system-level tests that stress the architecture, and implement stories.*

[Beck 2005], page 75.

This definition is clearly a provocation, since the tasks listed have little to do with what one traditionally expects from an architect: to define the architecture. Here something will be built initially, "the simplest that could possibly work", and the architect steps in only to **refactor** (that is to say, improve the architecture if it is *ex post facto* found unsatisfactory), test, and, like everyone else in the team, implement user stories.

Some authors accept, reluctantly, that there may be deliverables other than tests. Cockburn, for example, describes which actual results bring developers credit:

> **You get no credit for any item that does not result in running, tested code.** *Okay, you also get credit for* **final deliverables** *such as training materials and delivery documentation.*

[Cockburn 2005], page 98. Emphasis in the original.
→ See also "Definition of done", page 125.

Note the grudging "Okay": there can be a few exceptions, but code and tests remain the items truly worthy of interest.

Minimalism: an assessment

The insistence on minimal software, in the three forms just described, leads to some of the most absurd and damaging contributions of agile methods.

As always, there is some truth in the agile criticism of traditional projects, in this case their propensity to bloat. Projects and products do tend to include too many features. The criticism of paperwork and unnecessary documents is also partly justified. Many documents produced in companies applying rigid processes are already obsolete the day they are released, or serve little practical role. It is true, too, that in the end the code is what counts, not UML diagrams or Gantt charts.

None of this justifies renouncing upfront planning altogether.

First, many of the problems associated with bloat are just the result of bad management. A competent project manager knows to fight "creeping featurism" and constantly to ask whether this or that feature is really needed. The time-honored question, "*Do you want it all, or do you want it now?*", although really akin to blackmail, works wonders.

Classical requirements analysis — the kind of activity that, to the horror of agilists, takes place at the beginning of a project to make sure that we think before we shoot — is precisely intended to arbitrate between the needs of many different stakeholders and establish priorities. When you are faced with a long list of features and for every one of them a stakeholder claims it is absolutely essential, a trick that works well is to allocate everyone $100 in virtual money to stake on the features they want most. The truly critical ones quickly emerge.

The downside of a strategy of "building the simplest thing that can possibly work" is that it favors picking, at every stage, the low-hanging fruit: the features that can be implemented most easily, to produce a demoable result. Projects using this strategy work well *except at the end*. Throughout the development everyone is happy; the developers deliver feel-good demos and the customer is reassured. At the end, because some hard but incontrovertible problem has been put aside, it is impossible to deliver a satisfactory result.

> When the first "Obamacare" health exchanges started operating on 1 October 2013, they fell victim to their own success, to the delight of adversaries of the Affordable Care Act. Almost no one could get through, even less purchase insurance. High levels of activity were blamed, but that sounded like a lame excuse for lack of engineering; after all, many commercial sites routinely process far higher volumes and face higher complexity. Unless one assumes total incompetence, it is likely that during development and testing all the user stories must have seemed to work. There was simply not enough architecture and upfront thinking devoted to ensuring that the system would scale up.

Here is another illustration of the dangers of a piecemeal approach, in the agile tradition of enlightening anecdotes from fields other than software. The original deployment of Boeing's flagship 787 "Dreamliner" in 2013 was a disaster because of dangerous issues with batteries; the planes had to be grounded for several months. James Surowiecki had this to say in his analysis for the *New Yorker*:

> *Determined to get the Dreamliners to customers quickly, Boeing built many of*   [Surowiecki 2013].
> *them while still waiting for the Federal Aviation Administration to certify the*
> *plane to fly; then it had to go back and retrofit the planes in line with the FAA's*
> *requirements. "If the saying is check twice and build once, this was more like*
> *build twice and check once", [an industry analyst] said to me. "With all the time*
> *and cost pressures, it was an alchemist's recipe for trouble."*

These are only examples. But they confirm how naïve it is to expect that "refactoring", once you have something that works partly, can solve any problems that remain. These problems can be very hard, for example a major performance issue that cannot be corrected without a complete redesign. Empirical evidence confirms this suspicion. Boehm and Turner write:

> *Experience to date indicates that low-cost refactoring cannot be depended upon*   [Boehm 2004], page 40.
> *as projects scale up.*

and

> *The only sources of empirical data we have encountered come from*
> *less-experienced early adopters who found that even for small applications*
> *the percentage of refactoring and defect-correction effort increases with [the*
> *size of requirements].*

In software as in engineering of any kind, experimenting with various solutions is good, but it is critical to engage in the appropriate Big Upfront Thinking to avoid starting out with the wrong decisions.

Some of the worst project catastrophes I have seen were those in which the customer or manager was demanding to see something that worked right away ("*it doesn't matter if not everything is there, just show me an example run!*") and sternly reproached the developers who worked on infrastructure that did not produce immediately visible results — in other words, were doing their job of responsible software professionals. The managers got their demos, and then nothing else, since with the focus on delivering visible functionality the hard problems were repeatedly put aside. Each time the next functionality or scaling level was to be added, the team had to restart the design, since all efforts at generality and infrastructure had been shunned. Inevitably, morale sunk, stakeholders lost trust, and sooner or later the project was shelved.

Arguing for visible results is justified, but not if this concern comes at the expense of a fundamental engineering concern: *risk management*. It is the hallmark of a well-managed project that it identifies early the tasks on the critical path, those which will kill the project if not done right. A high-risk task may be a fundamental functionality, which can be demonstrated early, or it may be a scalability requirement (the web site will bear the load the day Oprah mentions your company on the air) that can only be addressed through in-depth design that will not be visible in early demonstrations. To focus on the visible at the expense of the essential is irresponsible.

Additive and multiplicative complexity: the lasagne and the linguine

In spite of the arguments for establishing a solid basis first, agile methods continue to promote the "get something running now" approach. As a typical example, an instructional video about Scrum shows a suit-and-tie manager type telling a developer type with a red scarf and aviator glasses:

> *I can live with something simple that works properly. The complexity can be folded in later.*

[Collabnet site], "scrum-meet-ings" page, at 6:26 in video.

The best one can say here is: well, if that is what you believe, good luck. Such luck will befall you if the complexity is in the form of details that can be added one by one. This is the first kind of complexity, and it does occur. We may call it *additive* complexity. It exists when the basic problem is simple, say compute tax as a percentage of price, and there are many special cases that can just be added one by one.

But there is also another kind, which we may call *multiplicative* complexity. It exists when the fundamental problem is already complex, and you will not get any acceptable solution until you have taken all the key elements into account. An example was cited earlier: support for a multi-language user interface is much harder to add as an after-thought than to integrate from the start.

← *"Agile methods and design", 3.3.2, page 39.*

Complexity in all cases comes from the accumulation of features to integrate. The difference is due to how they interact with each other (if you are reading this as lunch is approaching, I hope the picture below will not only whet your appetite but visualize the issue):

Additive & multiplicative complexity

- With additive complexity, the various features pile up on each other like the layers of a plate of lasagne; they are largely independent. Then it is quite all right to start thinking about the first few, and bring on the others as you go.

- With multiplicative complexity, the various features are entangled like the individual noodles in a bowl of linguine (or spaghetti).

Pamela Zave from AT&T, who has devoted much of her career to studying feature inter-action, starting with telecommunication software, writes:

> *Historically, developers of telecommunication software have had no effective*   *[Zave FAQ].*
> *means of understanding and managing feature interactions. As a result, feature*
> *interactions have been a notorious source of runaway complexity, software bugs,*
> *cost and schedule overruns, and unfortunate user experiences. Developers of*
> *other software systems are beginning to realize that they, too, have a*
> *feature-interaction problem.*

She gives a typical example:

> *Consider "busy treatments" in telephony, which are features for handling busy*
> *situations by performing functions such as forwarding the call to another party,*
> *interrupting the callee, retrying the call later, or offering voice mail to the caller.*
> *Suppose that we have a feature-description language in which a busy treatment*
> *is specified by providing an action, an enabling condition, and a priority. Further*
> *suppose that a special feature-composition operator ensures that, in any busy*
> *situation, the single action applied will be that of the highest-priority enabled*
> *busy treatment.*
>
> *In a busy situation where two busy treatments B1 and B2 are both enabled, with B2*
> *having higher priority, these features will interact: the action of B1 will not be*
> *applied, even though its stand-alone description of B1 says that it should be applied.*

Such cases are typical of why we cannot just assume that we will do "the simplest thing that can possibly work" then add features as needed. If we do so, we will keep finding collisions with what we have done before, and restarting the work. Imagine a standard agile, user-story-based approach to the problem. A user story in the recommended agile style would be

> (User story #1) As an executive, I want a redirection option so that if my phone   *The user story*
> is busy the call is redirected to my secretary.   *examples are*
>   *mine, not Zave's.*

A bit later as we think about priorities, we might concoct another story: *They use the*
   standard style
   described later

> (#2) As a system configurator, I want to be able to specify various priorities for   *in this chapter:*
> "busy" actions.   *"Express*
>   *requirements*

Then, as time goes, a couple more: *through scenar-*
   ios". 4.5.5.
   page 77.

> (#3) As a salesperson, I want to make sure that if a prospect calls while I am in a
> conversation, the conversation is interrupted so that I can take the call immediately.

> (#4) As a considerate responder, I want to make sure that if a call comes while my
> phone is busy I get the option of calling back as soon as the current call is over.

Others will follow. All are perfectly reasonable but, as Zave points out, you cannot just consider them independently. Some scenarios from the fourteen (!) she gives:

> *Bob has the "call-forwarding" feature enabled and is forwarding all calls to Carol. Carol has "do-not-disturb". Alice calls Bob, the call is forwarded to Carol, and Carol's phone rings, because "do-not-disturb" is not applied to a forwarded call.*

[Zave FAQ].

> *Alice calls a sales group. A feature for the sales group selects Bob as a sales representative on duty, and forwards the call to Bob. Bob's cellphone is turned off, so his personal Voice Mail answers the call and offers to take a message. It would be much better to re-activate the sales-group feature to find another representative.*

> *A new Mobility service is offered to office workers. When Alice signs up, her office phone number is forwarded to the Mobility service. On receiving a call for Alice, the Mobility service forwards it to wherever Alice's personal data dictates. However, whenever the data indicates that Alice is in her office, an incoming call enters a forwarding loop.*

These are typical examples of why a plain iterative approach, starting with a basic functioning system and adding features one after the other, can lead to disaster. And yet it is the agile mantra, expressed for example by this citation of Poppendieck that opens a chapter by Cohn:

> *These days we do not program software module by module, we program software feature by feature.*

Cited without further source in chapter 12 of [Cohn 2006].

For run-of-the-mill software, maybe. For complex stuff (of the multiplicative kind), a systemic approach is necessary. Such an approach involves Thinking, probably Big, and, like it or not, best done Upfront.

The agile belief that one can program features incrementally is not applicable to such sophisticated systems. Here we hit one of the principal limitations of the agile approach.

The role of documents

Taken literally, Poppendieck's dismissal of documents,

> *Once a working system is delivered, the user may care little about the intermediate consumables,*

← *See page 60.*

is pointless. Sure, a teenager sending a text message on her smartphone "cares little" about the requirements and analysis documents that were produced for the system's development, but that is also true of any other intermediate artifact, including the program code itself! We could just as well state that the user of a car and the inhabitant of a house "care little" about the "consumables" of the car and house production processes, but that does not mean these artifacts were useless. The question is not whether *users* care but whether *developers* do, for example those who have to maintain the system.

One may wonder whether Poppendieck meant "customer" rather than "user". But the same observation applies in either case. Developers are the relevant constituency.

The criticism of documents has to be based on better arguments. The key actual issue ← *See also "The change criticism", 3.2.4, page 35.* is **change**. Software, as the Agile Manifesto reminds us, will change. If the project produces requirements and design documents, they are difficult to keep in sync with the artifact that has the final word: the code. This observation is also what limits comparisons with other disciplines: software is unique in the speed at which we can change it, and in the absence of any *production* costs. One of the reasons car manufacturing cannot work without plans and documents is that once you have a design you produce many copies of it (cars); changing the design is a major decision, and a costly one, since you also have to update the production process. The "soft" part of the word "software" is there for a reason: we can change our program on a whim. If documents describe it, ensuring that they will always be updated is hard. In fact, most projects hardly ever try. That is the major problem with requirements, design and other documents.

Modern software technology has answers to propose, such as the "Single-Product Principle" which (in line with this book's avoidance of describing my own work) will not be discussed further here. Even without such techniques, however, the risk of change is not a reason to dismiss documents.

What is simplicity?

Another agile mantra worth further analysis is simplicity. In the previous subsections we studied specific consequences of the quest for simplicity: the injunctions to develop minimal functionality, no more than the product requested, and only code and tests. We saw the constant emphasis on "the simplest thing that could possibly work" and "you are not going to need it". To conclude this review of agile minimalism it is useful to take a closer look at the concept of simplicity and correct the confusion reflected in one of the "official" agile principles, which defines simplicity as *"the art of maximizing the amount of* ← *A10, page 50.* *work not done"*.

As anyone knows who has ever obtained a first solution to a problem of any kind, found it too complex, and tried to simplify it, achieving simplicity often means *adding* work, sometimes lots of it.

In a 1998 *Business Week* interview, Steve Jobs said it well:

> *That's been one of my mantras — focus and simplicity. Simple can be harder than complex: You have to work hard to get your thinking clean to make it simple. But it's worth it in the end because once you get there, you can move mountains.*

At www.business-week.com/1998/2 1/b3579165.htm.

A couple of generations earlier, Antoine de Saint-Exupéry, drawing on his observation of aircraft manufacturing, expressed a similar idea:

> *It seems that all human industrial effort, all the computations, all the nights spent working on the drafts, lead to a single visible result: simplicity — as if the experience of several generations was needed to extract, little by little, the curve of a column, of a keel or of an airplane's fuselage, until they reach the elementary purity of the curve of a breast or a shoulder. It seems that the work of engineers,*

From Terre des Hommes, *chapter III, "L'avion". My translation, emphasis added.*

designers, draughtsmen and technicians is only to burnish and rub out [until reaching] a perfectly blossomed form, freed at last from its crust, with the same spontaneous quality as a poem. **It seems that perfection is reached not when there is nothing more to add, but when there is nothing more to remove.**

If Michelangelo had equated simplicity with maximizing the work not done, he could just have left the block of marble alone, instead of hitting hard at it to bring out David (*"in every block of marble I see a statue as plain as though it stood before me, shaped and perfect in attitude and action. I have only to hew away the rough walls that imprison the lovely apparition to reveal it to the other eyes as mine see it"*). All right, I will stop throwing in citations by famous people from various centuries, lest you ask me to add "proof by citation" to the list of shady intellectual devices covered in an earlier chapter. ← *Chapter 2.* All these authors, however, express a fundamental observation: achieving simplicity is not the same as minimizing work. Both are worthy goals in software engineering, but they arise in different contexts and lead to different principles:

- Simplicity has long been advocated by the proponents of rigorous, elegant programming techniques, such as Dijkstra, Wirth, Hoare, Gries and Parnas. They often equate it with the use of simple *mathematical* models of programs, not a concern of agile authors.

- Avoiding unneeded work is, for its part, a key theme in the agile literature, as we have seen. It leads to such principles as "Eliminate waste" and "Decide as late as possible" → *"Lean Software's principles", 9.2.2, page 134.* in Lean Software.

The two views meet, but not necessarily in the way agile authors would like. Wirth published in 1995 a *Plea for Lean Software* — note the word "lean" — in which he criticized the accumulation of useless features in modern software products and advocated writing small, coherent systems. But to describe how to achieve such simplicity he wrote:

The experienced engineer, realizing that free lunches never are, will now ask: *[Wirth 1995].* *where is the price for this economy hidden? A simplified answer is: in a clear conceptual basis and a well-conceived, appropriate system structure.*

If the core — or any other module — is to be successfully extensible, its designer must understand how it will be used. Indeed, the most demanding aspect of system design is its decomposition into modules. Each module is a part with a precisely defined interface that specifies imports and exports.

In other words: you must think hard and think early. So much for deciding as late as possible and building the system one feature at a time.

4.4.5 Accept change

The world and our perception of it change; so do software system requirements. Directly involving customers in the project is likely to lead to even more change requests.

The Agile Manifesto talks of *"welcoming"* change, not just accepting it. This is an exaggeration. It is one thing to state that change is a normal phenomenon in software development, and quite another to start *hoping* for more changes. After all it always causes more work, when some functionality has been correctly implemented, to accept a requirements change than to stick with the original. For comparison, consider how successful the hotel booking service *booking.com* has become by letting customers change reservations without a penalty: it is hard to imagine that the company's employees come to work in the morning *wishing* that more customers will change their minds today! The policy may be profitable overall, but every change still causes hassle.

A sure sign that agile methods "accept" rather than "welcome" change, whatever the Manifesto proclaims, is that in practice they do limit change. Scrum, for example, has a strict rule — we will call it the *closed-window rule* — prohibiting the product owner, and everyone else, from adding or changing product requirements during a project development phase (sprint).

Scrum

→ *"The closed-window rule", 6.1.2, page 90.*

For all the abuse heaped on traditional methods and the "waterfall", Scrum appears to align itself here with standard software engineering wisdom. Contrary to the caricature found in agile texts, the software engineering literature has long recognized the necessity of change as a lifecycle-long process; it simply states that change must be properly managed. Only a naïve team would accept, let alone welcome, unbridled change at any time — and it would not deliver much software. Scrum uses its own specific rule for change management: accept change outside of sprints. This is a reasonable policy, entirely in the spirit of traditional principles and practices.

The enthusiastic acceptance of change is a refreshing departure from the mentality of many managers accustomed to a strict process-based approach, for whom the only good requirements are frozen requirements, and who treat change requests as nuisances. The spread of agile ideas has played a considerable role in changing that attitude.

The need to produce software that can easily be changed, called **extendibility**, is hardly a new concern. In fact it has been a core topic of software engineering discussions for decades. While the agile manifesto is right to promote a change-ready mindset, the main problem with extendibility is not psychological but technical: what software techniques can we apply to ensure that we do not need to redo everything from scratch when customers change their mind or some domain property changes?

The agile approach does have one important idea to contribute to advancing extendibility in practice: the Extreme Programming rule that **every piece of functionality should have an associated test case**. One of the impediments to change is the risk of breaking some previous function of the system, especially if the problem is found late. With a regression suite ready to be tested after every change, the risk decreases considerably.

Apart from that rule, however, the agile method offers little to help extendibility, and actually promotes techniques that go *against* it. Analyzing the agile attitude towards software change shows that, as they say of relationships on Facebook, "*it's complicated*". In grand declarations of intent, agilists proudly "welcome change"; but when it comes to technical issues they often take a scornful or hostile attitude towards ideas that do help produce extendible software.

An example of such an idea, in fact an entire software development method designed to support extendibility, is object-oriented software construction, with its enforcement of abstraction, information hiding, genericity, polymorphism, dynamic binding and other concrete mechanisms directly designed to facilitate software change. The Poppendiecks assert that OO does not deliver:

> While **in theory** OO development produces code that is easy to change, in practice OO systems can be as difficult to change as any other, especially when information hiding is not deeply understood and effectively used.

[Poppendieck 2010], page 52. Emphasis in the original.

but they do not suggest a better way to achieve extendibility.

Their comment is puzzling: what kind of "OO development" can there be without proper use of information hiding, one of the defining characteristics of the method? And any approach can be dismissed on the basis of bad results from people who do not "*understand it deeply*" and do not "*use it effectively*". Do we reject the idea of car transportation because there are bad drivers? Or should we reject Lean Software, the method promoted by the authors, if we come across someone who does not apply it right? Another example of bizarre agile logic.

The agile problem with change is not limited to such condescending and gratuitous comments. Some agile principles and practices directly damage extendibility. The most striking example is the campaign for minimal software, enjoining us, as described in the preceding sections, to build "only the product needed". We have been subjected to YAGNI, informed that it is "*a waste*" to include code "*not needed **now***", and ordered not to "*always handle the most general case*" but instead to program only for the here and now. This approach, however, is incompatible with the goal of supporting change. Change-aware developers try to think ahead and, whenever possible, to build more than strictly asked, in anticipation of likely evolutions.

← "Develop minimal software", 4.4.4, page 58.

Agilists seem not to have noticed this contradiction between the noble ambition of supporting change and the imposition of principles and practices that hinder it.

As in other cases, the agile criticism of some common practices is correct: programmers should not engage in unbounded and unwarranted generalization. But it does not justify rejecting the sound professional practice of trying to handle, if not the "*most general case*", at least a case more general than the one at hand.

Beyond the negative effect of such exaggerated advice, the fundamental issue governing change in software is architectural. Ease of change does not come out of thin air: it requires *designing the architecture for change*. Good textbooks teach you how, but such Big Upfront thinking is precisely what agilists reject.

Agile advocacy of change is the right goal — and only a goal.

4.5 TECHNICAL PRINCIPLES

We come to a set of software-specific techniques that lie at the core of agile approaches.

4.5.1 Develop iteratively

Agile development is iterative development. Agilists have little patience for water-fall-style processes — practiced or imagined — that devote weeks or months to activities such as requirements and design before they produce any code. In the agile view, the proof of the pudding is in the coding. Deliver early and often.

Produce frequent working iterations

Iterative development, advocated in the software engineering literature ever since a 1975 article by Basili, takes various forms. An iterative process could, for example, produce *[Basili 1975].* successive subsystems, or *clusters*, of the future product, each focused on a technology layer required by the final system: the persistence (database) cluster, the networking cluster, the business logic cluster, the user interface cluster. In such an iterative approach we may say that the decomposition is "vertical".

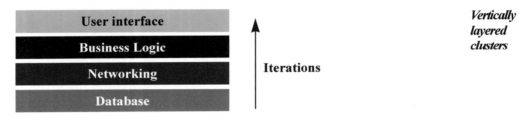

Vertically layered clusters

This is not the agile notion of iterative development. The agile decomposition will be horizontal: every iteration must yield a working system.

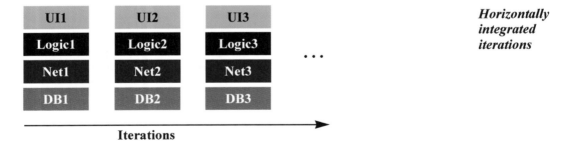

Horizontally integrated iterations

That system may offer, especially at the beginning, only a small subset of the full mechanisms; for example the database part might be primitive, or even just a stub (a place-holder module simulating the future functionality). But, in contrast with the vertical approach, it must be a functioning system that provides an end-to-end user experience, allowing the customer representatives in the project to try it and provide feedback.

The distinction between the vertical and horizontal forms of iterative development is related to the opposition between multiplicative and additive forms of complexity. In the presence of multiplicative ("linguine") complexity, establishing first an architectural basis common to all features will help disentangle feature dependencies. For additive complexity, a horizontal process is appropriate, adding features one after the other. This is the scheme promoted in agile development.

← *"Additive and multiplicative complexity: the lasagne and the linguine", page 63.*

Iteration length

All agile methods suggest that iterations should be short, typically a few weeks. They differ in the precise length they recommend. Scrum calls the iterations "sprints" and often (although not universally) suggests a duration of four weeks for each sprint.

Scrum

> I have found it useful to follow the Scrum recommendation but explicitly to base iterations on calendar months. Talking of (for example) "the October release" focuses everyone on the current milestone, simple and clear: the end of the month. The length differences between months (28 to 31 days) are immaterial; the actual development time is shorter anyway, to leave time for sprint planning at the beginning and sprint review at the end.

Such iterative development is time-boxed: the duration of an iteration is fixed in advance. If at the end of the allotted time some of the expected functionality is not completed — according to a "definition of done" agreed in advance — the functionality gets pushed to the next iteration, or dumped altogether, but the deadline does not change.

→ *"Definition of done", page 125.*

The time-boxing principle is more important than the exact length of iterations. Since missing deadlines is so common in the software world, it may take some time to convince a team that deadlines are firm and that if something has to go it will be the functionality, never the iteration's end date. Once everyone has realized this rule is for real, it has a healthy effect on the project: predictions become more realistic, since developers know they will not be allowed any extra time, and customers realize it makes no sense to ask for unfeasible goals. In my experience, the rule also has the effect of galvanizing the team: even though it is in principle possible to dump some functionality, the case does not happen much in practice: it does not look good, so developers, having made sure the plan is doable, do strive to implement the promised functions in time.

> Agilists sometimes invoke the time-boxed nature of iterations as an excuse to refuse to commit to both delivery time and functionality in deployed releases. The excuse does not hold, of course. External customer constraints still apply. We will encounter this "either-what-or-when" fallacy in the discussion of transitioning to agile.

→ *"The either-what-or-when fallacy", 10.2, page 146.*

Freeze requirements during iterations

Agile methods, as we know, promote acceptance of change, but in any realistic approach change has to be controlled. Here we are indebted to Scrum for a strict rule: functionality can only be added in the sprint planning phase. Once the sprint has actually started, meaning the team is implementing some of the retained functions, no one is permitted to add anything until the end of the sprint. The prohibition is strict and applies to everyone in the project and outside of it, managers included.

This idea is embodied in the "closed-window" rule, which we will review as part of → *"The closed-window rule", 6.1.2, page 90.* the detailed study of the notion of sprint. It is one of the most interesting contributions of Scrum.

Iterative development: an assessment

We should separately assess the two ideas reviewed: frequent working iterations; requirements freeze during sprints.

The most important property of frequent working iterations is that they are frequent. The software industry has understood over the past couple of decades that a "Big Bang" approach, where the various teams go away on their separate parts of a project and try a few months later to reconvene, does not work. Divergence is simply too hard to fix; people make inconsistent assumptions about the rest of the system, and the longer you wait to find out the harder it will be to reconcile them. This is the reason why early on Microsoft introduced the "daily build' process: compile and run a version of the system → *"Daily build and continuous integration", 7.1, page 103.* every night, and anyone who introduced a show-stopping bug does not get to go home until fixing it. A development cycle based on units of a few weeks has become the norm today, thanks in no small part to agile popularization of the idea.

What about the insistence that the frequent iterations must be *working* iterations? Here the assessment has to be nuanced. We saw earlier in this chapter the negative con- ← *"Minimalism: an assessment", page 61.* sequences of demanding a working system at every step, and refusing iterations whose purpose is to build infrastructure. Good engineering requires solid foundations; a competent manager will sometimes just refuse to show something that works, or pretends to work, and will instead build the core technology that will make the rest of the project efficient and scalable. Insisting on an executable system at every stage can be a waste of resources, and an irresponsible policy.

> When builders are constructing a house, for a long time they have little to show to the layperson for their efforts. They are working on the foundations, the piping, all the stuff that will make the house sustainable. You drive by every morning and think "What on earth are they doing in all that time? I see nothing at all!" Then one day you spot something that looks like the beginning of an actual house, and from then on it progresses amazingly fast, because the appropriate basis has been prepared. Of course the engineer had planned things that way all along; the layperson is the only one amazed.

> Imagine what an agile process would be here. Right from the first iteration we would insist on something that can be shown to the "user" and that looks like a house. We would need some floors and some walls. Maybe a roof, although we are in summer and that can wait until the second sprint. Then — oh yes, do we not need to connect to the sewage system? Maybe. Electricity? Let's add it now. Oh yes, foundations! Admittedly, it would be too bad if the house sunk into the ground. No problem, we can always at some point move the house to the next yard, dig a hole, set up the foundations, and move the house back.

> What, this is Southern California and we should think of earthquake resistance? That would be a lot of refactoring. Come to think of it, how many users of the house are really going to encounter earthquakes? The last really big one was, like, a hundred years ago! *You Are Not Going To Need It.*

Now we all know that software engineering is a different kind of engineering from construction engineering. But not entirely different. The benefits of thinking hard — and *upfront* — about infrastructure show up in all kinds of engineering. The obsession with delivering a working system at every step can be a damaging distraction.

Once again we see an important agile insight damaged by unfettered generalization. The insight is that developers can become so engulfed in the internal details of the technology that they forget the big picture: they forget that they have a customer who has signed up not for technology but for solutions. What the customer wants is a system. There is always a tradeoff between how much the system will do and when it will become available. A partial system that appears too early and is not scalable to a satisfactory result is bad; but so is a system that promises perfection but is always promised for later.

The order of tasks

Any iterative approach to development raises the question of how a team determines, in the course of an iteration, the order of individual development steps. XP was the first to provide an agile answer: start with "the simplest thing that can possibly work".

All agile approaches promote a similar view. Cockburn, for example, criticizes the "***Worst Thing First***" strategy on the grounds that

> [1] *If the team fails to deliver, the sponsor has no idea where the failure lies: Is the team not good enough to pull off this project? Is the technology wrong, or is the process wrong? In addition, the team members may get depressed or start arguing with each other.*

[Cockburn 2005], page 48. Number added.

and suggests instead the following for beginning and experienced teams, respectively:

> [2] *[For] teams that haven't worked together before and are tackling a new problem with new technology, I prefer **Easiest Thing First, Hardest Second**. The team [...] and the sponsors get the confidence of an early victory. If the most difficult problem is still outside the team's capabilities, I look for the **hardest thing the team can succeed with** as the second task.*

Same source, emphasis in the original. Numbers added.

> [3] *Once the risk of team and technical failure abates, a good strategy is **Highest Business Value First**.*

The rationale for the first advice [2] is convincing; it simply transposes to software the obvious observation that a new team of alpinists is not going to start with Mount Everest and a new orchestra with Stravinsky's *Rite of Spring*. But the main benefit of the proposed policies are for the team, not the project. What if the "*hardest thing*", initially postponed, turns out to be beyond the team's reach? The earlier effort will have been wasted, and the initial success will have produced a deceptive impression. It is easy to transpose Cockburn's above criticism of the "Worst Thing First" strategy [1]:

"If the team succeeds in delivering the '*Easiest Thing*' or the '*Hardest Thing it can Succeed With*', the sponsor has no idea what the success means: Is the team only good enough to pull off this part of the project? Is the technology right for the more difficult parts, and does the process scale for them? In addition, the team members may get over-confident and start congratulating each other prematurely, not realizing that the true challenges are yet to come."

Imitated from [1] on the previous page.

Cockburn's recipe for well-jelled teams, "Highest Business Value First" [3], is the usual agile recommendation, fundamental in particular to the Scrum strategy of picking the next available user story at every step of a sprint. Such a discourse is sure to resonate well with some manager types, but it can also be irresponsible. A product is successful if it offers not only one deciding benefit but a host of supporting features. After the highest-value item come the second-highest and all the others. What if the first one is implemented impressively, but with architecture choices that prove terrible for its successors? From the initial elation the project will quickly transition to delays and frustration.

Here again there is no single solution. We should note in particular that the conditions are often different at the beginning of a project and in its subsequent phases. This observations leads to the suggestion of dual development.

Dual Development

Resolving the tradeoff between infrastructure work and user-visible functions is one of the core issues of software development; no simplistic recipe — such as "deliver a working system at every iteration, generalize and solidify later", but also the other extreme, "build a perfect foundation first" — holds the solution. One policy that I have seen to work distinguishes between the early and late parts of a project:

- **Early on**, infrastructure is key. While mockups, experiments and prototypes can of course be useful, to simulate the future end-to-end user experience, what matters most is to analyze in depth the fundamental constraints on the system and to make design decisions that will guarantee success; not only initial success in the sense of a first delivery, but an extendible and scalable system whose architecture allows growth and adaptation. Everything else is a diversion.

  If at that stage a consultant tells you that it is impossible to make such decisions because agile methods say so, and that the only way to proceed is to start building "the simplest thing that could possibly work", only one reaction makes sense: fire the consultant. Any amateur developer can build such a mockup. The professional is the one who knows how to make the fundamental decisions even under incomplete information — and get most of these decisions right the first time.

- **Later**, however, when the key decisions have been made and the essential infrastructure built, the risk stressed by agile advocates becomes serious: the project could turn into a sterile, inbred development focused on perfecting internals rather than delivering value. Then it is time to bring in the relentless focus on delivering working systems regularly and to start hanging oversized banners in the development rooms:

Monthly sprints, built on the infrastructure developed in the first phase but now delivering working instances of the system, are now the order of the day, each providing user representatives with an ever closer idea of what they will get, and enabling them to give the developers the direct feedback they need.

It is also possible to apply these two approaches concurrently rather than in sequence. If you have a nervous customer who is anxious to see something running early on, you can assign part of the team to build the fundamental architecture, and the other part to deliver functionality that immediately works. This second task also functions as a prototyping and experimentation effort, to try out various possible solutions. The two parts inform each other: from the experiments follow lessons as to how to build the fundamental architecture; from the architecture come out pieces that the specific functions can use. It can be delicate to set up such a policy; in particular, the team must be ready to throw away unsatisfactory attempts at functionality when something better becomes available. But it can be the solution to producing visible results right from the beginning without sacrificing the system's long-term integrity, extendibility and scalability.

For such a combination of approaches — either one after the other or in parallel — we may use the name *Dual Development*.

→ *See also*
*"User stories",
8.3, page 119
and "Combining
a priori and a
posteriori
approaches",
7.4.4, page 113.*

4.5.2 Treat tests as a key resource

The search for software quality is at the heart of software engineering. It is easier, however, to argue for quality than to provide concrete ways to guarantee it. There are many ways to approach quality; some, such as the CMMI practices, affect management processes; others are technical and include, for example, formal (mathematics-based) methods of specification and verification. For most of the industry, and for agile methods, the principal technical means to quality is testing.

Testing enjoys an interesting status in the software community. Almost everyone knows Edsger Dijkstra's verdict from the seventies (*"testing can show the presence of errors, never their absence"*), which seems to relegate testing to uselessness. But then everyone still tests software, and many developers know no other verification technique.

What Dijkstra meant is that testing cannot be exhaustive, and in fact can only cover a minute part of the possible cases. (He took the elementary example of testing a 32-bit-integer multiplication program: running and checking 2^{64} cases is beyond computer and human capability.) On the other hand, the normal reaction — at least, my reaction — when hearing about a technique that can "only" show the presence of errors is *"Yes! Yoo-Hoo! Give me one of those!"*. Surely we want to find all the "errors" we can put our hands on.

Agile methods consider tests a central resource of any project. The resource takes the form of a **regression test suite**: the set of tests tried so far, including tests that failed at some point, revealing a bug that has since been fixed. As the name indicates, the purpose is to prevent the phenomenon known as "regression": the reappearance of a bug that had previously been fixed. Regression is — to an extent that often surprises outsiders to the field — a common occurrence in software development; old bugs come back to haunt you. The reasons are diverse: the fix may have corrected the symptom, not the real mistake, which manifests itself again when some new part of the software is executed; it may be the result of wrong reasoning, which has consequences elsewhere; or some configuration management mistake may cause a new version of the program to use a pre-correction version of the affected module. Whatever the cause, the risk of regression is one of the reasons why any project should keep a regression test suite, including in particular every test that failed at any point in the process.

The progress of these ideas is supported by modern tools enabling programmers to:

- Describe every test as a simple script, specifying the testing configuration, the inputs, and an assertion describing the expected pass/fail criteria ("oracle").
- Run a set of tests, or the entire regression test suite, as an automated process.

This combination of facilities is usually called "automatic testing". Even though this term is an exaggeration (since the automation does not cover the most delicate and time-consuming parts of testing: generating test cases and oracles), the corresponding tools, pioneered by JUnit, have changed the practice of software development and made the agile emphasis on regression testing possible, by enabling a project to run all the regression tests at the push of a button. *On more extensive forms of automatic testing see [Meyer 2009a].*

The next two principles extend this fundamental role of tests in the agile world.

4.5.3 Do not start any new development until all tests pass

The most concrete manifestation of the agile emphasis on quality is to regard the integrity of what has been produced as more important than the addition of new elements: quality trumps functionality.

The dilemma is a familiar one to any manager: the task list is large and grows, but not all that has been produced so far works. Where do you put your resources? In an agile project this kind of decision belongs to the group rather than one person, but the question remains. The agile approach is clear: do not move on until all tests pass.

The discipline is laudable but sometimes life has its way of eluding intellectually simple schemes. In particular, there is bug and bug. A test that fails may reveal a blocking problem, in which case the agile discipline is right: until it is fixed, moving on to new functionality is irresponsible. But it may also affect functionality that is not essential at the current stage. Removing that functionality would do the trick; that is, however, a delicate task, which takes up developer time for little benefit and could introduce new bugs. We can also cheat by declaring the bug a feature, but that does not help in the long term, since a correct version will eventually be needed.

Any serious project has a classification of bugs into categories such as blocking, serious and minor. A large project should specify a policy defining which classes of non-passing regression tests (typically, blocking and serious) preclude new developments, and which are acceptable.

4.5.4 Test first

A more controversial principle is the idea of testing first, associated with the Extreme Programming method and underlying some of its key practices: test-driven development and test-first development. The discussion of practices will indeed be the best place to analyze it in detail, but here we can look at the basic idea.

→ *"Test-first and test-driven development",* 7.5, page 113.

Just reading the two words "test first" literally would suggest a fairly simple principle: never write code without first writing a test that exercises it. In an approach that shuns writing precise requirements specifications, tests are a key part of the replacement, so the idea is a natural one. But test-first in the Extreme Programming sense goes further. Beck describes it as: *Write a failing automated test before changing any code.*

[Beck 2005], page 50.

Some functionality is not present yet, and you want to add it. Instead of thinking about it in the classical style of defining requirements, write a test for it, and — this is the surprising part — run that test (after adding it to the regression suite). The test should fail, since the functionality is not yet supported. Then fix the code until the test passes.

> The test-first principle, like Dijkstra's observation on the role of tests, is related to the concept of falsifiability cited at the beginning of this chapter. In the same way that an interesting principle must be falsifiable, an interesting software function must have an associated test whose failure demonstrates that the product does not fulfill the function. (A *successful* test case, or any number of them, demonstrate nothing, in the same way that no set of successful examples can prove the validity of a theory or a principle.) Writing the test first helps clarify what the function is about.

← *"What is a principle?",* 4.1, page 49.

The most important argument in favor of test-first programming is, again in Beck's words, to avoid *scope creep*, the production of code implementing functionality that might or might not be really needed; remember "YAGNI". Test-first increases the entry cost of producing new code since you know you are not even permitted to start without first having the test; and writing the test forces you to imagine a usage scenario for the new feature. If you have trouble devising one, you may conclude that the extension is not needed and just discard it, saving time for more important functionality, and avoiding producing untested code that would probably be of dubious quality.

← *"Produce minimal functionality",* page 58.

The injunction to write the test before the code, considered essential in Extreme Programming, goes too far for some people, and is subject to serious criticism if it leads to using tests as a substitute for specifications. But we do have a major agile contribution here: the idea of never adding any functionality without also providing a test to go with it. Whether the test is written before, during or immediately after matters less than the fundamental rule: **no code without test**.

4.5.5 Express requirements through scenarios

Agile development rejects Big Upfront Requirements. But software development needs requirements, upfront or not, and agile methods particularly emphasize the need to produce software that actually meets user expectations and delivers ROI to the business.

In the previous sections we saw part of the agile answer to requirements: integrate constant testing in the development cycle. More is needed, since tests cannot completely replace requirements. The core requirement techniques recommended in agile approaches can be viewed as more abstract versions of tests: use cases (which predate agile methods) and particularly user stories. Both describe typical interaction scenarios between users and the system.

A use case is coarse-grained and typically describes an entire walk through the system; for example, ordering a product on an internet site.

A user story describes an elementary unit of interaction. A standard scheme for user stories, previewed in earlier examples of this chapter, has emerged in the agile world:

As a [role], I want to [action] so as to [goal].

(The last part may be missing.) For example, in a graphical game product:

As a player, I want all pieces of the winning shape to blink or glow so that I can see the winning shape.
[Cohn 2006], page 270.

Let us use the term "scenario" to cover both use cases and user stories.
→ See also "User stories", 8.3, page 119.

The principle of using scenarios for requirements specification is one of the most widely practiced agile concepts, and one of the most damaging. (We continue our ride on the roller coaster of good, hyped and ugly ideas.) A specification is general: it says what should happen in all cases. A use case or user story, like a test, is specific: it tells you what should happen in one case. Ten user stories give you ten cases; they still lack the abstraction of a specification. If I tell you that I have a function that for the input 1 yields 1, for 2 yields 4, for 3 yields 9, and for 4 yields 16, I am really not saying anything for other values.

I had some fun plotting these values into a curve-fitting program, throwing in, for good measure, the value 25 for 5, and looking at the results predicted by best-fit functions. Sure enough, one of the predicted values for 6 is 36, but it is not the only one; just as good are 34 and 35.6. See the blog article cited on the right.
[Meyer 2012].

On the other hand if I tell you that $f(x)$ is x^2 I have specified the function in a way that ends the story and removes any further questions.

It is unfortunately easy to experience first-hand the damage caused by the systematic use of scenarios as a substitute for requirements. Many web applications, in particular, are designed that way. They cover interactions properly as long as you stay exactly within the schemes that the designers have imagined, but fail you as soon as your needs deviate from the standard cases.

As a typical example, not long ago I watched a small-business owner grappling with a pension-plan system which offers perfectly mapped scenarios for plan members and for plan administrators. Trouble was, she is both, and obviously the authors of the program had not considered that particular scenario.

This is where a more traditional requirements effort wins: it forces you to go from the specific to the general and to abstract from individual examples. Of course there is no guarantee that it will catch all cases; but the very notion of writing a requirements specification encourages you at least to *try* to describe the problem and the solution framework — or, to use Jackson's better terminology, to specify the domain and the machine.
← "The domain and the machine", 3.2.5, page 36.

5

Agile roles

One of the most tangible and immediate effects of agile methods is to force a fresh look at the duties and privileges of project members. Agile development redefines in particular the roles of managers, customers, and the development team.

We will start with the manager's role, continue with the team and the customers, then examine other important roles specified by some or all of the agile methods.

5.1 MANAGER

The most striking prescription affects what agile managers do and particularly what they are *not* supposed to do. Much of the agile discussion of this topic is indeed negative; the manager does not:

- Assign tasks (in the non-agile world, perhaps the defining duty of a manager).
- Decide what functions to implement (also a traditional manager's privilege).
- Direct the work of team members.
- Request status reports.

Henry Ford and Steve Jobs need not apply.

The tasks listed, no longer the purview of managers, will have to be assigned to other actors as discussed in the next sections: mostly the team as a whole, but also new roles such as the Scrum Master.

What remains for the manager? Essentially, a supporting role. The tasks include:

- Establishing an environment that enables the team to work successfully.
- Ensuring a smooth interaction with the rest of the organization. In this role the manager is a **champion** of the team with higher management and other organizational units. Part of the difficulty of this task is to make sure that other divisions of the company, which may not have seen the full agile light yet, do not impede the progress of the agile project by applying old ways of thinking.
- Handling resources, including suppliers and outsourcing partners.

A popular way in Scrum circles to describe the shift is that the manager "plays guru" instead of "playing nanny".

B. Meyer, *Agile!*, DOI 10.1007/978-3-319-05155-0_5,
© Springer International Publishing Switzerland 2014

Scrum goes further by not including a manager role at all. According to Schwaber:

There are only three Scrum roles: the Product Owner, the Team, and the Scrum Master. All management responsibilities in a project are divided among these three roles.

[Schwaber 2004], page 6.

The next sections review these more specific roles. It is natural to ask about the consequences of removing the manager role, in particular the possible dilution of responsibility; the last section discusses this issue.

5.2 PRODUCT OWNER

Deciding on product functions is in Scrum the task of a member of the customer organization called the product owner. As stated by Pichler, the product owner *champions* the product, *facilitates* decisions about that product, and has the *final say* over these decisions.

[Pichler site], blog/roles/ one-page-prod- uct-owner.

Concretely, the principal responsibility of the product owner is to define and maintain the **product backlog**: the list of features. We are talking here of product-level units of functionality, not the individual tasks needed to implement them: these tasks will be defined by the team at the beginning of each sprint. The product owner is, however, crucially involved at the start and end of every sprint:

- At the start, to select user stories from the product backlog, and explain them in terms of their business role.
- At the end, to evaluate the result of the sprint.

The Scrum product owner role covers one of the traditional responsibilities of a project manager, deciding on functionality, but not the others: *enforcing rules* is the job of the Scrum Master; and *handing out individual development tasks* (to implement the selected user stories) is the job of the next character in our cast — the team.

The Product Owner idea is an important Scrum contribution. Its main benefit is to separate the job of defining project objectives and assessing their attainment from the day-to-day management of the project, and in particular of the tasks intended to achieve these objectives.

5.3 TEAM

The team is a group of people but, like the chorus in a Greek tragedy, can also be viewed as a single character. It takes over several traditional manager responsibilities, including the critical one of deciding, step after step, what tasks to implement.

5.3.1 Self-organizing

As we saw in the previous chapter, the team is not a group of people directed by a manager but is empowered and self-organizing.

← "Let the team self-organize", 4.4.2, page 53.

As an example *a contrario* of these principles, Schwaber reports on his visit to a company that thought it was applying Scrum but was not doing it properly:

The ScrumMaster invited me to attend "his Daily Scrum". An alarm went off in my head. Why was it "his Daily Scrum" and not "the team's Daily Scrum"? At the meeting, he went around the room, asking each person present whether he or she had completed the tasks he had written by their name. He asked questions like, "Mary, did you finish designing the screen I gave you yesterday? Are you ready to start on the dialog boxes today?". Once he had exhausted his list, he asked whether the team needed any help from him. They were all silent. How could I tell him what I thought of his methods?

[Schwaber 2004], page 26, excerpted and abridged. On the "daily Scrum" see page 91.

What he thought was less than flattering, of course, since they contradicted the idea of a team that decides by itself what it will do next, picking from the list of remaining tasks.

The team in agile approaches is *self-organizing*. Cockburn and Highsmith write:

Agile teams are characterized by self-organization and intense collaboration, within and across organizational boundaries. [They] can organize again and again, in various configurations, to meet challenges as they arise.

[Cockburn 2001].

Note the key benefit claimed here: the ability to adapt quickly to new circumstances. The main task of a self-organizing team is to decide what to do next. In Scrum this means picking from the task list ("sprint backlog") the next task to be implemented.

The agile literature goes to great lengths to explain that self-organizing does not imply rudderless: in some methods at least the manager still has a role to play, as discussed in the previous section, but this role does not include meddling in everyday decisions such as picking the next task.

5.3.2 Cross-functional

Another recommended characteristic for agile teams is to be cross-functional. The Poppendiecks write:

Agile development works best with cross-functional teams [which have] the skill and authority necessary to deliver useful feature sets to customers independent[ly] of other teams. This means that whenever possible teams should be formed along the lines of features or services.

[Poppendieck 2010], page 69.

The rejected alternative is a division into teams organized along areas of competence, for example a hardware team and a software team (for an embedded system), or a database team and an application logic team. The recommendation is instead to use a division along user-visible subsystems, each covering a subset of the functionality, in line with the reliance on user stories to define that functionality. For example part of the team might be in charge of the scenario "process a new purchase order" and another part in charge of "cancel purchase order", even if the basic infrastructure is shared.

Such an assignment implies only a temporary responsibility associated with a particular task, not a long-term specialization, even less any exclusivity. In a fully cross-functional team, any developer should be able to go to the task list and pick the next task, whatever it is, that the team has deemed to be of highest priority. The presentation of agile roles will discuss the benefits and limitations of cross-functional teams.

→ *"Collective ownership and cross-functionality", 6.12.2, page 102.*

5.4 MEMBERS AND OBSERVERS

The agile world and Scrum in particular make a distinction, for any project, between two kinds of participants: those who are truly *committed* to the project, in the sense that its success is critical for them, and those who are also *involved* but from the sidelines. The accepted terms are respectively "pigs" and "chickens", a terminology that comes from a vulgar joke repeated in a zillion publications and not worth including here. With or without zoology, the concept is hardly new: committees routinely distinguish between *members* and *observers*. Another possible terminology would be "core participants" versus "fellow-travelers".

The distinction matters in particular for daily meetings, where the roles of the two categories are delineated: the members should dominate the discussion, with observers standing on the side. The observers will give their opinion if invited to do so, but actual project decisions, such as including or rejecting functionality, are the privilege of members.

5.5 CUSTOMER

We have seen, as one of the method's principles, that agile methods put the customer at the center. A concrete consequence is to emphasize the role of the customer throughout the project and — in some cases — the role of the customer *as a member* of the project. ← *"Put the customer at the center". 4.4.1, page 51.*

Traditional development approaches also strive to build a system that will please its customers, of course, but they limit customers' involvement to specific phases at the beginning and end of the lifecycle; in the extreme form represented by the "V-model" variant of the waterfall, those would be the top-left and top-right phases.

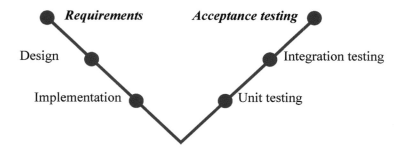

Simplified V-model of the software lifecycle

The simple V-model illustration shown here is not the most common one; usually implementation figures at the bottom, which makes little sense since it is the direct counterpart of (on the verification side) unit testing. In addition, some variants have more phases than shown here.

Even with an upfront requirements phase, many opportunities often arise later in the project for the developers to obtain more information from customers. Some project environments discourage such contacts or even prohibit them. Requiring that they happen through organized channels is reasonable, if only because — as mentioned in the discussion of the customer's role — different stakeholders have different views and you need to make sure you are talking to representative people. But *disallowing* any interaction between developers and customers is a sure way to obtain systems that do not meet customer objectives. Agile methods go further and *require* customer interaction.

← *Page 52.*

While the basic idea is common to all agile approaches, the level of customer involvement differs. Extreme Programming, as explained by Ron Jeffries, directs the team to include a customer representative, part of the "whole team" experience:

> *The team must include a business representative — the "Customer" — who provides the requirements, sets the priorities, and steers the project. It is best if the Customer or one of her aides is a real end user who knows the domain and what is needed.*

[Jeffries site], xpmag/whatisxp #whole.

This role does not appear explicitly in Scrum, since the product owner is the person responsible for representing users, as part of the more general task of conveying to the team the business goals of the project.

Once one accepts the idea of including customer representation in the team, the Scrum approach is superior to the XP notion of an embedded customer representative. There is evidence (anecdotal rather than based on systematic studies) that it is difficult to integrate even a well-meaning customer representative; sometimes the formula jells, but often the representative feels left out, since much of the interesting stuff occurs in technical discussions which he cannot easily follow; and a good deal of the time he just sits bored. In addition, a customer representative with no decision power can do harm as well as good. It is difficult to determine how much he represents the needs of the customer as a whole, and how much just his own. The odds are not good: think of the kind of person whom an organization would wish to assign full-time to a project but without any decision power (taxation without representation, as it were); is that going to be the most competent expert of the application domain? Probably not: such people are typically in high demand and very busy — with application domain tasks. Whoever has enough free time to be posted to a development group for many months may raise some suspicion: is the customer organization trying to help you, or to get rid of someone?

← *See "Put the customer at the center", 4.4.1. page 51.*

With the Scrum notion of product owner, you also get a customer representative, not necessarily full-time, but with a clearly acknowledged strategic decision role: defining the last word on what goes into the product and what does not. This role justifies putting at the project's disposal a product owner who truly understands the business and will provide operationally valuable input to the developers.

5.6 COACH, SCRUM MASTER

Agile methods raise frequent problems in their daily application and require enforcement, lest the team stray from the recommended principles. Sometimes the project manager plays this role, but the recommendation is to assign it to a specific individual: a *coach* in Extreme Programming; a *Scrum Master* in Scrum.

Larman encourages putting in place a "central" coaching team which advises many *[Larman 2010], page 399.* different groups. He also insists that the role of coaches should be to advise, not prescribe; this view is in line with the agile mistrust of consultants or managers who tell everyone what to do but are not ready to do some of the real work themselves.

"Coach" suggests a training role. Scrum Masters, in addition, take on a management role. The border can be thin; as Cohn writes:

> *A ScrumMaster may not be able to say "You're fired", but **can** say "I've decided* *[Cohn 2010], page 399.*
> *we're going to try two-week sprints for the next month".*

More generally,

> *The Scrum Master is responsible for making sure a Scrum team lives by the* *[Schwaber 2012], page 164.*
> *values and practices of Scrum.*

But the role goes beyond that of a political commissar; one of the primary tasks is to **remove impediments** identified by team members in daily meetings. An impediment is → *More on impediments in "Impediment", 8.12, page 129.* any obstacle, technical or organizational, that prevents the team from operating at full productivity (implementing as many user stories as possible). Some impediments are technical, such as a developer getting stuck because he does not know of an appropriate algorithm to solve a certain task; others are political or organizational, such as computers choking up on not enough memory or a subcontractor failing to deliver a component of the system.

The Scrum Master is also responsible for protecting the team from distractions and undue interference from the rest of the organization, since it is an agile tenet that developers should be able to concentrate on one task at one time.

The Scrum Master concept has met with considerable success. Some of that success is due to non-technical factors: to be worthy of consideration as a Scrum Master you should be a *certified* Scrum Master, meaning that you have followed appropriate training and paid your fee. This certification aspect of Scrum is good business. It provides a self-reinforcing loop: certified masters are natural advocates for the method, and the more companies they convince the more Scrum Masters will be needed.

For a new method, the basic concept of having a coach to help apply the method right is sound. More debatable is the expectation that a Scrum Master will do only that job, and will not be a developer. While staying away from absolutely ruling out such a possibility, agile authors clearly state that a Scrum Master should only be a coach; if the project is too small, rather than doubling up on other duties on the project, the Scrum Master should double up on projects, coaching several teams. Scrimshire writes of the risks of a coach who also programs:

> *Being directly involved in the work, being an agent in the system, being directly*   *[Scrimshire site].*
> *affected by difficulties arising in the team means the Scrum Master could lose*
> *objectivity. They could be too close to a problem to be able to coach the*
> *team effectively.*
>
> *As a developer, there is opportunity for directive or controlling behavior to creep*
> *in. Is the developer of sufficient character to be able to retain a sense of*
> *objectivity and unbiased questioning in the role coach or facilitator? If the*
> *developer had a differing technical opinion with the team would they be willing*
> *to accept the team's approach or mandate?*

My experience runs directly against this advice. I have seen too many times the sad spectacle of advisors who do not want to dirty their hands. That is what is so great about being a consultant: if the project succeeds it is thanks to your wonderful advice; if it fails it is for not following it properly. In the Scrum case, consultants make it even easier for themselves because the Scrum Master also stays away from programming but from the other core responsibility-laden task: management.

In traditional settings developers typically do not have much respect for advice-only consultants. There is still enough reverence around agile methods and Scrum that advice-only Scrum Masters are taken seriously. The hypnotism will not last forever, and companies will focus on work that brings real benefits. (Even the Red Army no longer needs political commissars.) Already today, not everyone buys the idea; a reader from India commented, à propos Scrimshire's article cited above:

> *I have seen the trend that organizations look forward to hire people with technical*
> *skills. Specially in India, they do not consider Scrum Master as [an] independent*
> *role but always club with developer (they call it technical scrum master).*

It is good to encounter some common sense, at least in India. A Scrum Master who also programs has the advantage of being close to the problem; "*too close*" perhaps, but it beats being too far. There is nothing like having to wrestle with the toughest part yourself to know how to advise the rest of the team.

Assigning the coaching role to a manager, rather than a developer, also makes sense. A good technical manager should be experienced enough to serve as coach; this is one of the traditional roles of managers, and there is no clear argument for not continuing it when the personalities involved fit the bill.

Harlan Mills developed long ago the concept of chief programmer: the project manager *[Mills 1971]*. who just happens to be the best programmer on the team and in addition has management capabilities and like a general who has risen through the ranks leads the team into battle. The chief programmer is a technical manager, but one who is not afraid to roll up sleeves once in a while and do the design and implementation for the toughest parts of the system. This technique is not for every team — if only because good potential chief programmers are few — but can be effective with the person and team. A good chief programmer will also play the role of coach.

5.7 SEPARATING ROLES

What should we make of the Scrum insistence on three and exactly three roles (Scrum Master, Team, Product Owner)? As usual, there is something to be taken and something to be left.

The most interesting idea is the separation of the *product owner* role from other management responsibilities. In many contexts it can indeed be helpful to hand out to two different persons (or groups, such as "the team" in Scrum) the tasks of :

• Directing the project, day after day.

• Defining what it must do for the business, and assessing whether it actually does it.

This distinction is applicable in projects where no one is equally at ease with the business and technical sides. Such a situation arises in enterprise-style projects ("business" or "commercial" data processing), the area from which agile methods seem to have drawn most of their experience. In a technical company, and particularly in a software company — Microsoft, Google, Facebook... — the classic distinction between "the software" and "the business" disappears, since the business *is* software and often the software is the business. In such environments one can often find an executive who is both thoroughly attuned to the business needs and perfectly capable of leading the project. If you intend to have a project manager — an idea anathema to Scrum and most other agile approaches — that person may also be qualified to serve as the product owner.

The argument *against* merging the manager and product owner roles is the risk of being, in Scrimshire's terms, "*too close to the problem*". He invoked that risk as a reason to separate the roles of *developer* and *coach*; we saw that there is in fact little cause for concern in that case, but the risk becomes more serious if we consider the roles of *project manager* and *product owner*. The manager could become so involved with the project — so "embedded" in it — as to develop a kind of Stockholm Syndrome and lose track of the needs of the business, which are the reason the project exists in the first place. A distinct "product owner" will not succumb to that temptation, and will provide an independent check on the project's real progress.

The decision — assign two people as manager and product owner, or keep the roles separate — is a tradeoff between consistency, favoring a single project manager defining a clear vision for the team, and independence, favoring the inclusion of a second viewpoint. Every project must examine that tradeoff in light of its own circumstances; there is no universal, dogmatic answer.

Many projects, especially when they have limited resources, consider other mergings:

- It may be legitimate — not just in India — to let one of the more experienced developers double up as coach (Scrum Master).

- The manager can also be the coach. This is particularly appropriate, and common, when the manager is a *technical* manager, in the "chief programmer" style, who has more experience than the rest of the team and is naturally qualified to serve as mentor and coach in addition to performing management tasks.

- On the other hand it makes no sense to merge the "coach" and "product owner" role (if the latter is distinct from "manager"). A separate product owner should represent the business needs and not meddle into how the team works.

More generally, while ensuring the presence of a method coach in the project is often a good idea, insistence on keeping it a separate role is not. No doubt it is a good business strategy for consultants; but businesses, their budgets and their projects are better off with doers than with talkers.

6

Agile practices: managerial

The agile principles imply, for a software development project, not only specific roles as studied in the previous chapter, but a set of concrete practices, such as the daily meeting, pair programming and test-driven development.

What, by the way, qualifies as a practice in software development? A practice has to be an activity or a mode of working, but with a special twist: repeated application. In the absence of repetition, we may have an interesting technique, but it is not a practice unless it is performed regularly (in the case of an activity) or enforced systematically (in the case of a mode of working).

Scrum also uses, for practices, the more picturesque name *ceremonies*.

We start in this chapter with practices affecting project organization and management. The following chapter will cover technical, software-specific practices.

6.1 SPRINT

One of the core principles of agile development is to work iteratively, producing frequent deliveries. All agile methods apply this idea, with various prescriptions for the duration of the individual iterations. To denote these iterations, the Scrum term "sprint" has come into wide use.

← *"Develop iteratively", page 70.*

The purpose of a sprint is to advance the project by a significant increment, working from a task list, known in Scrum as the sprint backlog. In most agile approaches each task on the list is defined as the implementation of a "user story".

6.1.1 Sprint basics

A Scrum sprint usually lasts one month. Many teams use other durations, and non-Scrum agile authors recommend iterations of varying lengths, although never more than a few weeks in line with the fundamental agile idea of short-cycled iterative development.

This idea of cutting up development into individual iterations lasting a month or so defines the notion of sprint, but a second property, particularly emphasized in Scrum, is just as important. It is the rule that *during a sprint, the task list does not grow*. The rule has to be absolute: no one, laborer, duke or emperor — or project manager — is permitted to add anything while the sprint is in progress.

B. Meyer, *Agile!*, DOI 10.1007/978-3-319-05155-0_6,
© Springer International Publishing Switzerland 2014

This rule is made realistic by the short duration of sprints. Clearly, if iterations lasted six months, it would be impossible to repress the customers' and managers' natural urge to add functionality. With a one-month period, once everyone has signed on to the policy, the project may enforce the strict ban on extensions. No exceptions are allowed, whatever the rank of the supplicant. If there is a really pressing need, it gets parked until the end of the current sprint, and will be examined for possible inclusion in the next sprint. If not having the envisioned feature is a real show-stopper, then the only solution is the extreme one (akin, in the execution of a program, to raising an exception): terminating the sprint early — a decision that, as we have seen, is the privilege of the product owner. It is a pretty drastic decision; unless the product owner feels things are so critical as to justify it, he will just wait, like everyone else, until the next sprint.

6.1.2 The closed-window rule

The rule barring additions of functionality during a sprint follows from one of the prin- ← *"Freeze*
ciples we saw in an earlier chapter. It does not seem to have received a specific name in *requirements*
the agile literature but it is so important that it deserves one. Let us call it the *during itera-*
closed-window rule: the window for changes is closed whenever a sprint is in progress. *tions", page 71.*

The closed-window rule addresses one of the biggest practical obstacles to successful software development: *disruptive feature creep*, more precisely disruptive customer- or management-induced feature creep. Customers and managers teem with ideas, and keep dreaming up new features. Giving them demos of early versions (in general a good practice, and strongly advocated in agile approaches) can make the phenomenon even worse by bringing to light what functionality is still missing. By itself the feature creep phenomenon is inevitable and in many respects healthy; a successful system will serve the business best if the key stakeholders have had their say. The problem is the disruptive nature of feature requests coming from a person carrying enough authority to change priorities. He or she comes up with a superb idea, so superb indeed that it has to be implemented right this minute at the expense of the currently scheduled tasks. Such interruptions can quickly derail a project: priorities get messed up, important work is delayed, and developers lose morale. But without a clear process such requests can be politically difficult to refuse.

The genius of the closed-window rule is that it neither ignores the risk of feature creep nor fights it head-on, but channels it into the limited framework of sprint planning exercises. A practical consequence is that a kind of natural selection takes place between feature ideas. Many a brilliant suggestion loses its luster when you look at it again after a few days, and when the time does come to select features for the next sprint it may no longer seem so urgent. Disruptions are avoided and noise takes care of itself. The ideas that were truly worthy of consideration are prioritized against all other tasks.

6.1.3 Sprint: an assessment

Two aspects are interesting to discuss: sprint duration, and the closed-window rule.

The one-month standard duration of sprints appears just right. In this book we often note that strict agile rules are too rigid, and sometimes see that the spirit is more important than the exact details; but in this particular case it appears that following the exact Scrum one-month prescription (including sprint planning and sprint review) works well. More precisely, Scrum specifies "thirty days"; I have found, as noted earlier, that it is ← *"Iteration length", page 71.* more effective to use a calendar month. Simplicity breeds focus.

The closed-window rule is an outstanding idea. While it contradicts the Agile Manifesto's principle A2, "*Welcome changing requirements, even late in development*", by ← *Page 50.* conceding that not all change is welcome at all times, it provides a framework for handling change (or "harnessing" change, as the principle puts it).

6.2 DAILY MEETING

A core agile practice is the daily meeting, also known as the "stand-up meeting" and as the "daily scrum". *Stand-up* because one of the original ideas was to make sure the meeting does not last long — fifteen minutes is the standard — by requiring everyone to stand; this requirement is impractical and usually not applied. *Scrum* because many groups use some approximation of the version fine-tuned by the Scrum method.

The rationale for meeting at the beginning of every workday is the general agile principle that direct contact is critical to project success. It meets here with the just as general agile distrust of heavy processes and such waste-inducing practices (think "lean") as long meetings. Hence the emphasis on both frequency and strict time limits. The method insists in particular on what a daily scrum is *not*: it is not intended to solve problems or engage in deep technical discussions. Its focus is precisely defined: answering the "**three questions**". What did you do on the previous working day? What will you do today? Any impediments?

The first two questions give the team the opportunity to catch up with each other on the progress of the project and its immediate future. They also help ensure that team members make realistic commitments and fulfill them, since today's answer to the second question, the promise, will meet tomorrow's answer to the first, the reckoning. As Cohn writes, the exercise is not a status update where a boss finds out who is behind schedule, but an opportunity for team members to make commitments to each other.

In the third question, an impediment is any obstacle that stands between a team member and the realization of his stated goals. There are technical impediments, such as problems with hardware or software products, and organizational impediments, such as the absence of a team member whose input is needed. The meeting should remove the → *"Impediment", 8.12, page 129.*

impediments when possible in the short time imparted, and otherwise assign responsibility for removing them. In Scrum, more specifically, removing impediments is one of the key responsibilities of the Scrum Master.

As emphasized by agile authors, one should be on the alert for practices that distort the purpose of the daily meeting and threaten its effectiveness. The two main threats are project members who go off into digressions, and the temptation to engage in deep technical discussions. Once you are aware of these risks, it is relatively easy to fend them off; the person in charge of enforcing good practices — in a traditional approach the project manager, and in Scrum the Scrum Master — can:

• Remind the ramblers to be concise; a more indirect technique is to enforce the time limit even (or *especially*) if this means that some people do not get to speak. It should not take more than one or two experiences of that kind for those who spoke too long to understand that they are the ones at fault. If it does, the team truly has a problem.

• If a technical discussion takes off on its own, intervene and suggest holding a separate meeting.

The idea of the daily meeting, with its focus on the three questions and the strict limitation of scope and duration, is brilliant. As with other agile ideas, you can stop listening to the advice when it becomes dogmatic. Some circumstances, such as geographically distributed projects, naturally lead to variations over the basic scheme:

• Setup time. A 15-minute meeting is fine for a resident team but generally not effective for a distributed team. Even with good technology and an experienced group of people, it can take a few minutes (*"Can you hear me?"*, *"Let's switch from Skype to WebEx"*, *"The video conference room is still occupied"*) to get down to business.

• Flexible working schedules. In many organizations, some employees come in at different times or occasionally work at home. Such practices contradict the agile insistence on direct personal communication, but they have other justifications, such as the desirability of a "sustainable pace", and companies may legally be required to allow them. ← *"Work at a sustainable pace", 4.4.3, page 56.*

• Time zones. Consider a group with some members in California and others in Shanghai. 7 AM for the former means (in the winter) 11 PM for the latter. You can ask people to be up late once in a while, but not every day.

• Meeting inflation. While there are good reasons for moving deeper technical discussions to a separate meeting, they should be balanced with the overhead of organizing separate meetings (*"Let's discuss this on Tuesday afternoon — Tuesday I am not here, can you make it Wednesday at 10? — Yes, but I think the meeting room is not available"* and so on), plus the context-switching time (the time for everyone to remember what it was all about). Sometimes when an issue can be solved by a 20-minute discussion it is just as simple to have that discussion then and there.

• Length variability. There is no reason to use the same limits regardless of team size. 15 minutes may be fine for a group of five people and too short for ten.

A distributed team I know, which works across three continents and has honed its process over several years, has two weekly meetings, Monday and Thursday, at a time that is acceptable in all time zones affected. Both last one hour for the reasons just mentioned. They have complementary goals:

- The Monday meeting is developer- and deadline-based. Its purpose is to check progress towards the next deadline. It is run in the spirit of a Scrum daily meeting: each member of the team presents his or her current status based on the "three questions". Since it uses a full hour, technical discussions are not prohibited as long as they remain short; anything that requires deeper analysis is moved to the Thursday meeting or some other medium (such as an email discussion, or an extraordinary meeting). The team long ago learned to make good use of the available time and never overruns the one-hour limit. There is no agenda for those meetings; they are organized around the task list, a shared document that everyone can consult (through screen sharing) during the meeting.

- In contrast, the Thursday meeting is agenda-based; it is devoted to the discussion of a list of issues collected in advance by the meeting secretary (a task that rotates between members of the group). Its decisions are recorded as "action items" in the minutes (produced in real time during the meeting), and copy-pasted to the agenda of the next meeting so that the first matter of the day is to check what has been promised, just as in a daily meeting.

This particular formula, obtained by trial and error (as well as reading agile and other software books) works well for that particular group. A team subject to different constraints will fine-tune its own variant of the daily meeting idea. Freed of dogmatism — adapted in particular to the multi-site, flexible-personal-schedule working style of modern companies — that idea, particularly its focus on the "three questions", is one of the principal contributions of the agile school. Some day, the whole industry will be practicing it and not even conceive that anyone could ever have been working otherwise.

6.3 PLANNING GAME

The next two practices to be reviewed (in this section and the next) address one of the toughest challenges of software management and development: estimating the cost of a system to be developed, or part of that system. The planning game comes from Extreme Programming, the planning poker from Scrum. Cost estimation, the goal in both cases, is only a subset of what "planning" normally covers; but this limited scope of the term is consistent with the rest of the agile creed, which does not like the idea of upfront tasks.

The unit of estimation has traditionally been a unit of work: person-month or, at a finer level of granularity, developer-day (one programmer working for one day). More sophisticated metrics have been developed recently, in particular the *story point*, which we will study in the discussion of artifacts. The discussion in this section and the next does not depend on the particular metric used. → *"Story points"*, *8.4, page 121.*

The XP planning game is a "game" not in the sense of a competition, with winners and losers, but in the game theory sense of a cooperative game, where two actors try to maximize different criteria and seek an optimal compromise between them. The two actors are "business" and "development" in Beck's term, or more simply the customer and developer groups. The customers seek to maximize functionality and minimize the time to obtain it. The developers understand the difficulty level associated with every element of functionality, and the incompressible time that it requires. In the game:

- Customers define the respective priority of a set of functionality elements — defined in agile style as user stories — for a project, or a particular iteration.

- Developers estimate the cost (person-days) of implementing each story.

In playing the game, the two groups perform these tasks repeatedly, engaging into negotiation over the estimates. Customers sort the stories on the basis of priority. The game terminates when the two sides have agreed to select the highest-priority tasks with a total cost that fits within the time allotted for the release and the number of developers. In a variant of the game, the result is not so strictly tied to a release cycle but simply consists of a prioritized list of user stories.

6.4 PLANNING POKER

Scrum's planning poker is another approach to the same problem as XP's planning game, how to estimate the cost of user stories in advance. Again the discussion does not depend on the choice of measurement unit, such as developer-day or story point.

The two ideas of planning poker are to:

- Rely on the collective judgement of a panel of estimators, iterating until they agree.

- Avoid pointless haggling over small differences by forcing the values to be taken from a sequence of clearly distinct values.

A sequence of values satisfying the last criterion is the Fibonacci sequence: 0, 1 (and 1 again), 2, 3, 5, 8, 13, 21, 35, ...

> I hear you: that is not the Fibonacci sequence! Indeed. The last number cited should be 34. Congratulations on your mathematical sophistication! But one agile consultant has had the brilliant business idea of producing and selling a deck of planning-poker playing cards. Trouble is, copyrighting the Fibonacci sequence is kind of hard, since it has been around since something like 1202 in Italy (and a couple of millennia earlier in India). Not to worry: just change one of the values. Not exactly as I did above — I am far too scared of a copyright infringement suit! — but you get the idea.

If estimates are done in person-days, the second value is sometimes replaced by 0.5 since some simple user stories may be implementable in less than a day. What matters is that the values differ sufficiently to avoid the estimators getting into a fight over insignificant differences, such as whether a particular task will take 11 or 12 days; the aim is rough-cut estimation rather than exactness.

Some variants of planning poker rely on an even smaller set of choices, in particular "T-shirt sizing" which offers five values from X-small to X-large. Most variants also include the value "?" for the benefit of an estimator who feels there is not enough information yet to propose an answer.

The panel of estimators is the development team, including the product owner and other customer representatives as appropriate. It applies a form of the "Delphi" expert-consensus decision method, which originated with the US military and has been in use for decades. It is also influenced by the more recent concept of "wisdom of the crowds", according to which a group can collectively reach a better decision than even the best individual experts in its midst. The goal is to arrive at a consensus, but to avoid reaching it through the intimidation of outlying thinkers by the initial majority. *[Surowiecki 2004]*

The process for estimating the cost of a functionality element involves the following steps:

1 Someone, typically the product owner, describes the feature.

2 The participants discuss it and ask questions as needed.

3 Every participant privately picks an estimate, from the preset sequence of values.

4 The choices are revealed. This where the process gets its name: as in a game of cards, you show your hand only when asked.

5 If the values agree, the process stops for this item and the common estimate is retained. (This is where it is important to have widely separated values in the sequence.)

6 If the values are not identical, a discussion takes place, with each member arguing for his or her choice. Then the process is repeated from step 3, on the basis of information gained in the discussion.

7 If the process does not converge quickly enough to a common value, the participants will have to abandon it and discuss what else to do, such as getting more information and postponing the estimation to a later date.

Cohn states that

> *Teams estimating with Planning Poker consistently report that they arrive at more accurate estimates than with any technique they'd used before*   *[Cohn site]*.

without, however, citing actual studies. My own experience, also individual and also not backed by studies, is less thrilling. The problem I have seen is the power of majority pressure. If you are truly an expert and you come up with an estimate that is widely different from those of the rest of the group, it is difficult to argue for long without appearing arrogant. To preserve group harmony you are naturally led to give up — at least if you know you are not yourself going to get the task of implementing the item. This outcome can be damaging to the project, especially when the expert knows how hard some task really is but is unable to convince the rest of the group, which has not performed such work before and thinks it will be a breeze.

6.5 ONSITE CUSTOMER

All agile methods, as we have seen, recommend involving customers or their represen- ← *Chapter 5,*
tatives in the project. XP in particular has the notion of an "active customer", also known *particularly 5.2*
as an embedded customer. This practice is mentioned here as a reminder since an earlier *and 5.5.*
chapter discussed the corresponding roles: "customer" and "product owner".

6.6 OPEN SPACE

Agile methods put considerable emphasis on the physical organization of the workspace.

Many development teams traditionally use, at least in the US, private offices for the
lead people and cubicles for everyone else. (Cubicles are less common in Europe, and
the more extreme formats are incompatible with local labor laws; some countries, for
example, require providing every office worker with access to daylight.)

Closed offices and cubicles are anathema to agile development. Because of the core
role of communication, it is a tenet that developers should work in an open space. Here
is a typical exhortation:

> *Use open working environments. Such environments allow people to*   *[Schwaber*
> *communicate more easily [and] get together, and facilitate self-organization.*   *2002], page 39.*
> *When I walk into open areas, I can immediately tell how the team is doing.*
> *Silence is always a bad sign. I know that people are collaborating if I can hear*
> *conversations. When I enter a cubicle environment, there is often silence*
> *indicating an absence of interaction. Cubicles are truly the bane of the modern*
> *workplace. They quite literally keep people apart and break teams up.*

In the recommended agile layout:

- The development area is a large room.

- Developers are seated at desks not too far from each other. If the team practices pair
  programming, there will be two developers at each desk, but in any case people should
  be able to hear conversations at neighboring desks and spontaneously join them.

- The walls are largely covered with whiteboards to support technical discussions.

- A quiet meeting room is available for technical meetings.

Many developers, in my experience, like this kind of arrangement, contradicting the ste-
reotype of programmers as inward-looking nerds. Many does not mean all; witness the
frequent practice of wearing noise-reduction headphones. Some agile authors recognize
the need for occasional isolation, "cones of silence" in Cockburn's terms.   *[Cockburn*
2003].

Indeed, while the basic idea is sound, and cubicles deserve all the scorn they get from
agile critics, it would be nice if everyone would follow Cockburn's example and refrain
from sweeping absolutes. Open spaces are not the solution for all people and all times.
It is impossible to take Schwaber's "*Silence is always a bad sign*" as a serious statement.

Software development is a challenging intellectual activity. There is the engineering part, which often requires "*communication*", "*collaboration*", "*interaction*" and "*conversation*", and the research part, which is in many respects akin to doing mathematics. There is a time for talking, and a time for concentrating. Some people think best by explaining their thinking to someone else, pair-programming style; some people think best while walking (like Napoleon); and some people think best by shutting themselves off from the world for a while. Most people think best by alternating between various models.

We have all met instances of the shy, introverted programmer who stays silent during meetings and one morning comes in with an impeccably designed and implemented subsystem, which all the "conversations" in the world would never have produced. It is part of the respect due to programmers (as advocated forcefully in the Crystal method) to accept that people are different and not to force a single scheme on them. Sure, you can gently nudge the silent genius, once in a while, to communicate a bit more. But if you start harassing him by enforcing a communicate-at-all-costs policy, all you will get is that he will soon take his talents to a more accommodating environment.

Crystal

The gentle nudging, by the way, may have to apply to both sides. An incessant chatterer may fulfill the agile ideal of "*valuing interaction*", as the Agile Manifesto has it, but may become a serious obstacle to the project's progress, and deserve an encouragement to stop talking and produce something for a change.

If silence is "*always a bad thing*", what of the reverse situation: a workplace where everyone is babbling all the time? It is just as alarming. A healthy environment, in my experience, is one in which sometimes people talk and sometimes they silently read, or write, or just think. When "*walking into*" a development space and seeing a programmer who is just staring at the ceiling, only a naïve (and mean, and incompetent) manager jumps to the conclusion that the programmer is wasting the company's money.

The need for flexibility comes not only from developers' personality traits but from the nature of the tasks at hand. Requirements definition calls for lots of interaction (although even here quiet thinking, to classify and abstract information, is essential); design and implementation call for lots of thinking (although even here communication, of the kind advocated by agile methods, is essential).

These reservations do not affect the essential soundness of the agile view: open spaces often work well. Just do not turn the idea into a dogma. Different people, different circumstances and different times during projects call for different solutions.

6.7 PROCESS MINIATURE

Agile training frequently uses a technique that Cockburn calls "process miniature": get familiar with a proposed software process by applying it to some non-software tasks over a short period, such as a day, an hour or even less. Scrum tutorial sessions, for example, are notorious for asking participants to design paper planes by applying the Scrum roles, principles and practices. Throwing the planes around is great fun.

[Cockburn 2005], page 91.

Process miniature can be a good way to visualize techniques that might otherwise appear abstract, and understand the dynamics of group interaction in a self-organizing team. One should not forget, however, that it is just a simulation, and that the most serious issues, technical and personal, will only materialize in the thick of a real project. Building paper planes is not quite the same as building planes.

6.8 ITERATION PLANNING

A number of agile practices take the form of regular meetings. We have already seen the "daily meeting", but there are others, codified in particular by Scrum.

At the start of an iteration (a sprint in Scrum) there should be a meeting to plan that iteration. The meeting should produce three main outcomes:

1   An **iteration goal**, describing what the team plans to achieve in the iteration, concisely — a sentence or two — and in terms understandable by ordinary stakeholders. A typical example (assuming a compiler project) is: implement the new functional-language extensions.

2   An **iteration backlog**: the list of tasks to be implemented. This outcome is primarily for the internal benefit of the team.

3   The **list of acceptance criteria** for each task.

Conspicuously absent from these goals are: the *assignment of tasks* to individual team members, which will be done at the "last possible moment" according to the rule of cross-functionality; and a list of *testing tasks*, since testing is done continuously as part of the implementation of user stories, not as a separate activity.

The meeting is primarily reserved for the team and the product owner. As the team will be responsible for implementing the backlog in the allotted time, the result represents a commitment on its part, normally ruling out the participation of observers.

← *"Members and observers"*, 5.4, page 82.

The definition of tasks (outcome 2 above) is a two-step process: select user stories from the backlog for the entire product; then, decompose each of them into tasks.

The process also requires estimating the cost of each task. This is where techniques such as the planning game and planning poker, discussed earlier in this chapter, come into play. Because the team is in the best position to size up tasks that it will have to implement, the product owner may at times be asked to leave the meeting while this estimation is in progress. Disagreements may imply repetitive application of the process.

To avoid endless discussions, the meeting has a time limit, generally a single day (eight hours), sometimes split into two parts, one for selecting user stories and the other for decomposing them into tasks.

6.9 REVIEW MEETING

Scrum

The review meeting mirrors, at the end of a sprint, the planning meeting performed at the beginning. Its purpose is to assess what has actually been done.

In the meeting, the development team presents to outside stakeholders, and in particular to the product owner in Scrum, the results of the sprint. It discusses what has been achieved, and not, against the original goals, cost estimates and acceptance criteria.

Such a review meeting is focused on results, not process. An end of sprint is also a good opportunity to reflect, beyond what has been done, on how it was done. In Scrum a separate meeting is reserved for that purpose: the retrospective.

6.10 RETROSPECTIVE

Scrum

A sprint retrospective reviews what went well and less well during the latest sprint, with a view to identifying what can be improved for the next one. The purpose is similar to what we find at level 5, "Optimizing", of the CMMI: integrating into the process (even *← "CMMI in* if this word is not welcome in agile circles) a feedback loop so that it can improve itself. *plain English", 3.6.1, page 44.*

Whereas a review meeting requires the presence of the product owner (or, outside of Scrum, other stakeholders representing the viewpoint of the customer), a retrospective meeting is inward-looking and hence should primarily include the team and coach (Scrum Master), although the product owner may attend.

6.11 SCRUM OF SCRUMS

Scrum

Basic agile techniques are intended for small teams, up to about 10 people. The question arises of how to scale up to larger projects. The Scrum answer is worth studying here. It is known as a "scrum of scrums", defined as

> *a daily scrum consisting of one member from each team in a multi-team project.*   *[Schwaber 2004], page 44.*

except that "daily" is according to Larman too high a frequency; two or three times a *[Larman 2010],* week is enough.   *page 200.*

The challenge confronting scrums of scrums is coordination. It manifests itself in two ways:

- Interface changes.

- Dependencies between sub-projects.

Regular meetings are an effective way to address the first problem; if you make sure that API changes that can break client code are clearly publicized (and, if possible, discussed in advance), you avoid a serious source of trouble.

On the second problem, the best agile answer that I have seen is that dependencies should be avoided. According to Schwaber:

> *Before a project officially begins, the planners parse the work among teams to minimize dependencies. Teams then work on parts of the project architecture that are orthogonal to each other. However, this coordination mechanism is effective only when there are minor couplings or dependencies that require resolution.*

[Schwaber 2004], page 44.

Quite true; dividing the project into "orthogonal" parts works only if the complexity is of the additive kind. But of course a large project is usually large because it is truly — that is, multiplicatively — complex, and then the dependencies will be tricky. Although the agile literature claims that Scrum, XP and other methods can scale up, and gives examples of successful large projects, it provides little guidance on how to tackle the issues. As described in its own texts, the agile approach mostly targets projects involving a small group of developers.

← *"Additive and multiplicative complexity: the lasagne and the linguine", page 63.*

6.12 COLLECTIVE CODE OWNERSHIP

We end this review of management-related agile practices with an agile prescription that could also be classified as a principle, although it enjoys neither the same importance nor the same general application as the principles of the previous chapter.

In many projects every software module or subsystem is under the responsibility of a specific person. A typical comment in dealing with teams at Microsoft is "*If you want to change something to that API, you will have to convince Liz, she owns that piece*". She does not "own" it in the sense of intellectual property but in the sense of technical authority: who decides whether to accept a request for change. Code ownership in that sense is not restricted to commercial software: many open-source projects, such as Mozilla, also enforce a similar model, where:

> *A module owner's OK is required to check code into that module. In exchange, we expect the module owner to care about what goes in, respond to patches submitted by others, and be able to appreciate code developed by other people.*

[Mozilla modules].

6.12.1 The code ownership debate

Individual code ownership has clear benefits: someone is in charge, and will feel responsible for ensuring the consistency of the software and its integrity. One of the worst risks in the evolution of a software system is a general degradation due to inconsiderate extensions ("creeping featurism"); having a clear point of responsibility helps avoid it.

Individual code ownership can have negative consequences as well, emphasized by agilists and in particular by proponents of Extreme Programming: balkanization of the system, where each part of the code becomes a little fiefdom; concentration in one person of the expertise about each part of the system, raising a serious risk if that person leaves; and barriers to change, as the owner of a particular element (even if still a member of the team) may not be available or willing when others need a change, or they may simply not dare to ask.

XP promotes collective code ownership:

[Beck 2005], page 66.

Anyone on the team can improve any part of the system at any time. If something is wrong with the system and fixing it is not out of scope for what I'm doing right now, I should go ahead and fix it.

This statement is in fact more nuanced than its predecessor in the first edition of the same book, which stated that "***anybody*** *who sees an opportunity to add value to* ***any*** *portion of* ***any*** *code is required to do so at* ***any*** *time*".

[Beck 2000], page 59, emphasis added.

Both versions surprisingly ignore the role of another core XP practice, pair programming, studied in the next chapter. In the actual application of XP as described by Cockburn, pair programming does temper the free-for-all:

XP has a strong ownership model: ***Any two people sitting together and agreeing on it*** [the change] ***can change any line of code in the system.***

[Cockburn 2005], page 216. Emphasis in original.

This restriction seems to be the minimum needed for making collective code ownership reasonable. Even in a competent and self-organized team, it would be dangerous to allow arbitrary changes without involving at least a second pair of eyes. The free-for-all policy may have made the success of Wikipedia, but only with safeguards such as a vigilant community of millions of editors and thousands of administrators, and with generally less momentous consequences. (A mistyped digit in the population figure for the Duluth entry, even if it takes a few hours before someone detects it, should cause no tragedies. Program bugs are a serious matter.)

The Crystal method takes a more moderate attitude:

Most of the Crystal projects I have visited adopt the policy "change it, but let me know".

Same reference as above.

In assessing the possible policies — personal ownership, collective ownership, and solutions in-between — it is important to note that preserving correctness is not the only issue. Agile methods require running the regression test suite regularly; so if as a result of a change-by-all policy someone messes up code that he does not completely understand, there is a good chance that the problem will be caught right away. A potentially more serious problem is degradation of the code, as described by Cockburn:

[If] everyone is allowed to add code to any class, [then] no one feels comfortable deleting someone else's code from the increasingly messy class. The result is [...] like a refrigerator shared by several roommates: full of increasingly smelly things that almost everyone knows should be thrown out, but nobody actually throws out.

Again from the same place.

Indeed a question more important than code ownership is change control. With modern configuration management tools it is possible to enforce specific rules automatically; for example you may prohibit committing a change unless at least one other person approves it. Google has such a rule. A more formal version requires a *review* of the code before it is committed; it is known as RTC, "Review Then Commit" and was Apache's initial policy. After complaints in 1998 that it was too constraining, Apache introduced the CTR option, "Commit Then Review", tempered by the possibility — seldom used but keeping programmers on their guard — of veto by any approved committer.

Every project should define its policy on this fundamental issue of change control, somewhere between the extremes of too much freedom, leading to code rot and bugs, and too much restriction, leading to an ossified process. The decision on code ownership should follow from this more fundamental policy, and also depends on other aspects of the company's or open-source project's culture. Once again a one-policy-fits-all rule, as prescribed here by Extreme Programming, does not survive objective analysis.

6.12.2 Collective ownership and cross-functionality

The extreme suggestion of letting anyone change anything becomes less surprising when viewed in light of another common agile practice: assigning the next task to the next available developer. Such an approach can only work if the developers are interchangeable; anyone can work on anything. This is the agile assumption of cross-functional teams: developers should remain generalists about the project, and not specialize in a narrow area. ← "Cross-func-tional", 5.3.2, page 81.

Arguments for and against cross-functionality are pretty much the same as those for and against individual code ownership. The risks of specialization are the emergence of jealously defended fiefdoms, and the dependency on individuals who may leave or be unavailable when the project needs them. On the other hand, a complex project will require highly focused competence in specific areas; it is inefficient to ask non-specialists to handle tasks in such an area, for which they will either botch the job or repeatedly disturb the expert. It is usually more productive to wait until that expert becomes available to do the job himself.

The application domain has a considerable influence on this discussion. When reading agile discussions, such as the recommendation of cross-functional teams, I sometimes have the impression that they are all based on consultants' experience with run-of-the-mill commercial developments for customers. In areas of advanced technical development, specialization is inevitable. If you are building an operating system and the next task involves updating the memory management scheme, you do not ask just anyone on the team. You ask the person who has devoted the last five years of his life to crafting the memory manager.

7

Agile practices: technical

Beyond the management-oriented practices of the previous chapter, agile principles have consequences on the techniques of software development. We now review the corresponding practices.

You may have noted a strong Scrum presence in the preceding chapter; in contrast, many of the practices below come from XP. The distribution of roles is understandable: Scrum is to some extent a generic management methodology, XP was designed by programmers for programmers.

The number of techniques in this chapter is not large; indeed many of the most striking contributions of agility are on the project management side, and relatively few core ideas are software-specific. But some of them are important, especially the last one discussed in this chapter, test-first development, which has already had a profound effect on the software industry.

7.1 DAILY BUILD AND CONTINUOUS INTEGRATION

Integrating a software project means taking the components of the software as written so far, compiling them together and running the tests (the regression suite).

Historically, large projects often had a long iteration cycle, of weeks or months. Worse than its duration is the nature of the process, which we may call the Big Bang approach, with the qualification that in software the Big Bang appears at the end, not at the start as in physics. In the traditional process, the various members or groups of the project would go off on their own at the start of a cycle, and start working on their respective parts. At the end of that cycle they would bring everything together (the Big Bang), or attempt to. Predictably — well, predictably if you have tried it once — such an attempt produces tears and blood. It is remarkable how quickly assumptions diverge and components become incompatible.

B. Meyer, *Agile!*, DOI 10.1007/978-3-319-05155-0_7,
© Springer International Publishing Switzerland 2014

Two evolutions in the practice of programming, respectively in tools and in methods, have contributed to today's much improved situation:

- Starting with tools such as the venerable "make" and RCS (followed by CVS, Subversion, Git), it has become possible to automate part of the task of putting components together and avoiding the awful configuration errors (today's version of module A combined with last month's incompatible version of module B) that have caused so many disasters. Since integration also involves running tests, the automated testing tools discussed later in this chapter also help significantly.

- Software projects have increasingly gone to much shorter integration cycles: not months or weeks but days or even hours.

The most visible initial step towards shortening integration times was Microsoft's famed "daily build", introduced in the nineteen-eighties. The idea was simple: at the end of each workday a system is built integrating all changes "committed" (that is to say, officially submitted) by developers; the system is compiled and run on the tests. As a Microsoft manager put it:

> *Doing daily builds is just like the most painful thing in the world. But it is the greatest thing in the world, because you get instant feedback.*

Cited in [Cusumano 1995], page 268.

The core rule of the daily build is what is sometime called the China Shop Rule: in a porcelain shop, you break it, you own it; in a software shop, you break it, you fix it. In the traditional Microsoft process, breaking it meant causing the overall system no longer to compile and link; the consequence for the culprit is some badge of shame (paying a $5 fine, wearing a goat horn) and, before that, staying at work until you have fixed the problem, however late that may be. Such measures do not go well with the agile principle of sustainable pace, but the idea of immediate check-in and integration remains.

← *"Work at a sustainable pace", 4.4.3, page 56.*

It may have been ground-breaking in the nineteen-eighties to demand that developers fix their code if it kept the system from compiling, but today the expectation goes even further: we also want the *regression suite* to pass. New developments in tools have supported this evolution. Today's tools include automatic program builders, which figure out the dependencies between software modules and bring together all the parts that make up a system, as well as regression testing tools that automatically run an entire test suite and report any failed test.

Agile rules, particularly in Extreme Programming, go further than the daily build practice. XP recommends "continuous integration". Beck's rule is

> *Integrate and test changes after no more than a couple of hours.*

[Beck 2005], page 49.

Note the emphasis on tests. Many teams, including agile ones, do not follow this injunction; a daily build discipline is already trying. In addition, integrating too often has its own drawbacks since integration takes time; even if with modern tools you do not need to run the build and tests manually, you must still wait for the process to complete. The bigger the system and — even for a small system — the more tests, the longer it takes. Beck dismisses the problem, a bit too offhandedly, by stating that it provides an opportunity for the programmer pair to discuss long-term issues of the project while waiting.

The Poppendiecks' advice on integration frequency is more nuanced. They describe several strategies: every few minutes, every day, every iteration. They comment that

It is not always practical to integrate all of the code all of the time. How often you integrate and test depends on what it takes to find defects… The proof that you are integrating frequently enough lies in your ability to integrate rapidly at any time without finding defects.

[Poppendieck 2010], page 78.

This focus is the right one: it is less important to set an exact duration than to provide evidence that the project has found its pace and in particular maintains the right level of quality, as reflected by the number of bugs found at the time of integration.

The Poppendiecks' observation confirms my own experience that with a proper process and a focus on quality, integration does not have to happen so often; a weekly period, for example, can work well. What matters is that the team has learned to work together and to keep constantly in mind, when making a change, what impact it might have on other parts. The developers also run the regression test themselves before committing their changes, and in fact throughout the development process, so it becomes extremely unlikely that an integration test fails. With such proactive thinking, real conflicts are rare.

Regardless of the periodicity of updates, the methodology applied by competent teams has changed considerably since the days of Big Bang software project management. Agile methods and their emphasis on frequent integration have contributed to this fruitful evolution.

7.2 PAIR PROGRAMMING

Pair programming is one of the cornerstones of Extreme Programming; in the early days, when agile was largely equated with XP, all discussions of agile methods tended to gravitate towards this provocative idea. It triggered considerable controversy, and also a large number of empirical studies to assess its effectiveness against traditional techniques such as code reviews. Today pair programming is occasionally practiced (and enthusiasts still come up with new variants such as "mob programming"), but it has retreated from the limelight; other agile practices are considered more important.

→ "Mob programming", 7.2.3, page 107.

The controversy was largely a consequence of XP's insistence on imposing pair programming as the sole and universal way to develop programs. Beck wrote

Write all production programs with two people sitting at one machine.

[Beck 2005], pages 42-43.

As in other cases of agile injunctions that industry found, shall we say, a trifle extreme, few companies have applied pair programming to "*all*" their developments for very long. But many programmers have found some dose of pair programming beneficial, and the technique deserves to be known.

7.2.1 Pair programming concepts

The two partners "paired" should be closely involved in the work, one handling the keyboard to compose the program, all the time expressing his or her thought process and uncertainties aloud, and the other commenting and correcting. This is a peer process, so the partners should regularly reverse roles.

The advertised benefits include keeping one another on task, brainstorming on improvements, clarifying ideas, holding each other accountable, and enabling one partner to take the initiative when the other is stuck.

Again by [Beck 2005], pages 42-43.

Beck and other XP authors obligingly provide practical advice: "*Set up the machine so that the partners can sit comfortably side by side*", "*cover your mouth when you cough*", "*avoid strong colognes*" and so on.

I know of very few other software engineering texts that discuss personal hygiene. Another distinction of Beck's *Extreme Programming Explained* is that it also comes closest, of all the software books I know, to deserving an X rating: "*When programmers are not mature enough to separate approval from arousal*" (arousal helped by the strong cologne?), "*working with a person of the opposite gender can bring up sexual feelings*", which "*are not in the best interest of the team*" (whether or not they are in the best interest of the people involved — regrettably, the text does not say). This is indeed about software projects, so the team is what matters: "*Even if the feelings are mutual, acting on them will hurt the team*". Just to make sure we understand what is at stake, we are offered an illustration: in a photograph artfully deferred to the next page in Beck's book, "*the man has moved closer to the woman than is comfortable for her*". Please do not tell my wife, but I turned the page with trepidation. Some readers will be relieved and others disappointed: the picture is suitable for a family audience. The participants are long past eighteen years of age, fully clothed, seen from the back, and separated by a good two inches. Do buy Beck's challenging and insightful book, but not for the titillation. This is, however, stuff for a torrid, florid, lurid novel — or script (Hollywood, are you listening?). I am eagerly waiting for the first author who, turned on by the cited paragraph, will write *My Pair Lady*, *The Pair Karamazov* or *Fifty Shades of Pair*.

[Beck 2005], page 43.

Coming back to less romantic aspects, the reaction of many people who hear the idea of pair programming for the first time is that having two programmers do the job of one will halve the output. To this objection, XP proponents respond that if those two people produce software that is more than twice as good, then we get a productivity gain, not a loss.

This response is correct. After all, typical productivity figures in the software industry, measured in SLOC (source lines of code, a metric that everyone criticizes — and that everyone uses), are around 20 SLOCs per person per day. Since writing twenty lines of code takes only a few minutes, the explanation — clear to everyone in the field and confirmed by numerous studies — is that developers spend most of their time on other tasks, in particular on *thinking* about the code they will write, and *correcting* code that was not right the first time around. If pair programming truly is a superior process, it is not unreasonable to expect that the two programmers together will produce more than 40 SLOCs; if these lines are of equal or higher quality, the project benefits. So the trivial productivity argument against pair programming cannot be sustained without a rational analysis of costs and benefits.

Empirical studies, however, fail to give a resounding answer of support for pair pro- *See [Müller*
gramming. When assessed against traditional techniques of *code review* (which subject *2005], [Nawrocki*
a programmer's work to a collective inspection process) and PSP, pair programming *2001]. PSP was*
appears to give similar results in overall productivity and code quality. "Appears" because *page 46.*
no current study is definitive, but the general trend is clear: no breakthrough here.

7.2.2 Pair programming versus mentoring

A mistake often made in the industry's application of pair programming is to use it as a
mentoring technique by pairing a junior programmer with an experienced one, as a
training experience. Mentoring is a fruitful technique, but its primary purpose is education, not software production.

The naïve manager who hopes to kill two birds with one stone — get the advertised
benefits of pair programming, *and* train the junior programmer in the process — will be
disappointed. It is a lose-lose proposition. The junior member will slow down the senior
member, who instead of getting help for the most difficult challenges of the job will find
himself repeatedly explaining the *easiest* parts. And the would-be learner will not learn
that much because the supposed teacher, thinking of the expected result and the deadline,
will not explain more than strictly needed.

If you are looking for a good way to frustrate your best developers — possibly even
to turn them away from development — do try pairing them with greenhorns.

The idea of pair programming is that it is *peer* programming: you get feedback from
someone who is roughly at your own level of expertise. Mentoring is something else. Both
have their value, but confusing them means you lose on both counts: mentoring distorted
by the need to produce a serious program will not educate well; pair programming distorted
by the need to educate will not yield the expected productivity and quality benefits.

7.2.3 Mob programming

If more means merrier, why stop at two? Zuill and other XP enthusiasts recently intro- *See [Mob site].*
duced mob programming, defined as "*all the brilliant people working at the same time,
in the same space, at the same computer, on the same thing*". No more separation of
roles; the team thinks and programs as if it were a single person, like the battalion in
Donizetti's *La Fille du Régiment*.

Such proposals illustrate how agilists have become one of the most fertile communities
in the software engineering world, a laboratory teeming with new ideas. (For other examples, too fresh to warrant further analysis in this book, look up "thrashing", "programmer
anarchy" and "no estimates".) Some will survive and others not. It is too early to predict
the fate of this one; the assessment that follows limits itself to pair programming.

7.2.4 Pair programming: an assessment

To assess pair programming, as well as many other agile techniques, it is useful to
remember Beck's immortal words, cited on the previous page: we should be "*mature
enough to separate approval from arousal*".

Applied judiciously, pair programming can unquestionably be useful. Many developers enjoy the opportunity to program jointly with a peer, particularly to deal with a thorny part of an assignment. The basic techniques, in particular the idea of speaking your thoughts aloud for immediate feedback, are well understood and widely applied. (As a manager I regularly hear, from a developer, "*On this problem I would like to engage in a round of pair programming with X*", and invariably find it a good idea.)

What is puzzling is the insistence of XP advocates that this technique is the only way to develop software and has to be applied at all times. Such insistence makes no sense, for two reasons.

The first is the inconclusiveness of empirical evidence, noted above. Granted, lack of data is often used as a pretext to block the introduction of new techniques. When an idea is obviously productive, we should not wait for massive, incontrovertible proof. But here there is actually a fair amount of empirical evidence, and it does not show a significant advantage for pair programming. Pair programming may be good in some circumstances, but if it were always the solution the studies would show it. In the absence of scientific evidence, a universal move is based on ideology, not reason.

The second reason, which may also explain why studies' results vary, is that people are different. Many excellent programmers love interacting with someone else when they write programs; and many excellent programmers do not. Those of the second kind want to think in depth, undisturbed. The general agile view is that communication should be encouraged and that the days of the solitary, silent genius are gone. Fine; but if your team has an outstanding programmer who during the critical steps needs peace, quiet and solitude, do you kick him out of the team, or force him to work in a way that for him may be torture?

It is one thing to require that people explain their work to others; it is another, quite dangerous, to force a single work pattern, especially in a highly creative and challenging intellectual endeavor. When Linus Torvalds was writing Linux, he was pretty much by himself; that did not prevent him from showing his code, and, later on, engaging thousands of people to collaborate on it. Many more examples come to mind: Bill Joy and Berkeley Unix, Richard Stallman and Emacs, Donald Knuth and TeX. (On second thought, the idea of forcing Don Knuth to pair-program is brilliant. Someone should try.)

> Noting that pair programming implies "*too much togetherness*" for some people's taste, Cockburn proposes "side-by-side programming" whereby two people program separately, each with a personal workstation, but close enough to see each other's screen. This setup seems hardly preferable to a classical mode of operation in which people concentrate when they need to, with as little interference as possible, and talk when they need to.

[Cockburn 2005], pages 92-93.

The insistence on pair programming as the only true way has clearly embarrassed some of the agile proponents. Larman, for example, draws the line:

> *Pair programming is only an XP practice; it is not required in Scrum.*

[Larman 2010], page 416-417.

While the first comment is an exaggeration (since one finds advocacy of pair programming far beyond the strict confines of Extreme Programming), the refusal to commit Scrum to a dogmatic application of pair programming is clear.

It is to the credit of XP to have introduced pair programming, explained the rules, and added this technique as an important element of the modern programmer's toolset. The decree establishing it as the sole answer is uncalled for, and has been rejected by the profession even as it was adding pair programming to its catalog of useful practices.

7.3 CODING STANDARDS

Agile methods include the idea that teams should adhere to strict coding standards to help quality. In the original description of Extreme Programming, Beck writes

> *If you are going to have all these programmers changing from this part to that part of the system, swapping partners a couple of times a day, and refactoring each other's code constantly, you simply cannot afford to have different sets of coding practices. With a little practice, it should become impossible to say who on the team wrote what code.*

[Beck 2000], page 61.

Coding standards are hardly a new idea; every decent software development organization has known for a long time that you need to define precise style rules. What is worth noting in the citation above is the rationale it gives for coding standards: to ensure that one cannot find out who wrote a program. This is an old idea too, introduced in the nineteen-seventies under the name of "egoless programming". It used to be criticized as an attempt by Dilbert's-boss types to suppress the creativity and individuality of programmers, and it is interesting to see it reappear as part of a completely different ideology. One cannot but be surprised. All this agile emphasis on communication and collaboration is great, but in the end great programs are written by great programmers (such as Kent Beck). Linux bears the mark of Torvalds, Berkeley Unix the mark of Joy, TeX the mark of Knuth, xUnit the mark of Beck and Gamma; no one complains. Even projects involving lesser mortals naturally assign the most difficult parts to the best programmers.

Whether or not one agrees with a particular rationale does not, of course, affect the soundness of the exhortation to apply coding standards.

7.4 REFACTORING

The agile alternative to upfront design is to adopt a constantly critical attitude towards successive versions of the program, looking for design and code "smells" (unsatisfactory elements), and correct them. This process is known as refactoring.

The techniques of "generalization", introduced in [Meyer 1995], cover part of refactoring.

7.4.1 The refactoring concept

A typical example of *code smell* is duplication. It is always bad to have the same code, or almost the same, in two different places in the program: two places to debug, two places to correct if the need arises, two places to change when requirements evolve.

A typical *refactoring* to correct duplication is to abstract the commonality into a separate module: in object-oriented programming, move the duplicated code to a new class representing the common abstraction, and make the existing classes inherit from it.

This change is only one way to remove the duplication and is not always appropriate. Programmers perform refactoring by identifying code smells and finding out in each case whether a known *refactoring pattern* is applicable and desirable.

Some refactorings are less momentous but still useful; for example you may want to change the name of a feature (method, member) of a class for clarity or consistency.

Modern programming environments provide tools for performing refactoring changes automatically.

Not every pattern of program change can yield a refactoring pattern. Two conditions are required:

- A refactoring **must not change the semantics** of the program.
- A refactoring must **improve the quality** of the code or the architecture.

The first condition means that the program should perform in exactly the same way after the refactoring as before. Refactoring is neither about bug fixing nor about fiddling with functionality, not even for just improving the user interface. Those kinds of changes are also necessary, but refactoring is only about improving the quality of the architecture.

← Remember that by convention we use "design" for the process and "architecture" for its result (page 37).

Both the need for refactoring and the role of automated support follow from this constant-functionality requirement. Even a change conceptually as simple as renaming a routine is not only tedious but error-prone if performed manually, since the name must be changed not only in the routine's definition but in all of its calls and other uses throughout the program. In other words the advantage of refactoring tools is that they can perform changes not only automatically but also safely.

Ensuring the second above condition requires defining quality for code and, more importantly, architecture. While there is no single, enforceable definition, the software design literature provides many criteria. It is clear, for example, that a class with just one routine, or a deep and narrow inheritance hierarchy (where every non-root class has exactly one parent and every non-leaf class exactly one heir, as pictured on the right), are potential signs of bad quality — design smells. (Tellingly, it is usually easier to point to such examples of non-quality, also known as "anti-patterns", than to provide a positive definition of quality.)

Beck actually has a more specific condition: a refactoring must "*make the design simpler*". His notion of **simplicity** includes no duplication, minimum number of classes and minimum number of methods.

[Beck 2000], pages 106 and 109.

7.4.2 Benefits and limits of refactoring

Drawing attention to the importance of refactoring has been one of the most visible effects of agile methods, and specifically of Extreme Programming. Refactoring has become one of the principal tools of the modern programmer.

As with many other ideas, the positive contribution ("use this technique") is more interesting than the negative one ("this technique is a replacement for traditional ones"). The mindset of always looking for possible improvements in an architecture is excellent. But refactoring is not an excuse for rejecting "Big Upfront Design". If you pay no attention to initial design, just building "the simplest solution that could possibly work", you could end up redoing the design again and again since the initial solution, while workable, was not adaptable. In describing the process, Beck also shows its limits:

> *Not all refactorings can be accomplished in a few minutes. If you discover that you have built a big tangled inheritance hierarchy, it might take a month of concentrated effort to untangle it. But you don't have a month of concentrated effort to spend. You have to deliver stories for this iteration.*
>
> *You have to take such a big refactoring in small steps (incremental change). You'll be in the middle of a test case and you'll see a chance to take one more step toward your big goal. Take that one step. Move a method here, a variable there. Eventually all that will remain of the big refactoring is a little job. Then you can finish it in a few minutes.*

[Beck 2000], page 107, slightly abridged.

A truly "big refactoring", however, is typically not a sum of small refactorings. In a compiler project I know, the team uncovered at some point the reason for a major performance overhead: the compiler was using an expensive data structure to keep track of the units of a system (classes and routines). It came up with a redesign identifying every unit by a plain integer instead of an object. This is a big system — thousands of classes, over two million lines of code — for which such a surgical refactoring is what everyone hates: tricky, painful changes affecting just about every module of the system, for no new user-visible functionality, the only benefits being a speed improvement and a more solid foundation for future developments. If you decide for it, there is no way to proceed by "*small steps*"; you cannot have one part using integers and the others using object identifiers. You have to accept that nothing happens, for "*a month of concentrated effort*" and possibly more. You might find that the result is not worth such a disruption, but if you do decide to go ahead it is all or nothing.

Beck's advice is yet another case of unwarranted generalization. Some changes can be carried out incrementally: do a bit here, a bit there, and one morning you wake up to the delightful finding that only a "*little job*" remains which you can "*finish in a few minutes*". Renaming classes and features for more consistency, locally rearranging the inheritance relations between a few classes, turning an attribute (a field) of a class into a local variable are typical examples. And some changes just cannot be carried out that way.

It would be nice to believe the mantra that starting from "*the simplest thing that can possibly work*" and incrementally improving the architecture yields great software. That is unfortunately not the case. The old GIGO principle applies: Garbage In, Garbage Out. As we noted in an earlier chapter, refactored junk is still junk. This observation is by no means an indictment of refactoring. It simply indicates that refactoring works best when:

- Applied to an architecture that is *already sound*, although not perfect.

- Combined with upfront design.

The next two subsections detail these two points.

7.4.3 Incidental and essential changes

There are two ways an initial design can lead to an imperfect architecture: incidental and essential. Incidental imperfections can be corrected through refactoring, but essential ones cannot. Inconsistent naming conventions are incidental; a wrong choice of abstractions is essential. The compiler issue cited above was an example of essential imperfection. Here is another common one.

You have a set of classes describing loosely related concepts, say jobs in a company. You also have lists of objects of these types. Several times as you were writing the program you realized that you needed some new functionality applicable to all objects in such lists. For example, you wanted to print the contents of a list, so you had to add a "print" routine to every one of the classes involved. Then you added an "encode" operation, to store objects compactly. The next time it was about producing an XML form.

These are functional changes, not refactorings, and you have performed them already. But you feel that more such cases will arise in the future, and you decide to put a stop to this constant modification of existing classes. (Maybe it will no longer be possible anyway, as some of the classes will be moved into a reusable library, not under your control.)

The technical solution is well known: use the *Visitor* pattern, which makes it possible to apply arbitrary operations to arbitrary instances of a class, where the operations are defined anywhere, not necessarily in the class itself. Adopting this solution requires making *one* change to all the affected classes: make them "visitable" by inheriting from a general *VISITOR* class with an appropriate *update* routine. You should also remove the kludge code that had been added as a temporary solution, and move it elsewhere. You decide that the long-term flexibility benefit is worth the short-term pain. *See [Gamma 1994], or the presentation in [Meyer 2009].*

This is a significant change. Maybe not a month of work, but at least several days depending on the number of classes involved and the consequences on other parts of the architecture. For best results it is not desirable to perform it one little step at a time: by switching contexts repeatedly you may forget the details and introduce inconsistencies. Better perform the operation in one sitting.

To avoid putting yourself in such situations, there is no substitute for careful upfront design. Even so, it is not always possible to have perfect foresight. When the case arises, it calls for an in-depth redesign, not covered by the kind of incremental refactoring promoted by XP and other agile approaches.

Understanding the difference between incidental and essential change is key to addressing the issue of software extendibility (changeability), and defines the limits of refactoring. The distinction is related to one that we studied earlier: additive versus multiplicative complexity. In general, a change is incidental when it affects additive elements: functionality with few dependencies on other parts of the system. If such dependencies exist (multiplicative complexity), the change is essential, and not amenable to simple refactoring. ← *"Additive and multiplicative complexity: the lasagne and the linguine", page 63.*

7.4.4 Combining a priori and a posteriori approaches

Refactoring, cast by agile proponents as an "either-or" technique, has its best use — like many other agile ideas that we review in this book — as an "and" technique. It works best when combined it with the ideas against which agilists artificially set it, in this case upfront design.

No amount of refactoring is going to correct a flawed architecture. The primary responsibility of any designer is to identify the fundamental abstractions that will provide the backbone of the architecture. Do it right, and you still have a lot of work to do; but do it wrong and you will end up (choose your metaphor) patching leak after leak, extinguishing fire after fire, applying band-aid after band-aid.

If you have an *unsound* architecture, there is no choice but to recast it, whatever effort that takes. ("If it is baroque, fix it".) If you have a *sound* architecture, you are not out of the woods yet because it is probably not perfect, and imperfections will creep in anyway as you refine it. This is where refactoring helps.

Agile methods have taught us that we should never lose our readiness to criticize our own work; we should remain alert to the possibility of design and code smells, identify them, and fix them on the fly.

See also "User stories", 8.3, page 119 and "Dual Development", page 74.

7.5 TEST-FIRST AND TEST-DRIVEN DEVELOPMENT

The final technical practice reviewed in this chapter is a somewhat extreme consequence of the central role of tests emphasized by agile approaches starting with XP. The idea, previewed in the discussion of principles, is test-driven development, or TDD for short, with its corollary of test-first development (which we may call TFD for convenience, although unlike TDD this abbreviation is not widely used).

7.5.1 The TDD method of software development

TDD is not a testing technique but a full-blown software development method. At the beginning of the book that introduced the idea to its full extent, Beck defines it as the repetition of the following basic cycle:

TDD cycle
1   Quickly add a test.
2   Run all tests and see the new one fail.
3   Make a little change.
4   Run all tests and see them all succeed.
5   Refactor to remove duplication.

From [Beck 2003], page 1.

That is it — including at the beginning, when you "add a test" to a still empty project base. The process thus defined has four major implications.

The first implication is that you always write the tests before you write the corresponding program elements. If we stop there we get TFD (**test-first development**), which is a subset of TDD — and only a subset, since it omits parts 2, 4 and 5 of the basic TDD iteration.

The second implication is that the process is extremely incremental: **one new test** at a time, exercising one new functionality or one previously unhandled case.

Without step 5 we would have a pure hacking-style process: handle one input value; add another, update the code accordingly; and so on. We might end up with a huge "if… then… elseif… else…" with one branch for every value that has been encountered in the tests. TDD is smarter, of course, and step 5 is key: **refactoring**. Once the tests run you are not necessarily happy yet; you want to ascertain the quality of the architecture and, if it is not good enough — using Beck's criterion, not *simple* enough, for example because it tries cases one after the other instead of unifying them — fix it before you move on.

The fourth consequence is a rule that we reviewed in the discussion of agile princi- ← *"Do not start any new development until all tests pass", 4.5.3, page 76.* ples, expressed here as step 4 of the basic cycle: **do not move on until all tests succeed**. This is the second secret (along with refactoring) to preventing the method from turning into hacking. If you make an inconsiderate change just to satisfy the latest test, chances are it will break some of the previous tests, causing a *regression*. All tests will be kept in the test regression suite, which every step must exercise in its entirety; the suite grows along with the project, providing an ever bigger guarantee of quality if you apply the rule that all the tests must always pass.

The wording of step 2 may be surprising at first: why should we *expect a test to fail*? It is, however, consistent with TDD as a software development method: since the method forbids you from implementing a new functionality before writing a test for it first, a new test should not be covered by previously implemented functionality, and hence should fail. The most obvious example occurs at the very beginning of the process, when you are not supposed to have any code written yet; for any test, an empty program will fail. Later on, it is in principle possible that a new test would succeed just because it happens to be covered by what has already been implemented, but in a strict TDD view such a test is not interesting since it breaks no new ground.

What is a test, by the way? TDD only makes sense with modern testing technology, which provides mechanisms for preparing numerous tests, each described by inputs and expected outputs, and running the whole collection of these tests (the regression suite) automatically. Tools collectively known as "xUnit" — developed in part, not surprisingly, by some of the people who also originated XP, and reviewed in the chapter on arti- → *"Tests", 8.2, page 117.* facts — make it possible both to describe the input and to specify the expected properties of the result, known as an oracle, in the form of the conditions they must satisfy, known as assertions. The tools can then automatically run hundreds or thousands of precisely defined tests and evaluate the oracles.

7.5.2 An assessment of TFD and TDD

The TFD and TDD techniques have made an important contribution to the state of the art in software engineering. Let us leave that contribution for last and start with the aspects that are more subject to criticism.

The most debatable idea is not explicitly stated in TDD but underlies the entire approach: it is the assumption that tests are all we need to specify programs. This is a very bad idea. Much of the earlier analysis of why *scenarios* such as user stories are not general enough for specification applies here, and indeed more strongly, since tests are even more specific than user stories. What is missing is abstraction; this was the difference (mentioned then) between stating that f has values 0, 1, 4, 9 and 25 for the first few integers, and telling you that $f(n)$ is n^2 for every integer n. *← "Express requirements through scenarios", 4.5.5, page 77.*

It is true that the larger the test suite grows, the more unlikely it becomes that some case will behave wildly. But unlikelihood is not impossibility, and many software malfunctions are due to a special case that escaped testing. Writing a specification means abstracting from specific cases and looking for general rules. Another way of stating this observation is to note that one can generate tests from specifications (there is an entire line of software verification research in this direction) but not the other way around.

Another aspect of TDD raises questions, but for entirely different (and almost contrary) reasons: the requirement that all tests must pass before the team moves on to any new functionality. The pros and cons of this principle were discussed earlier. *← "Do not start any new development until all tests pass", 4.5.3, page 76.*

In practice, few organizations apply the strict TDD process in the form of the repetition of the sequence of steps described above. The real insight has been test-first development and, more specifically, the idea that **any new code must be accompanied by new tests**. It is not even critical that the code should come only after the test (the "F" of TFD): what counts is that you never produce one without the other.

This idea has come to be widely adopted — and should be adopted universally. It is one of the major contributions of agile methods.

8

Agile artifacts

To support their practices, agile approaches have defined a number of artifacts, some of them concrete such as "story cards", others virtual, that is to say, of a purely conceptual nature. We start with the main virtual artifacts: working code, tests, user stories, story points, velocity, definition of done, product backlog. Then we move on to concrete artifacts: working space, story card, task and story board, burndown chart. We conclude with five artifacts, four of them virtual and one concrete, which figure prominently in agile discussions, albeit negatively, as pitfalls to avoid: impediment, technical debt, waste, dependencies, and dependency charts.

8.1 CODE

Code is at the center of the agile universe; specifically, *working* code, which can be executed as part of the system under development.

The emphasis on code is part of the agile quest to shift the conversation in software engineering from processes and plans to the concrete results that matter most to the success of a software project.

8.2 TESTS

Along with code, tests are the main product endorsed by all agile approaches. Extreme Programming was the approach that rehabilitated tests as a core software engineering concept. Two kinds of artifact are in fact involved here (the latter one made of a collection of instances of the former): unit tests and regression test suites.

A **unit test** is the description of a particular test run and its expected results. The process of unit testing has been profoundly reshaped by the appearance of the so-called "xUnit" testing tools, such as JUnit for Java. As noted in the previous chapter, it is not a coincidence that Beck, the most prominent figure behind XP, was (along with others such as Erich Gamma) one of the authors of these tools. A unit test in the xUnit style takes the form of a class and includes:

B. Meyer, *Agile!*, DOI 10.1007/978-3-319-05155-0_8,
© Springer International Publishing Switzerland 2014

- A routine (method) which executes the test.

- Set-up and tear down routines, to prepare for the test and reset the context. It might for example be necessary to open a connection to the database prior to the test and to restore the database's original state afterwards.

- An **assertion**, defining the condition (also known as an "oracle") for the test to succeed. Consider for example an operation that processes a request to rent a car and, if it deems it acceptable, sets the variable *age* to the driver's age; a test for that operation might include the assertion *is_accepted* **implies** (*age* >= 18 **and** *age* <= 75).

This standardized approach to defining tests has been one of the significant advances in the state of the art in software engineering over the past two decades, including for many projects that do not specifically use an agile approach.

There is an even better approach. Instead of treating the code and tests as separate artifacts, and associate assertions with tests only, we may view assertions as a **specification** mechanism and write them as an integral part of the code, in the form of class invariants and routine preconditions and postconditions. This is the method of Design by Contract as used in Eiffel; it also makes it possible to generate the tests automatically from the code and assertions. All this, however, is for another discussion. *[Meyer 1997]; [Meyer 2009a].*

The **regression test suite** is a collection of unit tests. It includes any test that has, at some point in the project, been found to fail. A particular phenomenon of software development is that old bugs can reappear (because of version control errors, of incomplete bug fixes, but also simply of continuing to use the same flawed thought patterns). This phenomenon is known as regression, and part of the purpose of a regression test suite is to avoid it through the practice of continually running the tests, as part of continuous integration. *← "Daily build and continuous integration", page 103.*

There is in fact no reason to limit the regression test suite to previously failing tests. We have seen that one of the important contributions of agile methods (originally of XP) is the rule that every element of code should have at least one associated test. The regression test suite includes all such tests. Ambler notes that

Agilists are at least doing regression testing if not TDD, *[Ambler testing].*

confirming that the regression test suite is one of the defining agile artifacts, just as continuous integration is one of the defining agile practices, even for teams that shun the more extreme ideas such as test-driven development.

The regression suite is a key asset of any well-managed software project. Part of its attraction is that it is a truly incremental product. We have seen that the incrementalism advocated by agile approaches does not always work when applied to development. But the regression suite is incremental by nature; it can start small and, if everyone sticks to the discipline of never adding a piece of functionality without also adding a test for it, grow quickly and become a core project resource.

8.3 USER STORIES

User stories provide the basic unit of requirements in agile methods.

A user story is the description of a fine-grain functionality of the system, as seen by its users. The more general notion is use case, developed extensively in a well-known book by Jacobson. A use case can be big: it describes an entire interaction scenario, for example the process of ordering an item on an e-commerce site. A user story is much smaller. *[Jacobson 1992].*

A standard style has emerged in agile circles to describe user stories. In that style a user story consists of a triple: [*category of user, goal, benefit*]. For example:

"*As a* staff member, *I want to* cancel a booking *so that* reasonable requests for policy exceptions can be accommodated.*"*

Although some projects impose such a fixed style, many variants are possible.

The flagship property of user stories as a tool for describing system functionality is that each story describes a unit of functionality from the user's perspective; more precisely — since there is no such person as "the user" — from the perspective of a particular category of users. "*Change from a relational database to a no-SQL solution*" is not a user story. To integrate such an architectural change, you would have to define it as a task for a user story that describes a benefit visible to users, for example "*As a marketing manager, I want to create new customer offers without having to fit an existing scheme, so as to react more quickly to market opportunities*".

The benefit of relying on user stories as the basis for development is to keep the team looking outward for what customers really want, rather than inward for how to develop the existing code further. But in this very benefit also lies the principal deficiency of the approach. The size of a user story as implied by its description gives little clue. Consider the following two examples, each adding a function to an airline booking system:

1 "As an airline customer, I want to enter a discount code at the end of a reservation rather than at the beginning, so as to avoid having to restart the procedure from scratch if I did not think of it at the beginning."

2 "As an airline customer, I want to use the same interface for purchasing a flight and for booking it by redeeming frequent flyer miles, so as not to have to restart the procedure from scratch if I did not decide at the beginning." *[Poppendieck 2003], page 127. On Lean Software's "integrity" see "Lean Software's principles", 9.2.2, page 134.*

Story 2 is inspired by an anecdote told by Poppendieck, complaining that her airline was violating the Lean principle of "integrity" by providing different systems for flight purchases and redemption of frequent flyer miles.

These two stories look similar but are of far different complexity. Implementing story 1 is probably a routine task, taking a day at most. Assuming that (as in Poppendieck's anecdote) the systems for purchasing a ticket and redeeming miles are currently distinct, story 2 involves merging these systems and may be a major endeavor. Although it is normal that different user stories require different amounts of implementation effort — this is the reason for sizing them up in "story points", as discussed in the next section — here we are talking about efforts of entirely different kinds: one is an incremental improvement, the other a major surgical rework. Expressing both tasks in user-story style obfuscates their fundamental difference of nature. Even if it never hurts to justify any program change by a user need, it is more effective to specify the change corresponding to story 2 as what it is: an architectural redesign.

The lack of such a perspective can lead to brittle designs and useless work. One can easily imagine some user stories, in the early days of the airline projects, about the need to allow users to redeem miles; these stories were implemented, leading to a separate system, to which new user stories were repeatedly added. At some point it became as complex as the ordinary booking system and someone realized that the two should be merged. The proper approach, to avoid duplication and waste of effort, would have been to take an architectural perspective and realize early on that the airline needed a **domain** ← *"The domain* **model** covering all its flight reservation concepts, such as purchase and redemption; both *and the machine",* systems would have relied on it. Such an approach requires abstracting from individual *page 36.* user stories and the superficial system views they imply, and concentrating instead on the essential properties, which often will lead to working on an architecture first — in particular a domain model — that supports many different user stories, those envisioned initially and many others that will emerge later.

The advice to look at the whole problem rather than individual details is, by the way, exactly what another of Lean Software's principles, "See the whole", is about. But Poppendieck gives no indication of how this principle might fit with the reliance on user stories to guide development. It does not.

Lean ▶

It has been a significant agile contribution to bring user stories to the forefront. They do have a role — but not the one that agile development assigns to them. As a basis to development they lead to piecemeal systems, built to handle one function after the other without sufficient attention to the infrastructure. True, infrastructure work is unglamorous, and shunned in agile approaches because it does not immediately bring new user-relevant visibility. Replacing a relational database by a no-SQL solution does not add functionality, but may be critical to the scalability of the system. Replacing a tree-based data structure by one based on hash tables is even more of a geek thing, leaving the impatient customer wondering what in the world those developers are doing this week. No user story here; and yet it may be a key step for the project.

In the same way that a test, or a million tests, cannot replace a specification, user stories (and use cases) cannot replace requirements and designs. Their unique role, like that of tests for specifications, is as a validation mechanism for requirements and designs. Higher-level requirements have the advantage of abstraction and generality, but run the risk of impracticality: of missing cases that are important to users. Listing user stories is not a replacement for writing general requirements, but is an important step to make sure that nothing has been forgotten. They describe particular walkthroughs that, while not sufficient to describe the system, are necessary if the system is to succeed.

> A colleague of mine was once asked to consult on a fancy new computer architecture, full of great concepts, object-oriented and all. His first reaction after hearing the enthusiastic presentation by the designers was: *very impressive, thanks, but how do I do a load and a store*? These are typical user stories. As checks on a proposed system, they are invaluable. As a way to build the system (who would devise a new computer architecture on the basis of load and store?), they are insufficient.

As noted in the earlier example, user stories detract from the task that is critical for all applications, and particularly for the kind of business application that agile development often targets: building the domain model. The domain model is (assuming an object-oriented approach) a set of classes covering the fundamental concepts of the envisioned system — flights and frequent flyer miles, employees and paychecks, customers and credit-cards, paragraphs and fonts, phone calls and text messages... — with the associated operations and relations (inheritance, client) between them. The domain model is focused on the business aspects of the system, not computer-only aspects such as database access and user interfaces. As a result, building a domain model does not deliver user-accessible functionality; a solid domain model will, however, serve as a backbone for successful system development.

There can be too much of a good thing: the risk exists of fine-tuning the domain model forever and neglecting that users need visible functionality. This is where user stories come in, as a reality check. The **dual development** technique introduced in an earlier chapter has its role here, enabling us to mix the approaches in one of two ways:

← *"Dual Development", page 74*. **See** *also "Combining a priori and a posteriori approaches", page 113.*

- Sequential: give the priority to the domain model in the first phase of system construction, so as to establish a solid basis, then move to a focus on regular delivery of user-visible functionality, informed by user stories.

- Parallel: work at the same time on both aspects, constantly informing one by the other.

Relying exclusively on user stories as the source of requirements, on the other hand, is not sufficient for the design of solid systems. This narrow focus is one of the main limitations of agile methods.

8.4 STORY POINTS

Successful project control requires both *estimation* of effort, in advance of an iteration, and *measurement* of progress, during the iteration and at the end. We saw estimation techniques in the discussion of the planning game and the planning poker; measurement of what actually happens once the project has started is just as important.

← *"Planning game", 6.3, page 93; "Planning poker", 6.4, page 94.*

For both estimation and measurement, teams need units of progress. The artifacts of this section and the next provide the basic agile answer.

Traditionally, the software industry has counted in person-months (or person-days). This measure is good for human resources and accountants, to prepare paychecks and determine IT costs, but as a project effectiveness metric it is not so useful. Beyond what is spent, we want to know what is achieved. (Anyone who has ever had to deal with parents complaining about a student's bad grade because "*he worked so hard and for so long!*" will be familiar with the difference.)

"Source lines of code" counts (LOCs, SLOCs) are still widely used. They are easy to measure, but that is almost the only argument in their favor. Even if they were a good proxy for functionality (a contentious assertion), it is difficult to estimate in advance the future SLOC count of a system under construction; as a result SLOCs are also not convenient for measuring progress in the absence of a solid reference against which to assess them. (Thanks for telling me that the project produced 85,000 lines so far, but does this means we are 90%, 50% or 10% done?)

A generally better measure is **function points**, which estimate the number of individual functions of the system, but they are also difficult to estimate in advance, and not always appropriate in developments using modern object-oriented techniques, where data abstractions are just as important as functions (which are attached to them).

In the agile world the basis for measuring progress will come from the standard mode of specifying functionality: user stories. We cannot simply count user stories, however, since they vary in difficulty. Hence the notion of *story point*. A story point is simply an integer that estimates the difficulty of a user story.

The unit can be a day of work, but other conventions are possible; for example a project can take as its story point unit the difficulty of its easiest user stories. Then all others are evaluated relative to that basis. In Cohn's words:

> *The beauty of this is that estimating in story points completely separates the* **[Cohn 2006], page 40.**
> *estimation of effort from the estimation of duration. Of course, effort and schedule are related, but separating them allows each to be estimated independently. In fact you are no longer even estimating the duration of a project: you are computing or deriving it.*

(Cohn's emphasis in this extract is on estimation, but the observation applies equally to a-posteriori measurement.)

Story points have three important properties:

- As the last observation indicates, they are **relative** indicators, not absolute time values. You could take the story point estimations and measurements for a given project, multiply them all by 5, and not significantly affect the process. Within a given project, however, the estimations should be consistent, making it possible to define and predict velocity as discussed in the next section.

- In measures of already achieved results, story points can only be counted for **implemented** user stories; incomplete work, such as user stories that have not been fully implemented, does not count. This rule is in line with the agile rejection of "waste", a category that includes any code that is not actually delivered.

- More generally, **any non-delivered artifacts will not count towards progress**. ← *See "Develop only code and tests", page 60.* Examples may include documentation, plans, and requirements, all of which are generally considered waste in the agile view, although such artifacts may be taken into account if made explicitly part of the *definition of done* as discussed below. Note that tests, while definitely not waste, are not counted in story points.

Story points are a fairly recent addition to the collection of agile artifacts. Extreme Programming initially used absolute measures of time: *ideal programming time*, the number of days required to implement a story assuming full-time work and no distractions, to be weighted by a *load factor*, the ratio of actual time to ideal time, "*typically 2 to 4*" (Beck). A criticism was that estimators used the load factor in practice to fudge the estimation, indeed an obvious temptation given the magnitude of this range. XP moved in 2002 to "pure programmer weeks". A trend then emerged to abandon the reference to precise units of time, and work instead with dimension-less numbers, which do not mean anything in the absolute; to emphasize this property, the affectionate term "gummi bear" is sometimes used as a synonym for story point. *[Beck 2000], page 178. On the history, see [Agile 2011].*

Within a project, story points do have a meaning, since they enable the project to compare progress from one iteration to the next using a consistent measure. Cohn again:

> There is no set formula for defining the size of a story. Rather, a story-point estimate is an amalgamation of the amount of effort involved in developing the feature, the complexity of developing it, the risk inherent in it, and so on. *[Cohn 2006], page 36.*

The planning poker (as well as its earlier variant the planning game) is one of the accepted agile techniques for obtaining such estimates. You will remember that the planning poker used values taken from a sequence of integers, for example Fibonacci-like values 0, 1, 2, 3, 5, 8, … With such a practice, 1 simply denotes the smallest significant user story cost, and all other values are understood relative to it. You might decide that this smallest unit corresponds to two hours or a half-day of work, although, as Cohn's citation on the previous page explains, the exact choice for that correspondence is not critical in the estimation process.

8.5 VELOCITY

Once the user stories have been given individual cost estimates and an iteration starts, the same measures can serve to assess progress. This is where *velocity* becomes useful.

This notion addresses a crucial need which, surprisingly, has been often ignored in pre-agile software development: to provide a clear, measurable, continuous estimate of the speed at which a project is progressing.

The field of software development abounds with jokes about projects that are "90% complete" after a few weeks, and remain there for a very long time. But the question "*how far are you?*" is a legitimate one for managers and stakeholders to ask.

The term "velocity" is, in ordinary language, just a synonym for speed. Speed is a ratio of advancement over time: for a moving object, d / t where d is the distance traveled and t the time it takes. This property also applies to velocity in agile project management, where the numerator (d) is nowadays measured in story points, but the denominator, the time, does not appear explicitly because the convention is to use an iteration, such as a sprint in Scrum, as the unit of time. So velocity in the agile world denotes the *number of story points achieved in the current project iteration.*

Velocity thus defined is a measure of work accomplished. This concept gives further credence to the policy of choosing relative rather than absolute values. It may be difficult to know ahead of time whether a particular task will take two hours, a half-day, a full day or two days. Instead, the story point methodology directs you to abandon hopes for perfect time accuracy and focus instead on assessing the difficulty of all tasks in comparison with each other. If you apply this methodology consistently throughout the project, the relative predictions (story points) will start giving more and more accurate absolute values (durations).

Concretely, assume that you have made two estimates:

- The first sprint will cover 30 story points.

- A story point corresponds to a day of the team's work

The second of these may be far off, although you hope the first one is better. Now assume that the 30-day sprint actually manages to complete 20 story points. Assume further that this pattern continues over a few more sprints: the ratio of time to story points (remember the "load factor" of early XP techniques) hovers around about 1.5, instead of 1 as anticipated. If that pattern remains stable for a while and the team continues to get better, as it should, at estimating story points, that correspondence (time per story point) becomes ever more precise and credible. This is what Cohn's first above citation called the ← *Page 122.* "beauty" of a relative metric.

Such techniques, which use continuously refined measurements to improve the precision of initially rough predictions, are an example of a more general software engineering concept originally introduced by Boehm: the "cone of uncertainty". The cone defines the estimated range (and, at the end, a measured value) for a certain project property; as time progresses and the project learns more, the range shrinks.

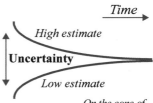

On the cone of uncertainty see [Boehm 1981] and [McConnell 2006].

As noted, velocity is usually measured over a full iteration. A finer level of granularity might be useful: although it makes little sense to compare yesterday's velocity to today's, tracking velocity on a continuous basis may give good indications to the project.

Velocity is one of the most interesting concepts popularized by agile methods. While the underlying metric is subject to the reservations made at the beginning of this chapter on the value of user stories as the basic requirement unit, the insistence that projects keep a precise record of their progress by tracking their velocity is sound and useful advice.

8.6 DEFINITION OF DONE

Scrum

The agile emphasis on delivering actual functionality and avoiding waste, reflected in the strict definition of progress as the number of delivered story points, requires stating and applying rigorous and consistent criteria to determine whether a task is actually completed. This is known in Scrum as the "definition of done", in the sense of explaining what you mean when you say that you are done.

Consistency is particularly important in the definition of done: we may or may not require that the completion of a user story include the completion of the corresponding user manual entry, but we must make the decision for all user stories. Otherwise we cannot fairly measure progress.

Sutherland cites the following example definitions of done:

[Sutherland 2013], **page 182**.

- Releasable. (The simplest.)

- Unit- and integration-tested; ready for acceptance test; deployed on demo server.

- Acceptance-tested; release notes written; releasable; no increased technical debt.

"Technical debt", discussed below, includes complications to the code or design deficiencies that are likely to cause unjustified future work.

→ *"Waste, technical debt, dependency, dependency charts"*, 8.13, page 129.

8.7 WORKING SPACE

Extreme Programming argued from its origins for grouping programmers in open spaces with no physical separation, also known as "bullpens", as a way to foster communication. Beck wrote:

> *XP wants to err on the side of too much public space. XP is a communal software development discipline. The team members need to be able to see each other, to hear shouted "one-off" questions, to "accidentally" hear conversations to which they have vital contributions.*

[Beck 2000], page 79.

The idea has been widely adopted by other agile approaches and you can safely replace "XP" by "Agile methods" in this advice.

The communal space is not meant to exclude offering privacy when needed. Beck's recommended layout also includes "*little cubbies*" (small personal areas) around the outside of the communal space, so that:

> *The team members can keep their personal items in these cubbies, go to them to make phone calls, and spend time at them when they don't want to be interrupted. The rest of the team needs to respect the "virtual" privacy of someone sitting in [his or her] cubby.*

Same source.

Cockburn's Crystal method also devotes considerable attention to office layout and its contribution to ensuring "osmotic communication" between members of the team.

→ *"Crystal's Big Idea"*, 9.5.1, page 141

While everyone knows that the practical organization of offices has an effect on team efficiency (as *PeopleWare* already convincingly argued), we should not exaggerate the role of programmer comfort. After all, many of the most successful Silicon Valley projects were started in garages. What is most interesting in the agile contribution here is the assumption that there *is* an office to lay out: a place of work for the full team. Increasingly, this assumption cannot be guaranteed: more and more projects are *distributed* across several sites.

← On People-Ware see "Work at a sustainable pace", 4.4.3, page 56.

Companies adopt a distributed development model for good reasons as well as some bad ones. Many agile books propose adaptations of their basic models to the case of distributed teams, but one finds little of general value in these discussions. The real agile contribution here is rather the opposite: by emphasizing the value of direct communication, agilists highlight how much more effective it is to have everyone in one place. For example the most interesting part of a chapter by Larman about agile multi-site development is this remark at the beginning:

> *The product development expert Don Reinertsen told us (and wrote) that he has informally polled thousands of people over the last decade and not once has he found a hands-on group that, having had both the contrasting experience of co-located versus distributed development, would choose the latter again.*

[Larman 2010], pages 415-416.

Although I have been involved for a decade in a successful and sustainable multi-site product development project (EiffelStudio at Eiffel Software), and teach at ETH a distributed software engineering course where students from universities around the world collaborate in building working software, I can state that our experience fully confirms this statement. One of the first sentences in our course's first lecture is:

se.ethz.ch/dose.

"Here is the basic law of distributed development: don't do it."

If you have a choice, that is. Sometimes you do not have a choice. But agilists remind us that the everyone-under-one-roof model, when practicable, beats all others.

8.8 PRODUCT BACKLOG, ITERATION BACKLOG

Individual requirements, as we have seen, are covered in the form of user stories. What about "the requirements" as a whole? (In software engineering, "a requirement" means the description of a property of the system, and "the requirements" is not just the plural of "requirement" but denotes the overall description of the system.) Agile approaches reject, of course, the traditional notion of a comprehensive "requirements document".

The replacement for such a document is a collection of user stories or tasks. More precisely:

- The collection of user stories for the project as a whole is the **product backlog**.
- The collection applicable to a particular iteration is the **iteration backlog**, or sprint backlog in Scrum, a collection of tasks associated with user stories (that is, each user story involves a number of elementary tasks).

Some other elements may appear; Cohn gives the examples of bugs, technical work and knowledge acquisition.

The term "backlog" highlights the particular way such a collection is used. The practice, associated with Scrum but widely used, is to divide the backlog into three parts, containing respectively the user stories or tasks that:

- Remain to be implemented.
- Are being implemented (in progress).
- Have been implemented.

Some teams add the category "to be verified".

It is useful to visualize the backlogs. The artifacts of the following three sections serve this purpose.

8.9 STORY CARD, TASK CARD

From tools of a conceptual nature we now move to tangible artifacts.

The systematic use of user stories as units of requirements calls for a standardization of the form in which they are written. The low-tech version uses "story cards": standard-size note cards, each recording a user story as in this typical example:

Story card

Numerous tools on the market provide software equivalents, although many people are comfortable with the paper version.

8.10 TASK AND STORY BOARDS

With the constant focus on velocity — delivering the best customer value in the least possible time — it is important in the agile approach to keep the team constantly aware of what has been done, what is in progress and what remains to be done. A visible reminder helps several agile goals, in particular:

- Supporting the basic development step of picking a task associated with a user story and assigning it to the next available developer.
- Keeping track of velocity (the number of story points implemented per iteration).
- Boosting team morale: one of the best ways to cheer up developers is to display vividly the progress of tasks from to-be-done to being-done to under-test to done.
- Discouraging waste: work that does not result in deliverable functionality is not shown.

The visual representation usually takes the form of a board, with columns representing the possible states of the tasks involved in the implementation of a user story. The states can be to-do, in-progress, under-test and done. The most common technique uses a whiteboard and post-it notes that move left to right as tasks get selected and processed:

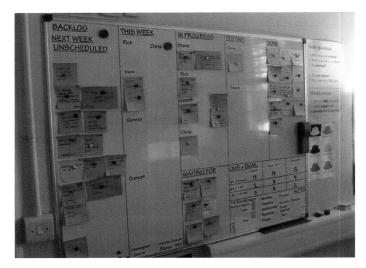

Task Board

(See also the figure on page 12.)

Details vary; sometimes the under-test state is merged with in-progress.

The Kanban method of production management uses similar boards.

→ *"Kanban", 9.2.4, page 136*

Numerous software tools are available to replace this physical artifact. They are particularly used by distributed teams; for a team that is physically located in a single place, it is hard to beat the simplicity and visual impact of a whiteboard with paper stick-ons.

The task board is a clever way to keep the team's attention focused on progress and velocity, especially when complemented by the burndown chart.

8.11 BURNDOWN AND BURNUP CHARTS

The burndown chart is a visual representation of the team's progress (velocity). The idea, introduced in the overview chapter, is simple: plot, against project time, the number of remaining units of work for the current iteration. Time is usually measured in working days; units of work can be story points or some other appropriate measure. The curve (red in the figure on the right) is normally decreasing. The blue line serves as a reference, describing ideal progress with a constant number of story points discharged every day.

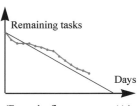

(From the figure on page 11.)

Cockburn's variant in the Crystal method uses a "burnup" chart which shows progress rather than remaining work, and also displays the units completed:

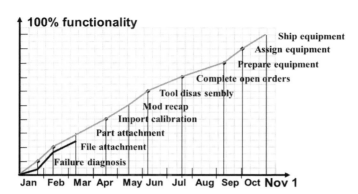

Burnup chart

(From [Cockburn 2005], page 99.)

Common to all variants is the rule that one should only count work that is both:

- *Deliverable* work, including code and tests, as well as other deliverables such as training materials and user documentation, but excluding results that have an internal role only, such as a plan or a design.

← *"Story points", 8.4, page 121.* **See also** *"Develop only code and tests", page 60.*

- *Finished* work, which for code means that it is fully tested.

Here again various tools are available to offer software support for maintaining and publicizing the chart.

The burndown chart is an important practical agile contribution, enabling teams to keep track of daily progress in a vivid form accessible to all.

8.12 IMPEDIMENT

We have seen that a constant concern in Scrum, and in particular a core task of the Scrum Master, is to remove *impediments*. An impediment, per the earlier definition, is any matter that damages the progress of the project, whether technical or organizational. Typical examples include unavailability of some necessary hardware resource such as a workstation, another team's delay in producing a module needed by the project, and interference by outsiders to the project.

The notion of velocity suggests a more concise definition: an impediment is simply any factor that reduces velocity.

8.13 WASTE, TECHNICAL DEBT, DEPENDENCY, DEPENDENCY CHARTS

Our last three artifacts do *not* belong to the agile approach, although they do belong to agile discussions, in a negative role: as obstacles to be avoided.

The fight to avoid **waste** is at the center of the Lean method, but is a concern in all agile approaches. Waste is not a single artifact but includes all the products, material and virtual, not delivered to customers. A design document is waste, unfocused meetings are waste. The agile insistence on code and tests as the only products worthy of consideration implies that waste takes many forms, which agile teams must always fight.

Technical debt denotes code elements of unsatisfactory quality that can accumulate in a project, like barnacles attached to a ship's hull, initially ignored because their effect is hardly noticeable, but growing to a point where they can bring the whole vessel — the whole project — to a halt. The principal agile tool to fight technical debt is refactoring: identifying code and design *smells* and remove them.

← *"Refactoring",* *7.4, page 109.*

Dependencies are constraints between development elements, such as tasks or user stories, expressing that to develop B it is necessary to have completed A. In a compiler project, for example, B might be "implement the parser" and A might be "specify the interface of the lexical analyzer". Dependencies stand in the way of the basic agile process of picking the next task in the list and assigning it to the next available developer in a cross-functional team, where tasks are ordered by business value. Clearly, if B depends on A but has a higher business value, we cannot apply this technique. Hence the standard agile advice of *minimizing dependencies*, a goal easier to state, however, than to achieve.

> The discussion of feature interaction has shown how intricately the functions of a system can be connected with each other. This phenomenon of feature interaction is one of the reasons we cannot realistically hope to get rid of dependencies.

← *"Additive and multiplicative complexity: the lasagne and the linguine",* *page 63.*

Another obstacle to the agile scheduling policy is the presence of *developer* constraints. It is commendable to aim for cross-functional teams, but in practice people have special skills and expertise. If for the next-highest-business-value task one of the team members has much higher competence than anyone else, but is busy with some other task, it is often better to defer the task until that person becomes available.

← *"Collective ownership and cross-functionality",* *6.12.2, page 102.*

Waste, technical debt and dependencies are virtual notions. The last item in this list of agile rejects can have a physical representation, although it is also used as a purely virtual artifact. It is the notion of **dependency chart**, often taking a form (illustrated on the facing page) that attracts the particular scorn of agilists, the **Gantt chart**, which serves as the basis for such project management tools as Microsoft Project. The basic process of using such charts and tools (in traditionally managed projects) is simple:

- List the tasks, their estimated durations and dependencies (in the sense defined above).

- List the people available to perform the tasks. Usually it suffices to list the number of people and their available time.

- Deduce a possible scheduling and assignment of the tasks, compatible with the constraint. This is where tools are useful.

Typical agile criticism of Gantt charts is expressed by Cohn:

> *Rather than a detailed command-and-control plan based on Gantt charts, the agile plan's purpose is to lay out an investment vision against which management can assess and frequently adjust its investments, lay out a common set of understandings from which emergence, adaptation and collaboration occur, and establish expectations against which progress will be measured.*

[Cohn 2003].

Note the "command-and-control" accusation and the vagueness of the proposed replacement. Cockburn does offer a concrete substitute:

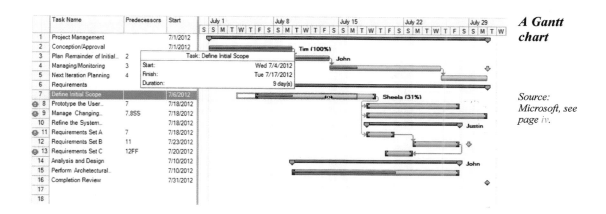

A Gantt chart

Source: Microsoft, see page iv.

The organization might adopt some of the ideas [of the Crystal method] *to simplify or improve their work product set (replacing the Gantt schedule charts with earned-value or burnup charts would be a good start).*

[Cockburn 2005], pages 252-253.

(Burnup charts are, as seen a few pages back, a variant of burndown charts; earned-value charts are an earlier, non-software-specific form.) The suggestion is surprising since burndown and burnup charts are a way to track progress and offer little help in planning.

Being always on the alert for waste, detecting and correcting technical debt, and minimizing dependencies are all worthy goals. Where the agile approach takes a bizarre turn is in its rejection of Gantt charts and tools for dependency-based scheduling. While Microsoft Project itself is not the greatest tool of the 21st century — it shows its age and is heavy to use — it serves only as a red herring here: a profusion of modern tools exist, many of them available in the cloud, to manage dependencies in an effective way. In any complex project dependencies exist, some of them subtle but as a result even more important, since if you detect them too late they will disrupt progress. You can minimize dependencies but (as agile authors admit, at least in print) you cannot eliminate them. Gantt charts and similar mechanisms are powerful engineering tools in the modern manager's bag of tricks. To renounce them is either to pretend that dependencies do not exist (they will take their revenge when a task stalls because it needs the results of another which has not been completed yet) or to accept handling them manually, with all the resulting tedium and risk of error.

Here Agile turns Luddite. There is no reason to bar agile projects from using concepts and tools which help address an issue that most of them face: ensuring that the scheduling of tasks is compatible with their interdependencies. The effective manager disregards ideology and picks, for every project, all the tools that help.

9

Agile methods

An Agile Method, such as Lean Software (with its Kanban variant), Extreme Programming, Scrum and Crystal, is a particular combination of some of the components presented in the previous chapters: principles, practices, roles and artifacts. Not just an arbitrary mix, but a reasoned construction with its own distinctive view of software development. In this chapter we review the key characteristics of the four methods cited.

The methods surveyed share the distinction of being documented by books written by their respective creators. In each case the method and the corresponding books are intricately connected; the books, marked by the strong personalities of their authors, set the spirit of the methods. As a consequence, each method description in this chapter includes a brief review of the associated foundational texts.

9.1 METHODS AND METHODOLOGY

We start with a clarification of the underlying concepts.

9.1.1 Terminology

You will see "methods" such as Scrum, XP and consorts also called "methodologies"; there is nothing wrong with this term since, along with the meaning of "methodology" as "the study of methods" — the topic of this chapter — the dictionary also accepts "a methodology" to mean a combination of methods. For the present discussion, "method" is shorter and just as appropriate.

> If this chapter is about methodology, the present section must be about the methodology of studying methodology. But do not fear; we will stop the escalation here and stay away from any word beginning with "meta".

9.1.2 The fox and the hedgehog

Each method consists of "many small ideas": principles and practices. We will in each case see a selection of these ideas, but such enumerations do not suffice to define what the methods are about. The discussion will identify, for each of them, **"one Big Idea"**, which stands behind all the method's components.

The section for a method starts with the method's Big Idea, continues with the list of its components and ends with an assessment of the method.

B. Meyer, *Agile!*, DOI 10.1007/978-3-319-05155-0_9,
© Springer International Publishing Switzerland 2014

9.2 LEAN SOFTWARE AND KANBAN

Lean

Prompted by the success of the Japanese carmakers and particularly of Toyota's hailed manufacturing process, methods of "lean manufacturing" have enjoyed considerable attention in many branches of industry. They seek to make industrial production more efficient by not building any unneeded part or product, delaying production of needed items until customers or other production steps actually require them (just-in-time production), minimizing unnecessary communication, and reducing waste at every step. Mary and Tom Poppendieck have transposed the ideas to software, using the term "Lean Software Development".

As we saw in an earlier discussion, Wirth wrote a *"plea for lean software"* in 1995. Lean Software as a general development method is, however, the Poppendiecks' creation.

← [Wirth 1995]; see "What is simplicity?", page 66.

This section will conclude with a short review of Kanban, a production method featuring analogies with Lean Software.

9.2.1 Lean Software's Big Idea

The obsession in Lean is to:

> **Reduce waste**

"Waste" in software is anything not delivered to the customer. The Lean approach is about making sure that software projects concentrate on what matters to customers, and setting aside any distractions from that goal, in particular any artifacts that do not yield a tangible business value.

← "Develop minimal software", 4.4.4, page 58.

9.2.2 Lean Software's principles

The Lean Software method promotes seven principles:

> **Lean Software Development principles**
>
> 1 Eliminate waste
> 2 Amplify learning.
> 3 Decide as late as possible.
> 4 Deliver as fast as possible.
> 5 Empower the team.
> 6 Build integrity in.
> 7 See the whole.

Principle 1, eliminate waste, is the most important. It includes, under "waste", many traditional products and activities of software development. Waste *products* are: detailed requirements documents which no one will read; partially done work (any code that was started to implement a certain functionality, but does not deliver it); extra features, which few users will ever need (bloat); defects (bugs). Waste *processes* are: unnecessary tasks, such as long requirements processes mandated by obsolete regulations; task switching (better to let programmers concentrate on one well-defined task at any time); waiting (for a module developed by another team, for resources, for information, for decisions); motion (transfer of artifacts from one group or person to another); needless management activities.

Principle 2, amplify learning, directs project to seek quality throughout, and programmers to learn from experience. It rejects the "do it right the first time" approach in favor of a "try-it, test-it, fix-it" process.

Principle 3, decide as late as possible, is derived from "just in time" techniques of production engineering. It promotes avoiding Big-Upfront-Design decisions, which will cause high costs if a change must be made down the road, and instead making design choices as late as possible, when all the necessary information is available.

Principle 4, deliver as fast as possible, is common to all agile approaches: produce a working system at every iteration, get the users to try it, and benefit from the feedback.

Principle 5, empower the team, is also an agile staple. The idea is to stay away from the practice of managers giving orders, and instead motivate the team to take its future and the success of the project into its own hands.

Principle 6, build integrity, covers the need for maintaining the consistency of a system's design. It is closely related to the notion of simplicity built into XP.

Principle 7, see the whole, is about concentrating on what is really important, the whole picture, and not to sweat the small stuff. Examples of small stuff that should not be sweated include:

- Intermediate deadlines: optimizing the overall progress of the project is more important. (With hindsight it is unfortunate — and an illustration of the danger of meta- *[Poppendieck phors and anecdotes — that the supporting example is Lance Armstrong's brilliant 2003], pages series of victories in the Tour de France, hardly the most inspirational model given 155, 157.* what we now know.)

- Monitoring individual performance on a continuous basis.

- Business contracts, in line with the Agile Manifesto's motto of "*valuing customer col- [Agile 2001]. laboration over contract negotiation*".

9.2.3 Lean Software: an assessment

Lean Software is not a cradle-to-grave method that tells you step after step how to organize your project and develop your software. It is rather a philosophy made of a set of general observations about what is important and not in software development.

The working hypothesis of the method, that software can benefit from ideas taken from industrial production, has both considerable attraction and built-in limits. Attraction because so many successes have followed from applying sound principles in, for example, automobile engineering. Limits since, as the creators of lean software themselves state, software does not have production, only design. Many of the improvements that made the success of Toyota and other innovative companies apply to production. Some of the analogies work, for example describing incompletely implemented software functionality as waste, comparable to inventory in traditional industries. Others are more far-fetched, such as "motion" (in software development people may have to move to see each other, but this phenomenon is nowhere close to the complexity of moving parts between factories).

The style of the lean books also complicates making direct sense of the method. They are eclectic, full of anecdotes and never boring for a minute, but by hopping madly from topic to topic and story to story, software-related or not — over two typical pages, video tape manufacturing then software testing then Lance Armstrong — they make it tough for the dizzied reader to derive precise rules for software projects.

[Poppendieck 2003], pages 156-157.

One should not turn to Lean Software for a comprehensive software development method, or expect its authors to be always right. Their contribution, however, is significant. By emphasizing that software engineering is engineering and can benefit from some of the same recipes that have worked in other fields, and in particular by reminding us always to be on the lookout for waste of any kind, Lean Software provides software developers and particularly project managers with a solid set of useful principles.

9.2.4 Kanban

Although distinct from Lean Software, the Kanban approach draws from the same source: the Toyota production process, where it evolved from observation of supply management in supermarkets. Kanban has gained some popularity in software circles, as a complement to Lean or Scrum.

Kanban's Big Idea is to minimize *work in progress* by ensuring just-in-time production, driven by demand. "Kanban cards" serve to keep track of needed materials and trigger a signal when the production system runs out of a needed part. A "Kanban board", similar to a Scrum task board, visualizes the progress of parts and products in the production process as they go through the stages of "to do", "in progress" and "done".

← "Task and story boards", page 127.

There is — so far — no explicit Kanban method for software, but teams have found Kanban principles of work-in-progress minimization useful, for example to help identify impediments in Scrum and focus software teams on the most productive tasks.

On Kanban for Scrum see e.g. [Kniberg 2010].

9.3 EXTREME PROGRAMMING

Extreme Programming is the original agile approach, in the sense that its introduction in the late nineteen-nineties was the event that brought agile ideas to the fore of the software engineering stage.

Extreme Programming is less visible today, much of the limelight having moved to Scrum. But this change of fashion hides the reality of the method's continuing influence: the most constructive XP principles and practices have been integrated into other approaches and many projects apply them, whether or not project members are aware of their provenance.

9.3.1 XP's Big Idea

The Big Idea of Extreme Programming can be understood as follows:

> **Increment then simplify**

This is the basic cycle, repeated until the team and the customer are happy: add functionality (induced, in Test-Driven-Development, by a new test that would fail under the previous version); when it works, look for any damage the new code has caused to the simplicity of the design; apply *refactoring* if needed to restore that simplicity.

This process is practiced by a small, self-organizing group of developers, working in pairs and maintaining at all times a close connection with representatives of the customer organization.

9.3.2 XP: the unadulterated source

An observation about the *descriptions* of Extreme Programming will help readers who want to study XP in depth beyond the presentation in this book. Although various authors, particularly Jeffries and Cunningham, have written good articles and books about XP, the reference is Beck's *Extreme Programming Explained*. The book has two editions, 2000 and 2005, and contrary to expectations I find the earlier version (still in print) a better source. The impression one gets about the second edition is that the author was piqued by some comments on the first:

> *Critics of the first edition have complained that it tries to force them to program in a certain way.*

[Beck 2005], page xxii.

(Strange: how can someone who buys a programming methodology book complain of being enjoined to "*program in a certain way*"?) He appears as a result to have toned down the message, going from concrete and hence criticizable assertions to more ethereal but less interesting generalities. Take for example the beginning (starting with the second paragraph) of the first edition's preface:

> *To some folks, XP seems like just good common sense. So why the "extreme" in the name? XP takes commonsense principles and practices to extreme levels.*   *[Beck 2000], page xv.*
>
> • *If code reviews are good, we'll review code all the time (pair programming).*
>
> • *If testing is good, everybody will test all the time (unit testing), even the customers (functional testing).*
>
> • *If design is good, we'll make it part of everybody's daily business (refactoring).*

(followed by four more bullet points, each citing another practice traditionally considered beneficial and stating that XP pushes it to the limit). Clear, engaging, challenging. In the second edition, the corresponding paragraph starts:

> *There are better ways and worse ways to develop software. Good teams are more alike than they are different. No matter how good or bad your team you can always improve.*

Sure, such a succession of gentle platitudes will not offend anyone, but what is "extreme" about them, and what are we learning? I benefit more from the in-your-face simplicity of the first edition. We are talking here about substance, not style. Although the second edition cites agile practices, it often does so in abstract terms; to get a precise description of the practices you need the original book.

Some of the comments of the second edition reflect a more balanced view resulting from a few extra years of experience, but they tend to dilute the essence of the ideas. Unless you want to read the two editions (you will have noted that the present book cites from both), you may expect to find more value in the first.

9.3.3 Key XP techniques

Many of the principles and practices discussed in previous chapters were originally introduced by Extreme Programming. The XP books include long lists of practices; the essential techniques (including, in the terminology of this book, not just practices but also principles and artifacts) are:

• Short iterations (as in all agile methods).

• Pair programming.

• User stories.

• Refactoring.

• Open workspace.

• Collective code ownership.

• Continuous integration.

• Test-first (or test-driven) development.

The last two elements constitute Extreme Programming's most lasting technical contribution to the practice of software development.

9.3.4 Extreme Programming: an assessment

Extreme Programming provided the initial jolt that brought agile methods to the attention of the programming world. The word "extreme" was intended to convey the decision to take the best development practices to their full extent, as explained in the excerpts from the first edition's preface quoted on the previous page ("if P is good, we'll apply it all the way", for a whole range of practices P). "Extreme" also characterizes the method's general assertiveness, its insistence that the techniques it offers are not just possibilities but obligations: for example, everyone should pair-program.

One can characterize this assertiveness as dogmatism, but it also leads to one of the method's main strengths, its consistency. XP reflects a strong view of how programming should be practiced, leaving little room for compromise. This stance has hampered the overall adoption of XP by the community. But many of the individual techniques promoted by XP have made their mark on the industry, and not just on teams that explicitly follow an agile process. If nothing else, Extreme Programming has convinced the world of the indispensability of the last two techniques mentioned above: projects should not let branches diverge, but integrate code all the time; and they should treat tests as a key resource, not letting any code be developed without tests to go with it, and running the regression test suite all the time. These two contributions alone would be enough to ensure XP's place in the history of software engineering.

9.4 SCRUM

Scrum

Scrum has come to dominate the agile scene. The numerical results of various studies differ, but the general trend is inescapable: Scrum has taken over from Extreme Programming as the agile method of choice, even if we cannot see the situation entirely in competitive terms since Scrum is more of an organizational technique and many teams that practice it add concepts from XP on the software-specific technical side.

There is a considerable literature on Scrum including several books from the creators, Schwaber and Sutherland. The authors and the Scrum Alliance have generously made available many documents, such as tutorials and lecture notes, which provide more concrete details. Cohn and Larman have also authored helpful Scrum books.

[Scrum Alliance].

9.4.1 Scrum's Big Idea

The most distinctive characteristic of Scrum is the "closed-window" rule encountered in previous chapters:

← *"Freeze requirements during iterations", page 71 and "The closed-window rule", 6.1.2, page 90.*

> **Freeze requirements during short iterations**

This is not the idea most highlighted in presentations of the method — you will hear about the "three roles" and the "four meetings" and Scrum Masters and "pigs" and "chickens" and various practices — but it is at the core of the method. It addresses one of the principal challenges of software engineering: how to handle change.

The Agile Manifesto naïvely states that agilists "welcome change"; but no serious development can have a policy of taking in any change at any time. The Scrum answer is to accept changes without letting them disrupt the current iteration, imposing the rule on everyone, regardless of rank and station. It is sustainable because the iterations are short, so any rejection is temporary; in addition it gives people the opportunity to cool off, and possibly to refine or withdraw a request for functionality.

> If out of my long immersion in agile methods for the preparation of this book I had to retain just one idea, that would be it. The principle is innovative, applicable, and effective.

9.4.2 Key Scrum practices

The iterations of Scrum follow practices studied in previous chapters:

- Sprint planning at the beginning.
- Closed-window rule, allowing requirements change but in a controlled way.
- User stories, decomposed in tasks, as the definition of work to be carried out.
- Daily Scrum to track progress and isolate impediments.
- "Definition of Done" to make sure what is claimed as progress truly is.
- Task board and burndown chart to assess velocity.
- Sprint review to reflect on the previous sprint and prepare the next one.

These are only some of the most important elements; many other Scrum techniques appear in earlier discussions.

9.4.3 Scrum: an assessment

Scrum has conquered the mind of many in the software industry; numerous projects are clearly finding its rules useful. Scrum has in particular turned the general idea of iterative development into a precise discipline, with rules codifying the goals, duration and management of individual iterations. The resulting iteration model, the sprint, is quickly becoming the industry standard, beyond teams that explicitly apply Scrum.

Scrum has been well-served by a savvy marketing operation, in particular by a certifying process (through the Scrum Alliance) that turns Scrum learners into Scrum supporters. It has also been well served by the first Scrum books, insightful and filled with reports from projects the authors advised. For software practitioners, however, these books also limit the method's applicability, since they are advocacy pieces with little room for nuance and less for self-doubt. Scrum clearly needs better presentations, more analytical, even-handed and rigorous.

Scrum's primary contribution affects the organizational aspects of projects, rather than software technology per se. (Some people go so far as to promote Scrum to manage any project, technical or not.) The need remains open for a method that would retain the best aspects of Scrum and address the unique demands of software development.

9.5 CRYSTAL

The name *Crystal* denotes an array of methods developed by Alistair Cockburn. We can take the word "array" literally: with projects characterized along two dimensions, criticality and size, each featuring four levels, we get a matrix of 16 elements. The names are color-coded. Understandably, only a few of the slots have been filled by detailed method descriptions. The Crystal Clear method covers smaller projects; Crystal Orange was the first to be developed and addresses larger projects.

9.5.1 Crystal's Big Idea

Crystal puts particular emphasis on the interactions with the team through a principle that makes a group jell into a single unit:

> ## Osmotic communication

With osmotic communication, *"questions and answers flow naturally and with surprisingly little disturbance among the team"*. From this goal follows a strong emphasis on an office space layout favoring open communication. The method treats such matters as core issues of software development, since projects can face major costs and impediments from bad communication between team members, delays in answering questions, and questions that were simply not asked because of some practical obstacle, of which poor office layout is an example.

This definition of osmotic communication is the Crystal Clear version. For larger groups, or groups split across different locations, the concept generalizes to "core communication".

9.5.2 Crystal principles

Crystal defines seven principles, a bit of a mixed bag.

"Frequent delivery" of *"running, tested code to real users"* is the *"single most important property of any project"*. This idea is common to all agile methods. *All citations (in italics) are from [Cockburn 2005].*

"Reflective improvement" requires the team, *"once a month, or twice per delivery cycle,* [to] *get together in a reflection worskhop or iteration retrospective to discuss how things are working"*. The idea is reminiscent of the "Optimizing" level in a model coming from a different corner of the software engineering scene: CMMI. The specific practice is also related to Scrum's "retrospective".

"Osmotic communication" promotes, as noted, a constant and free flow of information between team members.

"Personal safety" is Crystal's take on the agile idea of sustainable pace. The principle states that team members should be free to speak up, without fear of reprisal or other unpleasant consequences, when they feel they have to, for example to point out that a schedule is unrealistic. *← "Work at a sustainable pace", page 56.*

"**Focus**" defines the conditions under which developers can perform their jobs unimpeded. In particular, they should not be asked to: perform many tasks at once, preventing them from devoting to each task the attention it requires; handle side tasks, not relevant to the project goals; cope with frequent interruptions; or be denied knowledge of the organization's priorities. "*With two hours of guaranteed focus time each day, and two days in a row on the same project, a developer who otherwise is being driven to distraction may get four full hours of work done in a week.*"

"**Easy access to expert users**" is Crystal's variant of the general agile principle of customer involvement. The method does not prescribe embedding a user in the team, XP-style, or defining a product owner as in Scrum (although it does not preclude either technique), but requires a realistic guarantee of access to knowledgeable user representatives. "*Even one hour a week of access to a real and expert user is immensely valuable*". This recommendation is typical of Crystal's realism: as we noted in earlier discussions, real experts are in high demand and unlikely to be made extensively (even less full-time) available to a project; but it is essential to demand from higher management a guaranteed minimum level of access.

← "*Put the customer at the center*", page 51.

"**Technical environment with automated tests, configuration management and frequent integration**" is a long name for a principle, but clear enough: programmers should be given modern tools. Hardly a subversive idea today, except perhaps for some project managers born in the age of crinoline petticoats, but worth repeating.

9.5.3 Crystal: an assessment

Like Lean Software, Crystal is not a comprehensive method telling you what to do step by step either on the management side (as Scrum does) or in technical development (as XP does). Rather, Crystal is a concentrate of software development wisdom, much of it healthy.

What most distinguishes Crystal from other agile approaches is its refusal of dogmatism and its acceptance of some of the classical software engineering principles. The provision for variants of the method adapted to various kinds of projects, critical or not, large or small, is also a refreshing initiative.

The multi-method idea reflects the wide variety of project circumstances. It seems, however, unrealistic to fill a 4 x 4 matrix with individual method descriptions, each with its specific characteristics, reference book and training materials. More unrealistic still is the expectation that a project would choose one of the methods against the others based on a determination of its size and criticality; even if the decision is right, projects change as they go, and they should evolve smoothly rather than have to change methods in mid-stream. It would be more effective for Crystal to identify the universals of software development and present a single method that addresses them, while accounting for gradations in project parameters.

In the history of the field, Crystal could end up being only an episode. But if we consider — in terms of moment of acceptance rather than moment of creation — that Extreme Programming embodied the first generation and Scrum the second, Crystal, with its attempt to integrate the best ideas of software engineering regardless of their source and to provide a realistic framework for projects large and small, could grow into a real method, defining precise techniques of software management and development, and emerge as a first step towards agile methods of a third generation.

10

Dealing with agile teams

Before we move to a final assessment, some observations are in order on how to deal with groups that adopt agile ideas in your organization.

10.1 GRAVITY STILL HOLDS

We have seen numerous examples of agile authors asking us to suspend disbelief. A 2012 book distributed under the aegis of IBM summarily dispels various objections: *[Ambler 2012].*

> [Objection: agile is unsuitable for regulated environments]. [In such environments] *organizations are audited from time to time for compliance with regulations. With agile, these organizations can feel confident when they endure these audits. They benefit from faster delivery of data and higher quality of their output.*

> [Objection: agile means we don't know what will be delivered.] *Because agile is an iterative process, it provides the opportunity not just for greater control but better control over building the right things in the lifecycle.*

> [Objection: agile does not scale] *Agile definitely scales. Large teams must be organized differently. Large agile teams succeed by using products like IBM Rational Requirements Composer for requirements modeling.*

And so on. Trust us, agile solves everything. This is not very good advice to give to managers, who are entitled to more caution from such a venerable company.

The truth is that software engineering has laws that limit what we can expect. An example of such a law goes back to Boehm's work in the nineteen-eighties and has been confirmed by numerous studies since then. It states that for any IT problem there exist a "nominal" cost and a nominal development time, and that solutions cannot deviate from them by much. The following figure illustrates it: *See e.g. [Boehm 1981] and page 226 in [McConnell 2006].*

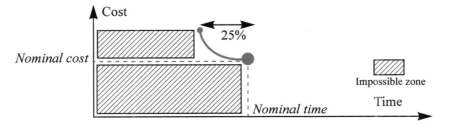

Nominal values and possible deviations

B. Meyer, *Agile!*, DOI 10.1007/978-3-319-05155-0_10,
© Springer International Publishing Switzerland 2014

The big red dot represents the nominal point. According to these studies, it is possible to get a shorter delivery time by spending more (hiring more developers or managers, or better ones), as represented by the curve, but that curve stops at about 75% of the nominal time. The grayed area is an impossible zone: you cannot get the results for less money, or in less than 75% of the nominal time.

> Studies differ as to what happens to the *right* of the nominal point. Some suggest that you can save money by taking more time, for example with fewer developers, and others that you will end up both late and over budget.

When we talk about such "laws" of software engineering we are not at the level of rigor and universality of the laws of physics; they are simply observations supported by credible empirical studies. They reflect, in addition, the technology of the moment. Laws defining the limits of what ships can do ceased to hold when steamboats replaced sailing. In software too it is quite possible that a technology leap radically alters the rules of game. Before you believe that it increases productivity — not for a particular flagship project or group but for everyone — at a level that established software engineering wisdom deems infeasible, you had better be careful. Gravity still holds.

The very IBM-sponsored study that touts agile as ready for deployment anywhere *[IBM 2012]*. found that 54% of organizations surveyed have "*tried and rejected at least one agile approach*". Characteristically, the conclusion it draws from that finding is that the methods it promotes (Scrum, Kanban, Lean) are superior. To any unbiased person, the statistic will serve instead as a warning: an invitation to approach agile methods with caution.

Agile methods clearly have many benefits to offer (otherwise this book would have no reason to exist). But expecting miracles will not help. It is preferable to set realistic goals and strive to achieve them.

10.2 THE EITHER-WHAT-OR-WHEN FALLACY

We have seen that iterations in agile development are time-boxed: if something has to   ← *"Iteration* give, it will be the functionality, not the iteration's end date. We also saw that this prin-   *length", page 71.* ciple is excellent. But the idea applies to the internal steps of a project. The customers' world has its own constraints, and they are often not negotiable.

When January 1st, 2002, was chosen as the date of monetary unification for twelve countries, with the provision that the previous currencies would cease to be legal tender only two months later, it was pretty clear that the IT infrastructure would have to be ready for the changeover to the euro by that first day of the year. It was.

It is indeed one of the defining rules of software development that delivery date and functionality are equally important. Yet the agile world has promoted the idea that one cannot promise both. You can commit to the what, or to the when, but not both. Beck articulates this notion explicitly:

> *Write contracts for software development that fix time, costs, and quality but call*   *[Beck 2005],* > *for an ongoing negotiation of the precise scope of the system. Reduce risk by*   *page 69.* > *signing a sequence of short contracts instead of one long one.*

You can move in the direction of negotiated scope. Big, long contracts can be split
in half or thirds, with the optional part to be exercised only if both parties agree.
Contracts with high costs for change requests can be written with less scope fixed
up front and lower costs for changes.

Clever, especially if you are a consultant. I can promise what it will do. I can also promise that you will have it by next June. Choose one.

For most customers, of course, this either-what-or-when trick will not do. Customers
want to know the when as well as the what. Agile authors suggest "educating" customers
so that they understand the harsh realities of life. Most customers, of course, will skip the
trip to the re-education camp; they will not fall for that trap, even if that means being
labeled as "mediocre hierarchical bureaucrats" in the terms of an author we encountered $\leftarrow$ *"Intimida-*
in an early chapter. Call us bureaucrats all you please, but we have a set amount of money   *tion", 2.2.3,*
to spend, set business results to achieve, and a set time to achieve them.   *page 23.*

This issue is what distinguishes competent software teams (and competent consultants) from the rest. The definition of a competent team is that over the years it consistently delivers appropriate functionality on time and within budget.

The agile mystique can temporarily hide this fundamental difference between the professionals and the amateurs, by providing the amateurs — those unable to deliver quality
results within time and budget — with fashionable excuses. Such pretense cannot last for
very long, since economic considerations will quickly put an end to the hype.

In a transitional period, however, the either-what-or-when pretense can cause trouble,
especially in environments where agile teams coexist with others using more classically
predictive techniques. The plan-oriented groups can find it hard to get precise commitments from the agile ones. They should not, of course, let them off the hook; and an internal division of the project into time-boxed iterations cannot translate into a refusal of
what-and-when deadlines for customer deliverables. But any organization adopting agile
methods should be prepared for such scenarios.

The difficulty of getting agile teams to commit is the most delicate issue in an organization's transition, total or partial, to agile development.

As usual, the indefensible agile exaggeration conceals an important and productive
observation. The reluctance to promise both what and when comes from bad experience
with projects featuring oversize goals and unrealistic deadlines.

The reasonable conclusion is that it is better to split such goals into intermediate steps:
better a bird in the hand four months from now than ten in the bush in two years. Define
tangible objectives that can be achieved at regular intervals. Achieving them will not only
yield partial releases that can already be deployed, but also boost the morale of everyone,
development team and customers, by providing a sense of continuous progress. But the
team should commit to these milestones: what the system will do, and when.

11

The Ugly, the Hype and the Good: an assessment of the agile approach

We have now studied the core principles, roles, practices and artifacts that make up the agile canon. It is time to assess the agile contribution: which of the ideas should be kept at bay, which ones do not really matter, and which ones truly help.

For the sections in this chapter, it is appropriate to reverse the order of the book's title (and to use not three but four categories, distinguishing the merely good from the brilliant). The flaws of agile methods are real enough, but the approach would not warrant our attention if it did not also include genuine advances, so it is important to end with these pearls.

11.1 THE BAD AND THE UGLY

We start with the worst in the agile approach: ideas that damage the software process.

11.1.1 Deprecation of upfront tasks

The prize undisputedly goes to the deprecation of "upfront" activities, in particular upfront requirements and upfront design.

Agile criticism of "Big Upfront Anything" includes some perceptive comments. It is true that one cannot fully comprehend requirements before the development of the system; that requirements will change; that the architecture will have to be improved as implementation proceeds. Those observations express some of the fundamental difficulties of software engineering, and the futility of trying to define everything at the beginning.

There is, however, no argument for shunning the normal engineering practice — the practice, in fact, of any rational endeavor — of studying a problem before attempting to solve it, and of defining the architecture of the solution before embarking on the details. The alternative proposed by agile methods is an ad hoc approach: identify some functionality, build it, assess and correct the result, repeat. It is no substitute for serious requirements and design.

Iterative development is great. Trying out ideas on a small scale before you make final decisions is great. Treating requirements as a living, changeable product is great. Reassessing design decisions on the basis of results is great. Insisting on regular deliveries (once the basic structure is in place) is great. Refactoring is listed at the end of this chapter as one of the significant contributions of agile methods. None of these ideas justifies forsaking the initial tasks of analysis and design.

B. Meyer, *Agile!*, DOI 10.1007/978-3-319-05155-0_11,
© Springer International Publishing Switzerland 2014

In other cases we can see the pros and cons of agile ideas. Here there is no place for equivocating: neglecting these upfront steps, as agile authors advocate, is guaranteed to harm your development.

11.1.2 User stories as a basis for requirements

As previous chapters have discussed on several occasions, user stories play a useful role as ways to check the completeness of requirements, but to use them as the basic form of requirements means forsaking abstraction. In addition, they ignore the critical Jackson-Zave distinction between the machine being built and the domain that constrains it. *← "The domain and the machine", 3.2.5, page 36.*

The resulting systems are narrowly geared to the specific user stories that have been identified; they often do not apply to other uses; and they are hard to adapt to more general requirements.

User stories are no substitute for a system requirements effort aimed at defining the key abstractions and the associated operations (the *domain model*) and clearly separating machine and domain properties. *← Pages 120-121.*

11.1.3 Feature-based development and ignorance of dependencies

A core idea of agile methods is that you can treat software development as a sequence of implementations of individual features, selected at each step on the basis of their business value. It would be great if such an approach were applicable, but it exists only in a land of make-believe. Difficult projects do not lend themselves to this scheme: they require foundational work (building core architectural elements, such as a communication or persistence layer) which extend across features; and the features interact through dependencies, causing complexity of the "multiplicative" kind. *← "Additive and multiplicative complexity: the lasagne and the linguine", page 63.*

11.1.4 Rejection of dependency tracking tools

The potential complexity of feature interactions requires a careful analysis of task dependencies; projects can skip this analysis only at their own risk. The advice to stay away from Gantt charts and dependency-management tools is not only naïve but detrimental. Such tools are not a panacea for project management but have proved their value over several decades of use. They can help agile projects just as well; dogmatic rejection of useful tools is a self-inflicted wound.

11.1.5 Rejection of traditional manager tasks

The self-organizing teams promoted by agile methods, with no manager having the traditional duty of assigning tasks, are the best solution for a few teams, and are inappropriate for many others. The picture of the manager as an incompetent control freak is a caricature. Many software projects have been brought to completion, and many projects on the brink of failure have been rescued, through the talents of a strong manager. Imposing a single management scheme on everyone is arrogant.

> Suggestions that management can exert its influence through "subtle control" make things worse. Developers are entitled to demand that any control to which they are subjected be explicit, not devious.

11.1.6 Rejection of upfront generalization

Agilist rightly note that the primary responsibility of a project is to deliver working software to its customers, and that too much early concern for extendibility (ease of change) and reusability (applicability to future projects) can hinder that goal, especially since it is not always clear initially in what direction the software will be extended and which parts will need reuse. But these observations are not a reason to reject the concept of generalization altogether. We have seen that such an attitude directly contradicts the professed agile principle of "welcoming change". Good software developers do not wait for change to happen: they plan for it by designing flexible architectures and solving more than the problem of the moment.

← *"Accept change", 4.4.5, page 68.*

11.1.7 Embedded customer

The XP idea of a customer representative embedded in the development team does not work well in practice, for reasons explained in an earlier discussion. The Scrum notion of a product owner, however, figures below in the list of excellent ideas.

← *"Onsite customer", 6.5, page 96.*

11.1.8 Coach as a separate role

The Scrum idea of a dedicated Scrum Master is good for Scrum, but not appropriate for most projects. Good development requires not just talkers but doers.

← *"Separating roles", 5.7, page 86.*

11.1.9 Test-driven development

Test-first development, and the requirement of associating a test with every piece of functionality, appear in the lists of good and excellent ideas below. So does refactoring.

Test-driven development is another matter. A software process defined as the repeated execution of the basic steps of TDD — write a test, fix the code to pass the test, refactor if needed — cannot be taken seriously. With such an approach one is limited to tunnel vision, focused on the latest test. An effective process requires a high-level perspective, considering the entire system.

← *"The TDD method of software development", 7.5.1, page 113.*

While test-driven development is extensively discussed in the literature, industry has made its choice: it is not broadly practicing this technique. (On the other hand, many companies have adopted user stories. One may only hope that they will realize that replacing requirements by user stories is the same as replacing specifications by tests.)

11.1.10 Deprecation of documents

Agile criticism of document-heavy processes that produce little real customer benefit is right on target for some segments of the industry — although in some cases, such as mission-critical systems, little can be done about the situation since the documents are legally required by certifying agencies. (And not just out of bureaucratic inertia. Even the most enthusiastic agilist might feel, when flying to the next agile conference, that it was not such a bad idea after all — not total *"waste"*— to assess the plane's software against a whole pile of certification standards.)

Outside of specific industries with high regulatory requirements, a strong case exists for lightening up the document infrastructure. It is true, as agilists emphasize, that "design" in software is not as remote from production (implementation) in other engineering fields. Modern programming languages help, because they make it possible to include some of the traditional design in the code itself. (Some of my own work has addressed this issue.) None of these observations, however, can justify the deprecation of upfront plans and documents. Software engineering is engineering, or should be, and sorely needs the benefits of a careful predictive approach, as well as the supporting documents. ← *"Is design separate from implementation?", 3.3.1, page 37.*

11.2 THE HYPED

The next category includes ideas that may have value but are unlikely to make a significant difference in matters that count: productivity of the software process and quality of software products. Under this heading we may include:

- **Pair programming**, hyped beyond reason. As a practice to be applied occasionally, pair programming is a useful addition to the programming team's bag of tricks. But there is no credible evidence that it provides major improvements to the programming process or that it is better than classical techniques such as code reviews, and no reason to impose it as the sole mode of development.

- **Open-space working arrangements**. There is no single formula for the layout of a working environment. What we do know is that it is essential to provide simple, obvious opportunities for informal communication. Beyond that, many office setups are possible which will not endanger a team's success. (A related point appears, however, under the "good" ideas of the next section: avoiding distributed development.)

- **Self-organizing teams**. A few teams are competent and experienced enough to manage themselves, like a conductor-less orchestra. Most are not. Each situation calls for its own organizational solutions and there is no reason to impose a single scheme on the entire industry.

- **Working at a sustainable pace**. All great advice; death marches are not a good management practice. But advice can only be wishful here; these matters are determined by economic and organizational pressures more than by good intentions. They are not specific to the programming world: like a company that is responding to a Request For Proposals, a researcher who is facing a conference submission deadline will work through the night to meet it. The most software methodologists can do is to argue that such practices should remain the exception.

- **Producing minimal functionality**. It is always a good habit to question whether proposed features are really needed. But usually they get introduced for a reason: some important customer wants them. It is easy to rail against bloat or heap scorn on monster software (Microsoft Word and Adobe Acrobat are common targets), but try to remove any functionality and brace for the screams of the outraged users.

- **Planning game, planning poker**. These are interesting techniques to help estimate in advance the cost and time of development activities, but they cannot be a substitute for more scientific approaches. In particular, they are open to the danger of intimidation by the crowd; the voice of the expert risks being smothered by the chorus of novices.

- **Members and observers**. In project meetings, the views of the people most seriously involved matter most. This trivial observation does not deserve the amount of attention that the agile canon devotes to the distinction between "pigs" and "chickens".

- **Collective code ownership**. The policy governing who is permitted to change various parts of the code is a delicate decision for each project; it depends on the nature of the team and many other considerations. It is pointless to prescribe a universal solution.

- **Cross-functional teams**. It is a good idea to encourage developers to gain broad competence and to avoid dividing the projects into narrow kingdoms of expertise each under the control of one person. Beyond this general advice, there is little a method can change here to the obvious observation that special areas require special skills. If one of your developers is a database expert and another is a concurrency expert, you will not ask the first, if you have a choice, to resolve a tricky deadlock issue, or the second to optimize queries. This observation is another reason why the agile scheduling policy of picking the highest-business-value task in the pipeline is simplistic and potentially harmful.

11.3 THE GOOD

Promoting **refactoring** is an important contribution of the agile approach, particularly of XP. Good programmers have always known that it is not sufficient to get something that works, but that they should take a second look at the design and improve it if needed. Refactoring has given a name to this activity, made it respectable, and provided a catalog of fundamental refactoring patterns. As a substitute for upfront design it is terrible advice, belonging to the "ugly" part of agile. But as a practice that accompanies careful initial design it is of benefit to all software development.

Short daily meetings focused on simple verbal reports to progress — the "three questions" — are an excellent idea. It need not be practiced in a dogmatic way, since distributed projects and companies with flexible work schedules must adapt the basic scheme, but is one of the practices that undeniably help software development, and deserves to be adopted even more widely than it already is.

Agile methods rightly insist on the importance of **team communication** ("osmotic" in Crystal terminology) to the success of projects. One of the consequences is to recommend co-located projects, whenever possible, over distributed development

The practice of identifying and removing **impediments**, in particular as a focus of progress meetings, is a powerful agile insight.

In a similar vein, Lean's identification of sources of **waste** in software development and insistence on removing them provides an excellent discipline for software projects.

11.4 THE BRILLIANT

Fortunately, in our review of agile ideas we have encountered a number of effective and truly inspiring principles and practices.

Short iterations are perhaps the most visible influence of agile ideas, an influence that has already spread throughout the industry. Few competent teams today satisfy themselves with six-month objectives. The industry has understood that constant feedback is essential, with a checkpoint every few weeks.

The related practice of **continuous integration** and the associated **regression test suite** artifact, while not agile inventions, have been popularized by XP and are major factors in the success of modern projects. The industry, or at least every competently managed project, has turned away from older "big bang" practices, and will never go back.

The **closed-window rule**, which prohibits everyone regardless of status from adding functionality during an iteration, is one of the most insightful and effective agile ideas. ← *"The closed-window rule", page 90.*

Time-boxing every iteration — not accepting any delays, even if some functionality has not been implemented — is an excellent discipline, forcing team members and customer representatives to plan carefully and realistically, and bringing stability to the project. (We have seen that it should only apply to iterations, not to an entire project, for which the customer dictates delivery dates.) ← *"The either-what-or-when fallacy", page 146.*

Scrum introduced the beneficial notion of a clearly defined **product owner** who represents the goals of the customer organization and has decision power over what goes into the product and what does not.

The emphasis on **delivering working software** is another important contribution. We have seen that it can be detrimental if understood as excluding requirements, infrastructure and other upfront work. But once a project has established a sound basis, the requirement to maintain a running version imposes a productive discipline on the team. ← *"Dual Development", page 74.*

The notion of **velocity** and the associated artifact of **task boards** to provide visible, constantly updated evidence of progress or lack thereof are practical, directly useful techniques that can help every project.

Associating a test with every piece of functionality is a fundamental rule which contributes significantly to the solidity of a software project and of the resulting product.

The ideas listed as good or brilliant are relatively few, but they are both important and beneficial; they deserve careful study and immediate application. They justify the journey, arduous at times, that we took through the land of agile methods. Once disentangled from the questionable part of the agile credo, they will leave a durable mark on the practice of software engineering, and find their place, along with earlier ideas such as structured programming, formal methods, object-oriented software construction and design patterns, in the history of major advances in the field.

Bibliography

All URLs checked January 2014.

[Agile 2001]
  Agile Manifesto, at agilemanifesto.org.

[Agile 2011]
  Agile Alliance: *Velocity* page at guide.agilealliance.org/guide/velocity.html, 2011.

[Ambler 2006]
  Scott Ambler: *Agile Adoption Rate Survey*, at www.ambysoft.com/surveys/agileMarch2006.html.

[Ambler 2001]
  Scott W. Ambler: *Agile Modeling and the Rational Unified Process (RUP)*, at www.agilemodeling.com/essays/agileModelingRUP.htm (part of Ambler's "agile modeling" site), 2001.

[Ambler 2010]
  Scott W. Ambler: *The Agile Maturity Model* (AMM), in Dr. Dobbs Journal, April 2010, available at www.drdobbs.com/architecture-and-design/the-agile-maturity-model-amm/224201005.

[Ambler 2012]
  Scott W. Ambler and Matthew Holitza: *Agile for Dummies*, Wiley, 2012. See also "IBM limited edition" available online at www-01.ibm.com/software/rational/agile/agilesoftware.

[Ambler testing]
  Scott W. Ambler: *Agile Testing and Quality Strategies: Discipline Over Rhetoric*, at www.ambysoft.com/essays/agileTesting.html#AgileTestingStrategies, undated.

[Anand site]
  Bachan Anand: *Conscires* site at agile.conscires.com.

[Basili 1975]
  Victor R. Basili and Albert J. Turner: *Iterative Enhancement: A Practical Technique for Software Development*, IEEE *Transactions on Software Engineering*, vol. SE-1, no. 4, December 1975, pages 390-396, available at www.cs.umd.edu/~basili/publications/journals/J04.pdf.

[Beck 2000]
  Kent Beck: *Extreme Programming Explained — Embrace Change*, Addison-Wesley, 2000. (First edition; see also [Beck 2005].)

[Beck 2003]
  Kent Beck: *Test-Driven Development — By Example*, Addison-Wesley, 2003.

[Beck 2005]
  Kent Beck, with Cynthia Andres: *Extreme Programming Explained — Embrace Change,*, Addison-Wesley, 2005. (Second edition; see also [Beck 2000].)

[Boehm 1981]
  Barry W. Boehm: *Software Engineering Economics*, Prentice Hall, 1981.

B. Meyer, *Agile!*, DOI 10.1007/978-3-319-05155-0,
© Springer International Publishing Switzerland 2014

[Boehm 2004]
  Barry W. Boehm & Richard Turner: *Balancing Agility and Discipline – A Guide for the Perplexed*, Addison-Wesley, 2004.

[Brooks 1975]
  Fred Brooks: *The Mythical Man-Month*, Addison-Wesley, 1975.

[Chromatic 2003]
  Chromatic: *Extreme Programming Pocket Guide*, O'Reilly, 2003.

[CMMI 2010]
  CMMI Product Team: *CMMI for Development, Version 1.3, Improving processes for developing better products and services*, Technical Report CMU/SEI-2010-TR-033, Software Engineering Institute, November 2010, available at www.sei.cmu.edu/reports/10tr033.pdf.

[Cockburn 2001]
  Alistair Cockburn and Jim Highsmith: *Agile Software Development: The People Factor*, in *Computer* (IEEE), vol. 34, no. 11, November 2001, pages 131-133.

[Cockburn 2001a]
  Alistair Cockburn: *Agile Software Development*, Addison-Wesley, 2001.

[Cockburn 2003]
  Alistair Cockburn: *The cone of silence and related project management strategies*, online article at alistair.cockburn.us/The+cone+of+silence+and+related+project+management+strategies, 2003.

[Cockburn 2005]
  Alistair Cockburn: *Crystal Clear — A Human-Powered Methodology for Small Teams*, Addison-Wesley, 2005.

[Cockburn 2010]
  Alistair Cockburn: *Vid of Alistair describing Shu Ha Ri*, video lecture, 7 July 2010, available at alistair.cockburn.us/Vid+of+Alistair+describing+Shu+Ha+Ri. See explanatory text (from 2001 book) at alistair.cockburn.us/Vid+of+Alistair+describing+Shu+Ha+Ri.

[Cohn 2003]
  Mike Cohn: *The Need for Agile Project Management*, online article at www.mountaingoatsoftware.com/articles/the-need-for-agile-project-management.

[Cohn 2006]
  Mike Cohn: *Agile Estimating and Planning*, Addison-Wesley, 2006.

[Cohn 2009]
  Mike Cohn: *Intentional Yet Emergent*, online article at www.mountaingoatsoftware.com/blog/agile-design-intentional-yet-emergent, 4 December 2009.

[Cohn 2010]
  Mike Cohn: *Succeeding With Agile*, Addison-Wesley, 2010.

[Cohn 2010a]
  Mike Cohn: *The Role of Leaders on a Self-Organizing Team*, online article at www.mountaingoatsoftware.com/blog/the-role-of-leaders-on-a-self-organizing-team, 7 January 2010.

[Cohn site]
  Mike Cohn: *Succeeding With Agile* site, www.mountaingoatsoftware.com.

[Collabnet site]
  Collabnet Scrum Methodology site, at scrummethodology.com.

[Cox 1996]
  Brad Cox: *Superdistribution: Objects as Property on the Electronic Frontier*, Addison Wesley. 1996.

[Cunningham 2004]

Ward Cunningham (interviewed by Bill Venners): *The Simplest Thing that Could Possibly Work*, at www.artima.com/intv/simplest.html.

[Cusumano 1995]

Michael A. Cusumano and Richard W. Selby, *Microsoft Secrets: How the World's Most Powerful Software Company Creates Technology, Shapes Markets and Manages People*, Simon and Schuster, 1995

[DeMarco 1999]

Tom DeMarco and Tim Lister: *Peopleware: Productive Projects and Teams* (Second Edition), Dorset House, 1999. (First edition was published in 1987.)

[DeMarco 2001]

Tom DeMarco: *Slack: Getting Past Burnout, Busywork and the Myth of Total Efficiency*, Dorset House, 2001.

[Deming 1966]

W. Edwards Deming: *Some Theory of Sampling*, 1966, reprinted by Dover Publications, 2010.

[Denning 2012]

Steve Denning: *The Case Against Agile: Ten Perennial Management Objections*, in *Forbes* magazine, 17 April 2012, at onforb.es/HQ8i6J.

[Derby 2011]

Esther Derby: *Misconceptions about Self-Organizing Teams*, online article at www.estherderby.com/2011/07/misconceptions-about-self-organizing-teams-2.html, 19 July 2011.

[Dhawan 2008]

Krishankumar Dhawan, *Geste Kopfschuetteln Indien* (Indian head-nodding), YouTube video (in English), 30 June 2008, , at bit.ly/dmIoGj (short for www.youtube.com/watch?v=3hCV2oO2akw).

[Dijkstra 1968]

Edsger W. Dijkstra: *Go To Statement Considered Harmful*, Communications of the ACM, vol. 11, no. 3, March 1968, pages 147-148.

[Evans 2003]

Eric Evans: *Domain-Driven Design: Tackling Complexity in the Heart of Software*, Addison-Wesley, 2003.

[Eveleens 2010]

J. Laurens Eveleens and Chris Verhoef: *The Rise and Fall of the Chaos Report Figures*, in IEEE *Software*, vol. 27, no. 1, Jan-Feb 2010, pages 30-36. See also S. Aidane, *The "Chaos Report" Myth Busters*, 26 March 2010, www.guerrillaprojectmanagement.com/the-chaos-report-myth-busters, and [Glass 2006].

[Gamma 1994]

Erich Gamma, Richard Helm, Ralph Johnson and John Vlissides: *Design Patterns: Elements of Reusable Object-Oriented Software*, Addison-Wesley, 1994.

[Fowler 1999]

Martin Fowler: *Refactoring: Improving the design of existing code*, Addison Wesley, 1999.

[Ghezzi 2002]

Carlo Ghezzi, Mehdi Jazayeri, Dino Mandrioli: *Fundamentals of Software Engineering*. 2nd Edition. Prentice Hall, 2002.

[Glass 2006]

Robert L. Glass: *The Standish Report: Does it Really Describe a Software Crisis?*, in *Communications of the ACM*, vol. 49, no. 8, pages 15-16, August 2006.

[Glazer 2008]
    Hillel Glazer, Jeff Dalton, David Anderson, Mike Konrad and Sandy Shrum: *CMMI or Agile: Why Not Embrace Both!*, Technical Note CMU/SEI-2008-TN-003, November 2008, available at www.sei.cmu.edu/library/abstracts/reports/08tn003.cfm.

[Gualtieri 2011]
    Mike Gualtieri: *Agile Software Is A Cop-Out; Here's What's Next*, blog article, 12 October 2011, at blogs.forrester.com/mike_gualtieri/11-10-12-agile_software_is_a_cop_out_heres_whats_next.

[Hadamard 1945]
    Jacques Hadamard: *Psychology of Invention in the Mathematical Field*, Princeton University Press, 1945

[Halliwell 2008]
    Luke Halliwell: *The Agile Disease*, blog article, 16 November 2008, at lukehalliwell.wordpress.com/2008/11/16/the-agile-disease.

[Humphrey 2005]
    Watts S. Humphrey: *PSP: A Self-Improvement Process for Software Engineers*, Addison-Wesley, 2005.

[IBM 2012]
    IBM-sponsored study by Project At Work: *Agile Maturity Report*, 2012, available online at www-01.ibm.com/software/rational/agile/agilesoftware.

[IEEE 1998]
    IEEE: Standard 830-1998, *Recommended Practice for Software Requirements Specifications*, 1998, available (for a fee) at standards.ieee.org/findstds/standard/830-1998.html.

[Jacobson 1992]
    Ivar Jacobson: *Object Oriented Software Engineering: A Use Case Driven Approach*, Addison-Wesley, 1992.

[Jackson 1995]
    Michael Jackson: *Software Requirements and Specifications: A Lexicon of Practice, Principles and Prejudices*, Addison Wesley / ACM Press, 1995.

[Jackson 2000]
    Michael Jackson: *Problem Frames: : Analysing & Structuring Software Development Problems*, Addison-Wesley, 2000.

[Jacobson 1992]
    Ivar Jacobson: *Object-Oriented Software Engineering: A Use Case DrivenApproach*, Addison-Wesley, 1992.

[Jeffries 2001]
    Ron Jeffries, Ann Anderson and Chet Hendrickson: *Extreme Programming Installed*, Addison-Wesley, 2001.

[Jeffries site]
    Ron Jeffries: *Xprogramming* site at xprogramming.com.

[Kniberg 2010]
    Henrik Kniberg and Mattias Skarin: *Kanban and Scrum — Making the Most of Both*, InfoQ, 2010.

[Kraft 1977]
    Philip Kraft: *Programmers and Managers: The Routinization of Computer Programming in the United States*, Springer Verlag, 1977.

[Larman 2010]
    Craig Larman and Bas Vodde: *Practices for Scaling Lean & Agile Development: Large, Multisite, and Offshore Product Development with Large-Scale Scrum*, Addison-Wesley, 2010.

[Leffingwell 2011]
Dean Leffingwell: *Agile Software Requirements — Lean Requirements Practices for Teams, Programs, and the Enterprise*, Addison-Wesley, 2011.

[Lutz 1993]
Robyn Lutz: *Analyzing Software Requirements Errors in Safety-Critical, Embedded Systems*, in ISRE 93 (Proc. Int. Symposium on Requirements Engineering), IEEE, 1993, also available at www.cs.iastate.edu/%7Erlutz/publications/isre93.ps.

[Madeyski 2010]
Lech Madeyski: *Test-Driven Development – An Empirical Development of Agile Practice*, Springer Verlag, 2010.

[Markham 2010]
Daniel Markham: *Agile Ruined My Life*, blog article, 7 September 2010, available at www.whattofix.com/blog/archives/2010/09/agile-ruined-my.php.

[Martin 2009]
Angela Michele Martin: *The Role of Customers in Extreme Programming Projects*, PhD thesis, Victoria University of Wellington, New Zealand, 2009.

[McBreen 2002]
Pete McBreen: *Questioning Extreme Programming*, Pearson Education, 2002.

[McConnell 2006]
Steve McConnell: *Software Estimation: Demystifying the Black Art*, Microsoft Press, 2006.

[McCracken 1982]
Daniel D. McCracken and Michael A. Jackson: Life cycle concept considered harmful, in ACM SIGSOFT Software Engineering Notes, vol. 7, no. 2, April 1982, pages 29-32.

[Meyer 1988]
Bertrand Meyer: *Object-Oriented Software Construction* (first edition), Prentice Hall, 1988.

[Meyer 1995]
Bertrand Meyer: *Object Success: A Manager's Guide to Object Orientation, Its Impact on the Corporation and its Use for Reengineering the Software Process*, Prentice Hall, 1995.

[Meyer 1997]
Bertrand Meyer: *Object-Oriented Software Construction, second edition*, Prentice Hall, 1997.

[Meyer 2008]
Bertrand Meyer: *Design and Code Reviews in the Age of the Internet*, in *Communications of the ACM*, vol. 51, no. 9, September 2008, pages 66-71.

[Meyer 2009]
Bertrand Meyer: *Touch of Class: Learning to Program Well, Using Objects and Contracts*, Springer-Verlag, 2009.

[Meyer 2009a]
Bertrand Meyer, Ilinca Ciupa, Andreas Leitner, Arno Fiva, Yi Wei and Emmanuel Stapf: *Programs that Test Themselves, IEEE Computer*, vol. 42, no. 9, September 2009, pages 46-55, available at se.ethz.ch/~meyer/publications/computer/test_themselves.pdf.

[Meyer 2012]
Bertrand Meyer: *A Fundamental Duality of Software Engineering*, 14 October 2012, blog article at bertrandmeyer.com/2012/10/14/a-fundamental-duality-of-software-engineering/.

[Meyer 2013]
Bertrand Meyer: *Apocalypse no!* (part 1, includes a link to part 2), 12 March 2013, blog article at bertrandmeyer.com/2013/03/12/apocalypse-no-part-1/.

[Meyer 2013a]
    Bertrand   Meyer: *What   is   wrong   with   CMMI*,   12   May   2013,   blog   article   at
    bertrandmeyer.com/2013/05/12/what-is-wrong-with-cmmi/.

[Mills 1971]
    Harlan D. Mills: *Chief programmer teams, principles, and procedures*, IBM Federal Systems
    Division Report FSC71-5108, Gaithersburg, 1971.

[Mittal 2013]
    Nitin Mittal: *Self-Organizing Teams: What and How*, at scrumalliance.org/articles/466-selforgani
    zing-teams-what-and-how, 7 January 2013.

[Mob site]
    Mob Programming site, at mobprogramming.org.

[Mozilla modules]
    Mozilla Modules and Module Owners, at www.mozilla.org/hacking/module-ownership.html.

[Müller 2005]
    Matthias Müller: *Two controlled experiments concerning the comparison of pair programming to
    peer review*, in *Journal of Systems and Software* 78, 2005, pages 166-179.

[NASA 1999]
    Mars Climate Orbiter Mishap Investigation Board Phase I Report, 10 November 1999, available
    at bit.ly/Ot7mJ8 (short for ftp.hq.nasa.gov/pub/pao/reports/1999/MCO_report.pdf). See also the
    CNN article at bit.ly/d51nla.

[NATO 1968]
    Peter Naur and Brian Randell (eds): *Software Engineering*, Report on a Conference Sponsored by
    the NATO Science Committee, Garmisch, Germany, 7-11 October 1968, republished in 2001 at
    homepages.cs.ncl.ac.uk/brian.randell/NATO/nato1968.PDF.

[Nawrocki 2001]
    Jerzy Nawrocki and Adam Wojciechowski: *Experimental evaluation of pair programming*, in
    European Software Control and Metrics (Escom), April 2001, pages 269-276.

[Nonaka 1995]
    Ikujiro Nonaka and Hirotaka Takeuchi: *The Knowledge-Creating Company: How Japanese
    Companies Create the Dynamics of Innovation*, Oxford University Press, 1995.

[Parnas 1986]
    David L. Parnas and Paul C. Clements: *A Rational Design Process: How and Why to Fake it*, in
    IEEE *Transactions on Software Engineering*, vol. 12, no. 2, February 1986, pages 251-257,
    available at y.web.umkc.edu/yzheng/classes/doc/IEEE86_Parnas_Clement.pdf.

[Pfleeger 2009]
    Shari Lawrence Pfleeger and Joanne M. Atlee: *Software Engineering: Theory and Practice*. 4th
    Edition, Prentice Hall, 2009.

[Pichler site]
    Roman Pichler Consulting: *Scrum* site at www.romanpichler.com.

[Poppendieck 2001]
    May Poppendieck: *Lean Programming*, in *Dr Dobb's*, two-part article, 1 May and 1 June 2001, at
    www.drdobbs.com/lean-programming/184414734 and www.drdobbs.com/lean-programming/184414744.

[Poppendieck 2003]
    Mary and Tom Poppendieck: *Lean Software Development — An Agile Toolkit*, Addison-Wesley, 2003.

[Poppendieck 2010]
    Mary and Tom Poppendieck: *Leading Lean Software Development*, Addison-Wesley, 2010.

[Poppendieck essays]
Mary Poppendieck, *Lean Essays* site, www.leanessays.com.

[Poppendieck lean]
Mary and Tom Poppendieck: *Lean Software Development* site, www.poppendieck.com.

[Reeves 1992-2005]
Jack W. Reeves: *What is Software Design?*, in *C++ Journal*, Fall 1992, available with two complementary essays (2005) at www.developerdotstar.com/mag/articles/reeves_design.html.

[Royce 1970]
Winston D. Royce: *Managing the Development of Large Software Systems*, in Proc. IEEE WESCON, 1970, pages 1-9, at www.cs.umd.edu/class/spring2003/cmsc838p/Process/waterfall.pdf.

[Schwaber 2002]
Ken Schwaber and Mide Beedle: *Agile Software Development with Scrum*, Prentice Hall, 2002.

[Schwaber 2004]
Ken Schwaber: *Agile Project Management with Scrum*, Microsoft Press, 2004.

[Schwaber 2004a]
Ken Schwaber: *Managing Agile Projects*, Addison-Wesley, 2004.

[Schwaber 2012]
Ken Schwaber and Jeff Sutherland: *Software in 30 Days: How Agile Managers Beat the Odds, Delight Their Customers, And Leave Competitors In the Dust*, Wiley, 2012.

[Schweigert 2012]
Thomas Schweigert, Risto Nevalainen, Detlef Vohwinkel, Morten Korsaa and Miklos Biro: *Agile Maturity Model: Oxymoron or the Next Level of Understanding*, in *Software Process Improvement and Capability Determination* (SPICE), Communications in Computer and Information Science vol. 290, 2012, pages 289-294, at link.springer.com/chapter/10.1007%2F978-3-642-30439-2_34.

[Scrimshire site]
James Scrimshire: *Hurricane Four* site, hurricanefour.com.

[Scrum Alliance]
Scrum Alliance site at scrumalliance.org.

[Shore 2008]
James Shore and Shane Warden: *The Art of Agile Development*, O'Reilly. 2008.

[Shore 2008a]
James Shore: *The Decline and Fall of Agile*, blog article, 14 November 2008, at www.jamesshore.com/Blog/The-Decline-and-Fall-of-Agile.html.

[Shore site]
Web site for [Shore 2008] at jamesshore.com/Agile-Book.

[Silver 2007]
Melanie Silver: *Am I, or Am I Not, Using Scrum? That is the Question*, Scrum Alliance site, 18 March 2007, www.scrumalliance.org/articles/41-am-i-or-am-i-not-using-scrum-that-is-the-question.

[Sobel 2007]
Dava Sobel: *Longitude: The True Story of a Lone Genius Who Solved the Greatest Scientific Problem of His Time*, Walker, 2007.

[Stellman site]
Andrew Stellman and Jennifer Greene: *Building Better Software* site, www.stellman-greene.com/.

[Stephens 2003]
Matt Stephens & Doug Rosenberg: *Extreme Programming Refactored: The Case Against XP*, Apress, 2003.

[Surowiecki 2004]
James Surowiecki: *The Wisdom of Crowds: Why the Many Are Smarter Than the Few and How Collective Wisdom Shapes Business, Economies, Societies and Nations*, Knopf Doubleday, 2004.

[Surowiecki 2013]
James Surowiecki: *Requiem For a Dreamliner*, in the *New Yorker*, 4 February 2013, available at www.newyorker.com/talk/financial/2013/02/04/130204ta_talk_surowiecki.

[Sutherland 2009]
Jeff Sutherland: *Self-Organization: The Secret Sauce for Improving your Scrum Team*, video at www.youtube.com/watch?v=M1q6b9JI2Wc.

[Sutherland 2010]
Jeff Sutherland, Carsten Ruseng Jakobson and Kent Johnson: *Scrum and CMMI Level 5: The Magic Potion for Code Warriors*, in Proc. 41st Hawaii Int. Conf. on System Sciences, 7-10 Jan. 2008, at ieeexplore.ieee.org/xpls/abs_all.jsp?arnumber=4439172&tag=1 (and bit.ly/17LZE2R).

[Sutherland 2012]
Jeff Sutherland, Rini van Solingen and Eelco Rustenberg: *The Power of Scrum*, CreateSpace, 2012.

[Sutherland 2013]
Jeff Sutherland: *Scrum: The Art of Doing Twice the Work in Half the Time*, tutorial notes, 2013, available at jeffsutherland.com/CSMjsv16.pdf.

[Wake site]
Bill Wake: *Exploring Extreme Programming* site at xp123.com.

[Wallace 2002]
Doug Wallace, Isobel Raggett & Joel Aufgang: *Extreme Programming for Web Projects*, Addison-Wesley, 2002.

[Waters site]
Kelly Waters: *All About Agile* site, www.allaboutagile.com.

[Weisert 2010]
Conrad Weisert, *Are Agile Methods and Reusable Components Incompatible?*, online article at www.idinews.com/agileReUse.html.

[Wells site]
Don Wells: *Extreme Programming* site, www.extremeprogramming.org.

[Wenzel site]
Joel Wenzel, *In Point Form* site, joel.inpointform.net.

[Wirth 1995]
Niklaus Wirth: *A Plea for Lean Software*, in IEEE *Computer*, Vol. 28, no. 2, February 1995, pages 64-68.

[Yegge 2006]
Steve Yegge: *Good Agile, Bad Agile*, blog article, 27 September 2006, available at steve-yegge.blogspot.com/2006/09/good-agile-bad-agile_27.html.

[Yourdon 2003]
Ed Yourdon: *Death March*, 2nd edition, Prentice Hall, 2003. (First edition published in 1997.)

[Zave 1997]
Pamela Zave and Michael Jackson: *Four dark corners of requirements engineering*, in ACM *TOSEM* (*Transactions on Software Engineering and Methodology*), vol. 6, no. 1, January 1997, pages 1-30.

[Zave FAQ]
Pamela Zave, *Feature Interaction FAQ*, at www2.research.att.com/~pamela/faq.html, with links to a page listing many publications on feature interaction.

Index

In the electronic version, clicking a page number will take you to the corresponding occurrence.